THE BRITISH TAX SYSTEM

FOURTH EDITION

J. A. KAY
M. A. KING

OXFORD UNIVERSITY PRESS
1986

Oxford University Press, Walton Street, Oxford OX2 6DP
Oxford New York Toronto
Delhi Bombay Calcutta Madras Karachi
Petaling Jaya Singapore Hong Kong Tokyo
Nairobi Dar es Salaam Cape Town
Melbourne Auckland
and associated companies in
Beirut Berlin Ibadan Nicosia

Oxford is a trade mark of Oxford University Press

Published in the United States
by Oxford University Press, New York

British Library Cataloguing in Publication Data
Kay, J. A., 1948–
The British tax system.—4th ed.
1. Taxation—Great Britain
I. Title II. King, Mervyn A.
336.2'00941 HJ2601
ISBN 0–19–877263–7
ISBN 0–19–877262–9

Library of Congress Cataloging in Publication Data
Kay, J. A. (John Alexander)
The British tax system
Bibliography: p.
Includes index.
1. Taxation—Great Britain. I. King, Mervyn A.
II. Title
HJ2619.K39 1986 336.2'00941 86–21755
ISBN 0–19–877263–7
ISBN 0–19–877262–9 (pbk.)

Printed and bound in
Great Britain by Biddles Ltd,
Guildford and King's Lynn

Fantastic grow the evening gowns;
Agents of the Fisc pursue
Absconding tax-defaulters through
The sewers of provincial towns.

Caesar's double-bed is warm
As an unimportant clerk
Writes I DO NOT LIKE MY WORK
On a pink official form.

From W. H. Auden, 'The Fall of Rome'
(*Collected Shorter Poems*, Faber & Faber, 1966)

Preface

With the fourth edition of *The British Tax System* it is time to take stock of the changes that have occurred to both this book and the tax system since the first edition appeared in 1978. We wrote the book initially as a result of our experiences as members of the Meade Committee on the Structure and Reform of Direct Taxation between 1975 and 1977. The impact which the contents of the Meade Report have had on our thinking is obvious, but any reader who believes that he will find here a substitute for reading that Report is quite mistaken.

The substance of parts of both this book and the tax system has changed since the first edition. New chapters have been introduced, others have disappeared, and almost all have been extensively re-written. Major changes have been made to tax rates, the taxation of investment income, company taxation, social security, and capital taxation, and reforms are planned for local and personal taxation. There has been much to discuss in successive editions. We are confident that further changes will necessitate new editions in the future.

Some common factors are, however, increasingly evident. One is that the process of tax reform in the UK is very unsatisfactory. Several years of inertia lead to a frenzy of ill-conceived change, after which torpor is restored: a cycle which has occurred four times in the last twenty years and which, in the absence of institutional change, is likely to recur as frequently in the next twenty. What is required is a strategy for tax reform. The warm reception initially given to the 1984 Budget, the most radical in intent for a decade, illustrates the extent of the demand for reform. But there was, in fact, no articulated strategy behind that Budget. If we sought to read one into it, it would be that of the comprehensive income tax—a strategy which could and would not work, for reasons which readers of earlier editions of this book, or the current one, should fully understand. A principal concern of this book remains the description of such a strategy, based on a personal expenditure tax and a cash-flow corporation tax.

Many people have helped us prepare the various editions. To

those thanked in earlier Prefaces we would like to add Debbie Clark, Chantal Crevel-Robinson, and Judith Payne.

In this edition we have brought the information up to date as of 1 January 1986.

Contents

List of Figures

List of Tables

Introduction

In this book we seek to use economic analysis to examine the problems facing the British tax system. We try to do this in a practical way by looking at real day-to-day problems. We were ourselves surprised that economics was useful to us not only in analysing the economic effects of taxes, but also in thinking about administrative problems. The reason for this is that much of the muddle and complexity of the present system derives from the absence of any clear view as to what principles do or should underlie it.

This is not to suggest that economics provides all the answers. Public finance is one of the most rapidly developing branches of economic theory, but we found much traditional theory of little help in dealing with the everyday problems of the British tax system and it is instructive to consider why. Much of this material is concerned with evaluating the economic effects of taxes, and this is quite properly done by contrasting the characteristics of different theoretical taxes. But the ways in which actual taxes differ from these theoretical taxes are often of much greater economic significance than the ways in which theoretical taxes differ from each other. We pursue in this book the question of whether income or expenditure should be the major component of the tax base: the extent to which savings should or should not be taxed. It is conventional to think of this in terms of how aggregate savings respond to changes in taxes. But there is little evidence to suggest that aggregate savings are likely to be very sensitive to tax changes. What is more significant is that the ways in which people save are very sensitive indeed to the ways in which different savings media are taxed. The present tax system, in effect, exempts some forms of saving from tax but not others; and this, we think, has more marked economic effects than a structure in which all forms of savings are taxed or one in which none of them is taxed. We pursue this argument, and others like it, in more detail below; but we note at this stage that the loopholes and anomalies in the tax system can often be much more significant in their effects on behaviour than the taxes themselves. The economist who thinks that because the main UK personal direct tax is called an income tax it has the same characteristics as income taxes he encounters in public finance texts is likely to be seriously misled.

These observations are not in any way intended to question the need for any analysis of applied economic problems to be rooted firmly in economic theory; indeed it is because we are convinced of this that we offer, in Chapter 1, a crash course in some simple, but central, economic concepts. We would like to stress that we shall only make proposals for change if we believe them to be practicable. It is necessary to spell out what this means. The most usual definition equates the impracticable with the unfamiliar. This definition is convenient for those who find adaptation to new ideas difficult or disturbing, but it is not very useful for a discussion of the tax system. It is perfectly clear that there are many other systems of all kinds which differ from those at present in operation which would work, and it would be surprising if some of them would not work better than existing systems. Those who believe that being practical involves confining attention to minor modifications of the *status quo* are simply showing that their minds, or the minds of those to whom they are reporting, are closed.

A related error is to confuse a practical outlook with an obsession with detail. As an example, the Inland Revenue in its memorandum on local income tax to the Layfield Committee was apparently exercised by the problem of people who live in caravans. It would be foolish to deny that there is such a problem. It would also be foolish to deny that the problem is, like the number of people who live in caravans, small. It is very unlikely that anyone would say 'I would be in favour of a local income tax if only I could think of a way of dealing with people who live in caravans'. Given that this is so, it is pointless to discuss the matter further at this stage. Not only is it unnecessary to consider the difficulty in advance of making basic decisions about the structure of such a tax (such as whether to have one); it is positively undesirable to do so, since this kind of problem can be more sensibly tackled in the light of other, more important, decisions that would need to be taken first. The enumeration of endless lists of unimportant objections is a common administrative tactic for resisting change, and the man who seeks to deal with it by answering them is lost. Since most people are—rightly—uninterested in the minutiae of hypothetical tax systems, we shall not take our description of alternatives beyond the point at which we are confident that we, or a competent firm of management consultants, could fill in the remaining details. It is extremely unfortunate that the Inland Revenue has cried wolf so often on the impossibility of administering reforms—including several which were subsequently implemented—that its views on what is and what is not feasible can no longer be regarded as reliable.

All this said, it must be recognized that administrative feasibility is an important constraint on tax policy, and we have given it due weight in our discussion. We shall regard measures as practicable if we believe they can be operated reasonably cheaply and simply in a manner which corresponds to the underlying intention of the measure. Most things can be made to work, after a fashion, if we are prepared either to spend a good deal of effort on policing them or to accept many *ad hoc* expedients and anomalies in their operation. Practicability is therefore a matter of degree (so that it is not easy to make firm statements about it) and we judge something to be impracticable if it would cost too much in one or other of these directions: too much administrative burden or too extensive compromise with the original objective. It should be clear from this definition that it is not only not necessary for a measure to be part of the *status quo* for it to be practicable; it is not sufficient either. There are substantial parts of the British tax system which do not work satisfactorily and could not, without great difficulty and expense, be made to do so. We shall return to this point in various specific contexts.

We begin our discussion in Chapter 1 with a brief explanation of some basic economic concepts which we believe to be of fundamental importance to an understanding of the tax system. The style of this chapter is necessarily rather different from the rest of the book and we suggest that if it poses difficulty the reader should move on to Chapter 2, referring back to Chapter 1 when necessary. Table 1 shows the ways in which different taxes contribute to overall tax revenue. Income tax yields the most revenue and it is with this tax that we begin in Chapter 2, which describes the evolution of income tax and the main features of the tax as it operates today. We describe how income tax is administered and the topical subject of the black economy. The economic effects of taxes on earnings are analysed in Chapter 3, and in Chapter 4 we discuss the taxation of investment income and the tax treatment of savings.

Table 1:   *Sources of tax revenue*

	1985/6 (£ million)	
Taxes on personal income		
Income tax	35,100	
National insurance contributions	24,330	
Advance corporation tax	3,800	
	63,230	(52.8%)
Taxes on company income		
Mainstream corporation tax/DLT	6,960	
Petroleum revenue tax/Gas levy	6,920	
	13,880	(11.6%)
Taxes on transfers of capital		
Capital transfer tax	890	
Stamp duties	1,230	
Capital gains tax	930	
	3,050	(2.5%)
Taxes on commodities		
Value added tax	19,300	
Duties on: oil and petrol	6,500	
tobacco	4,300	
alcoholic drink	4,200	
betting and gaming	730	
Car tax	880	
Vehicle licences	2,400	
Customs duties	1,200	
Agricultural levies	160	
	39,670	(33.1%)
TOTAL	119,830	

Note: The classification of taxes in this table is not intended to reflect any economic judgements about the effective incidence of particular taxes.
Source: *Financial Statement and Budget Report 1986–87.*

In Chapter 5 we examine the choice of the tax base and the possibility of a direct tax which is levied not on income but on personal expenditure. Chapter 6 explores how such a tax might operate.

Two of the most controversial of current issues are the interaction between taxation and social security benefits, and the role of indirect taxes. We discuss these issues in Chapters 7 and 8 respectively. Problems of rates, local authority finance, the taxation of companies, and the imposition of special taxes on economic rents are dealt with in Chapters 9–12. The final three chapters discuss the tax system as a whole. In Chapter 13 we consider the way in which inflation has influenced the development of the tax system. Chapter 14 looks at the question of the distribution of the tax burden among different groups and individuals in society and at how progressive the tax system should be. We conclude the book with a description of some reforms which are worth pursuing and others which are not.

There are two aspects of the tax system about which we shall have little to say: its use to stabilize fluctuations in the economy and relations with other countries. Following the Keynesian revolution much attention was directed to the use of fiscal policy as a way of controlling fluctuations in aggregate demand. Stabilization policy based on marginal changes in government expenditure and taxation was to be the means of eliminating the business cycle. Indeed Musgrave in his classic work on public finance (1959) explains that he began with the idea of producing a tract on 'compensatory finance' dealing with the question of how the public budget affected certain key macro-economic variables such as the level of unemployment. But the gaps in the theory of public finance which he discovered, many of which still exist today, lay in the more traditional areas of the effect of taxes on income distribution and economic efficiency. In the end stabilization policy occupied less than one-third of his treatise. This trend has continued. In a more recent book by the same author (Musgrave and Musgrave, 1976) only 100 out of 750 pages are devoted to fiscal stabilization.

Part of this decline in interest is due to the realization that macro-economic policy is more complicated than the simple textbook Keynesian models led us to believe and that 'fine-tuning' of the economy is considerably more difficult than we might have hoped. This is because there is uncertainty as to what will happen to the economy in the future in the absence of any change in policy, and because there are long delays between when a decision is made to alter taxes and when the desired effect on spending or unemployment becomes apparent. First of all there is the inevitable delay in collecting statistics, so we may only have an adequate idea of what was happening to the economy some months or even a year ago. Even when the government has looked at the statistics, deliberated, and then decided to, say, reduce taxes there are still more lags in the system. Individuals will take time to adjust their spending decisions and, at least initially, the impact will be felt on the level of stocks in shops. Producers will probably wait before increasing their output rather than running down stocks, and the extra output will be met by overtime working until firms are convinced it is worth expanding their labour force on a more permanent basis. These lags in conjunction with uncertainty about the future make stabilization policy a hazardous business.

It has been seriously argued that the net effect of British government policies has been to destabilize rather than to stabilize the economy, and that they have in any case been motivated more by electoral factors than by considerations of demand management ('the political business cycle'). (See Worswick, 1971; Nordhaus, 1975.) We shall not attempt to assess these views. For our purposes we may simply note that it is unlikely that the choice of the *structure* of the tax system will make these problems any easier. It is with the structure of the system that we shall be concerned and to say that we shall not answer every question is not to say that we shall not tackle the most pressing.

1

The economics of taxation: some basic concepts

Tax incidence

Economists have long been concerned with the question of who actually pays any particular tax—the *incidence* of the tax. At first sight, it may seem surprising that this is a problem. The house-owner who is required to write out a cheque in payment of rates to his local authority, or the employee who sees income tax deducted from his wages, knows very well who is paying the tax. But things are not really so simple. The tax on tobacco is paid by the trader who withdraws it from a bonded warehouse, at some intermediate stage of the process that turns tobacco leaves into cigarettes. But no one imagines that he really pays the tax, in the sense that he is personally worse off by the amount of the duty that he regularly pays over to the Customs and Excise. The tax is paid by those who ultimately smoke the cigarettes. There is no law that requires or even entitles the tobacco distributor to recover his liabilities from them—indeed in all probability he has no direct dealings with them and does not know who they are. He simply adjusts the terms on which he sells in order to reflect the tax that he is required to pay; so, in turn, do those who buy from him; and the final result is that the tax burden is passed on to the consumer.

We can therefore usefully distinguish the formal incidence of a tax from its effective incidence. The formal incidence falls on those who have the actual legal liability for paying the tax. The effective incidence identifies those who are, in the end, the people who are out of pocket as a result of the imposition of the tax. Naturally enough, it suits traders to encourage some confusion between the two. Suppliers will from time to time express regret that they are obliged to charge VAT on a particular invoice. But the truth of the matter is that they are not obliged to charge VAT at all: they are merely obliged to pay it, and in adding it to a bill they are seeking (as those who devised the tax intended they should) to pass that burden of payment on to someone else. The formal incidence of

VAT is on the supplier; the effective incidence (subject to some qualification) is on the purchaser.

Even where popular usage distinguishes the formal and effective incidence of tax, we tend to make 'all-or-nothing' assumptions about the incidence of a tax. Thus it is assumed that VAT is essentially a tax on consumers, and there is no doubt that this is basically true. But it is not completely true. When a special discriminatory rate of VAT was imposed on television sets and some other electrical goods in 1975, their prices rose and purchasers of television sets suffered accordingly. But the demand for television sets fell; so did profit margins in the manufacture and distribution of television sets, and the profits of companies engaged in these activities were reduced; the earnings of those who worked in these industries were lower, and some of them lost their jobs. Thus the major part of the incidence of the tax was on consumers, but some of it fell on the owners of, and workers in, activities related to the supply of television sets.

Income tax is assumed to be paid by those who earn the income, and this is a good first approximation to the effective incidence of the tax. But it is only a first approximation. This is especially true at higher income levels: when the board of directors ponders on the appropriate differential between the chief executive and his deputy it is unlikely that they are entirely oblivious to the fact that much of it will be absorbed in tax, and if this induces them to make the pre-tax margin a little wider than they would have done in the absence of the tax, then the company is sharing some of the incidence of the tax with its employee. (It is also, as we shall suggest later, likely to encourage them to think of some more efficient way of paying the chief executive.) Nor are these problems confined to higher income levels. When a householder meets a tradesman who offers to work for £100 in cash or £120 by cheque he is faced with a useful reminder that on taxable transactions part of the effective incidence falls on the employer rather than the employee.

Although the general notion of incidence is an indispensable concept in the analysis of taxation, it is one which cannot easily be given a precise meaning. The reason is that it implicitly requires a counterfactual hypothesis: what would have happened if the tax had not been imposed? It is not sufficient to say 'there would have been no tax', since public expenditure would have had to be financed in some other way. So we must specify either what other tax would have been imposed, or which item of public expenditure would have been reduced, or how the government would have met its borrowing requirements, and the answer to our incidence question will depend on the alternative assumption that we make. For this reason the issue is sometimes described as 'differential incidence' because we examine differences between alternative tax systems that raise the same revenue. Several different concepts of incidence can be found in the theoretical literature on public finance, each reflecting different counterfactual hypotheses; while empirical studies of tax incidence either make intolerably crude assumptions or become impossibly complicated.

Thus we noted above that a consequence of imposing a heavy tax on television sets was that some of those employed in their manufacture suffered reduced earnings, and others lost their jobs; had the same tax revenue been raised in some different way, other groups of workers would probably have suffered similar hardships. But without exploring these issues in detail—as a rigorous answer would require—we can say that a significant part of the incidence of this tax fell on those who were previously employed in making televisions.

What factors govern the incidence of any particular tax? We can set out two basic principles. First, the formal incidence of a tax is generally irrelevant to its effective incidence. It makes little practical difference to the incidence of the tobacco tax whether it is levied on importers, wholesalers, manufacturers, retailers, or individual smokers; and the sensible decision is to impose the legal liability at the point at which the tax can be collected most cheaply and conveniently. Second, the harder it is for someone to substitute other things for the taxed activity, the greater the proportion of the incidence of the tax which he will bear. VAT is imposed on most goods; and since there is not very much (except leisure) that can be substituted for consumption in general, most of the burden of VAT falls on consumers. But if a specially heavy rate of VAT is imposed on one or two items, as with television sets, the situation is rather different. Consumers can substitute other things for television sets, and if the price rises sufficiently they will tend to do so. Producers, on the other hand, are in the short term stuck with capacity for manufacturing television sets; and if the only way to sell them is to keep down the price and absorb part of the tax themselves then that is what they must do.

If the tax were more discriminatory still—if it were imposed on a single manufacturer of television sets in isolation, for example—then that manufacturer would have no alternative but to hold down his price, accept the resulting losses, and grin and bear it until in the long run he could try to move into a less adversely treated business. For most people, there is no alternative to work which is both attractive and feasible, and that is why the major part of the incidence of the income tax falls on the employee. But there are alternatives to effort, to overtime, and to increased responsibility; and to the extent that these are important and valuable components of the package which a particular employer is buying, that employer will have to pay the price, at least to some extent, by raising the gross wage that he pays to a level that takes some account of the burden of taxation on the employee.

The first principle—the irrelevance of formal incidence—is easy to understand in abstract, but has some wide-ranging implications. For instance, it suggests that it is a matter of no practical importance whether National Insurance contributions are levied on employees or employers (see pp. 23–5 below). It is not too easy to determine what the effective incidence of such a tax is—though the argument above has suggested that it mostly falls on the employee—but whatever it is, it will be the same for both kinds of contribution. When wages come to be renegotiated, the employer's concern will be with gross labour costs, inclusive of any pay-roll taxes to which he may be subject; and that will determine the level of employment that he will provide at any particular wage and the offer he will be prepared to make to avoid industrial trouble. On the other side of the table, the employee's interest is in his take-home pay, net of any deductions imposed on him; and that should determine the amount or quality of work that he will provide at particular wage rates and the minimum he will accept in preference to incurring the costs of a strike or other action against the employer. None of these calculations is in any way affected by the proportions in which a given tax is divided between employers' and employees' contributions, and this will therefore not have a significant effect on the final outcome.

Of course, none of this denies that the nature of formal incidence may have significant short-term effects. If a shift from employees' to employers' contributions were to be made, then next week workers would be better off and firms worse off. But this is simply to say that adjustments may take time, and that the incidence of a tax may differ in the short and long runs. In practice the restoration of net real wages to their initial level might come about as much through an uncompensated rise in prices as through a diminution in the rate of increase of money wages. But the proposition that effective incidence is independent of formal incidence in the long run is true generally. The invoice that says £60 + £9 VAT, or the pay-slip that says £60 less £15 deductions gives £45 net, may in the short run mean what they appear to say. However, it is erroneous to suppose that if these tax items were not there the price or the wage from which these computations start would necessarily remain unchanged, and it is likely that the price might be £64 or £66 and the wage £54 or £57.

Tax capitalization

The easiest way to see *tax capitalization* in operation is to start with a rather artificial example. Suppose there exist a range of bonds, each of which sells for £100 and yields 10 per cent in perpetuity; income tax on this yield is levied at 50 per cent, so that the after-tax return on each bond is £5. Now suppose that the government decides, for some reason, that among these bonds there is one particular one that should be tax-exempt. As a result, this bond—let us call it bond X—now returns £10 per annum after tax as well as before it. Because of this, it is worth twice as much to any taxpayer, and so its price rises to £200. Now look ahead a few years. By this time, most of the holders of bond X will be people who have purchased it since the tax concession was given—people who have paid £200 for it. They are only earning 5 per cent on their investment—which is the same as they could earn from other bonds—and are therefore no better off than if this concession had never been granted. In spite of this, however, they would suffer if the concession were withdrawn—if they intended to continue holding the bond, their after-tax income would be halved, while if they intended to sell the bond, they would discover that its capital value had halved. As a result of this, even people who are deriving and have derived no direct benefit from the concession would lose if it were repealed. The holders of such a bond might include some pension funds and charities, which do not pay tax and therefore gain nothing from the apparent concession (such groups would not find bond X especially attractive, but they might have other reasons for wishing to hold it). They too would suffer capital losses as the price of bond X fell if it became again subject to tax; although they obviously gain nothing from the concession, they would suffer by its withdrawal.

This is a simple case of a capitalized tax exemption. The only people who gain from it are those who hold the favoured asset at the date when the concession is introduced (and perhaps their descendants). In the example above, the fortunate holders of bond X on the critical day when the chancellor made his announcement saw the capital value of their asset double. Subsequent to that, no one derives any benefit from the concession at all. Nevertheless, later holders of the bond would lose if the concession were discontinued: in effect, they have bought the right to it from the former holders, and would have the part of their savings which they have invested in this form eliminated. Indeed, they would probably lose rather more than would be generally recognized. Not only would they be worse off by virtue of the extra tax they would themselves have to pay, but they would additionally be worse off because the asset they hold would fetch much less on resale. In other words, tax capitalization is a trap. In such a situation, almost everyone could agree that it would be better if the concession had never been given in the first place. But once it has been given, it is inequitable to withdraw it, and such a course is likely to cause real hardship. Thus the apparent beneficiaries of the concession will feel insecure: although their gains from it are small, their potential losses are significant and their position is anomalous and hence vulnerable. But once a concession of this kind has been made, there is not very much that can reasonably be done except to resolve not to fall into this particular trap in future. There is no point in considering the possibility of phasing out capitalized tax concessions, or any other method of retrieving the position. The chancellor who has made such a move is almost literally in the position of a man who has unwisely given his assets away. After the first flush of gratitude, the original recipients will have spread ownership far and wide, and there is no method, except theft, by which he can ever get them back.

Needless to say, there are numerous examples of capitalized taxes in the British tax structure. It seems useful to give two concrete examples here. One, and probably the most important, is the effect of tax concessions to owner-occupied housing. These are discussed in more detail below. For present purposes, we may simply accept that investment in housing is very favourably treated relative to investment in other kinds of asset. As a result, house prices are higher than they would otherwise be. This means that the interest and capital repayments being made by current house-buyers are substantially greater than they would be if there were no tax concessions, and hence the concessions are of little net assistance to them. Nevertheless, they would be seriously injured if, for example, relief on mortgage interest were reduced or withdrawn: not only would they find they had to pay more in tax every year but the anticipated capital gains on their houses would fail to materialize and might well be turned into capital losses. New purchasers are not gaining much from the present tax system, nor indeed has this ever happened; those who have gained have been those who have owned houses, over the thirty or forty years in which the favoured position of housing has been built up, who have seen substantial real appreciation in value of their assets. They have not benefited much either, since the gain one derives from living in the same house of ever-appreciating nominal value has very little practical utility.

This analysis is well illustrated by the effects of the withdrawal in 1974 of tax relief on mortgages in excess of £25,000. This change did not necessarily make it more difficult to buy expensive houses, since the loss of tax relief led to a fall in the price of such houses. The principal losers from the change were those who owned such houses in 1974. Moreover, people in this position lost whether they actually had large mortgages or not, since the fall in prices affected all property without reference to the personal tax position of the owner.

A second illustration of tax capitalization was provided at around the same time in the market for agricultural land. Under the pre-1974 estate duty, substantial reliefs were given for agricultural assets. Their nominal purpose was to assist working farmers. It is more likely that they damaged the interests of such farmers, since the capitalization of such concessions raised land prices to levels which were nonsensical in terms of any likely agricultural returns from the land and at which working farmers were squeezed out of the market by those avoiding estate duty. When the withdrawal of such concessions was proposed as part of the shift to capital transfer tax, land prices fell by a third or more. However, political pressures for the restoration of these reliefs were largely successful, and land prices have fully regained their earlier levels.

Tax and welfare

What are the costs of collecting tax revenue? Some costs are obvious. Any tax diverts resources from the taxpayer to the government, and leaves him worse off by that amount. Of course, that is not the end of the story; these resources are presumably used to provide public services, which may be more or less valuable to him than the possibilities for private consumption that he loses. But there are bound to be administrative costs to tax collection, since it is necessary to provide inspectors to receive the revenues and gaols to receive those who do not pay them. There will also be 'compliance costs' for taxpayers, who will spend time and suffer distress completing tax returns, and who may employ advisers to help them fulfil their obligations and suggest how to minimize them. All of these latter activities represent the necessary costs of tax collection and are pure social loss, simple subtractions from the total of goods and services—private and public—available to the community.

There is a less obvious cost, which has been called the 'excess burden' of taxation. Suppose I earn £2 per hour, and my employer is willing to give me as much, or as little, work as I require at this rate. However, a 25 per cent income tax reduces my take-home pay to £1·50 per hour, and given this I choose to work forty hours per week, thus paying £20 in tax each week. For £1·50 I do not think it worth working any more than this, but if I were paid a little more I might. (Premium payments for overtime often succeed in inducing additional effort.) In fact, for £2 per hour I would stay late on one or two evenings and put in an extra three or four hours' work a week. My employer would be better off—why else would he allow this overtime? I would be better off—why else would I stay? And if the £20 that I pay in income tax were levied, not as income tax, but as a weekly contribution to public revenue which I was obliged to pay regardless of how much work I did that week or whether I did any at all, then my net earnings from overtime would be £2 per hour and I would decide to do it.

But with an income tax, I turn this opportunity away. The problem results from the way the tax depends on how much I choose to work. These disincentive effects imply that the losses imposed by the tax are greater than the £20 that I have to pay—if I had the opportunity to do so, I would prefer to pay the £20 as a lump sum, and everyone would be better off. The idea that income taxes have undesirable disincentive effects is of course familiar, and the 'excess burden' concept is simply the economist's formal expression of it. But the idea is quite general, and commodity taxes impose losses of just the same kind. If a bottle of whisky costs £1 to make but, because of tax, sells for £6 then it is easy to imagine that I do not buy it because I am willing to pay only, say, £2. If I were able to buy it at that price, I would more than cover production costs, be able to contribute something (though less than the regular £5) to the Customs and Excise, and enjoy a warm inner glow myself. Because of the tax, none of these things happen. There is a disincentive effect here too— a disincentive to consume whisky—and this imposes an 'excess burden' or welfare loss of the same kind as disincentives to work.

It is very important to recognize that the magnitude of such effects depends on the impact of taxation at the margin—on the tax implications of a decision to work a little more or a little less, or to buy slightly more or less of a particular commodity—and not on the over-all or average burden of taxation. My reluctance to put in more effort to obtain higher earnings arises because the Revenue will take such a high proportion of these additional earnings. Thus there are two basic components to the welfare effects of a tax. There is an 'income effect', which reflects the reduction in the taxpayer's net income that occurs when part of it is compulsorily transferred to the government, and which depends on the average rate of tax. There is also an 'excess burden', which reflects additional losses arising from the way in which the tax is levied. This depends on the marginal tax rate and the way in which behaviour responds to that marginal rate. The total loss is the sum of these two.

Tax and incentives

We have considered the question 'How do the disincentive effects of taxation on effort affect welfare?' We now look at a different but closely related question: 'What effect would an increase in taxation have on the amount of work you do?' Any individual considering his answer would probably feel the influence of two conflicting pressures. On the one hand, he would realize that the tax change would make him worse off. As a result, given his commitments and expectations about the style of life that he aims to enjoy, he would feel some pressure to do more work in order to earn sufficient to live up to these expectations. This effect (the *income effect* of the tax change, so called because it results from the fall in his real income) depends on the *average* rate of tax: on the total size of the burden imposed by the tax structure. On the other hand, he will also be conscious that the tax change reduces the amount of additional consumption that he can enjoy as a result of additional work, so that increased effort becomes less attractive relative to idleness or staying at home and redecorating the bedroom. This effect (the *substitution effect* of the tax, so called because it implies a substitution of leisure for work) depends on the *marginal* rate of tax—on the proportion of any additional earnings that is absorbed in tax. The net impact of such a tax change on the work done by any individual therefore depends on the balance of these two factors: one, tending to increase effort, which is related to the average rate of tax; the other, tending to reduce it, which depends on the marginal rate of tax.

We can illustrate this by returning to the example above. We were able to eliminate the excess burden in that case by transforming the 25 per cent income tax which reduced gross earnings from £2 to £1·50 an hour into a fixed tax of £20 per week. This revision of the tax restored his overtime rate to £2 and persuaded him to do more work. In this way, we eliminated the substitution effect of the tax. We could now eliminate the income effect also by abolishing the tax of £20 per week. If we did, the worker would discover that he could achieve the same standard of living—which requires a net weekly income of £60—by working for thirty rather than forty hours per week. It is very likely that he would in fact respond by reducing the amount of work he did, and this would tend to offset the increase that had resulted from the reduction in the marginal rate of tax. Thus the net effect of complete abolition of income tax on the amount of work he does may be small, and may even lead him to reduce it. This observation does not, however, upset our excess burden analysis at all. The gains we made from eliminating the excess burden—from encouraging him to do work which both he and his employer wanted—remain. Adding in the income effect—conferring on him an opportunity to take out increased income in the form of greater leisure—raises his welfare further. The disincentive effects of taxation, which discourage additional work effort or other kinds of economic activity, make society worse off; the offsetting incentive effects, which force people to greater effort to maintain living standards reduced by taxation, do not make any one better off.

Care is therefore necessary in evaluating empirical evidence on the effect of taxation on incentives. In our normative analysis—where we asked how taxation affected welfare—there was an income effect and a substitution effect, and they both operated in the same direction. The income effect is the welfare loss that results from having to pay the tax—a loss which is offset by the benefits of public expenditure—and its size is determined by the average rate of tax paid. The substitution effect is the welfare loss that results from the disincentive effects of taxation at the margin and this depends only on the marginal rate of tax. This is a pure social loss, and there is no corresponding gain to any one. The sum of these two components gives the total loss which any tax imposes on the individual who pays it.

In our positive analysis—where we asked how taxation affected the quantity of effort—we also identified an income effect and a substitution effect, but discovered that they generally work in opposite directions. The income effect of taxation increases effort, the substitution effect reduces it, and the observed change in work effort is the net effect of the two. It follows that even if empirical studies show that tax has little effect on work effort, we cannot necessarily infer that incentive effects are not a matter for concern. Such an outcome might result from a small substitution effect offset by a small income effect, in which case our inference would be justified; or from large income and substitution effects, in which case the effects on welfare would be correspondingly large. More sophisticated analyses are required to enable us to discriminate between these possibilities.

We have used as an expository device the possibility that a person might be subject to a tax of £20 per week rather than a 25 per cent income tax on his earnings of £80. If such a tax were related to his earning potential rather than his earnings, it would take the form of a fixed weekly sum and would, as we have seen, have no disincentive effects at all. Economists have dreamt of such 'lump sum taxes' which eliminate the excess burden of taxation, but it is not easy to find taxes which have no disincentive effects. Nevertheless, they illustrate that it is possible to envisage a tax system where average rates are high but marginal rates are low. In practice, the easiest way to reduce marginal rates is to reduce average rates; but it is possible, by improving the structure, broadening the base, or altering the rate schedule, to achieve one without changing the other and hence to effect a more or less unequivocal improvement in the effects of the tax system on economic efficiency. We consider these effects and possibilities further in our discussion of particular taxes.

Fiscal neutrality

In discussing these issues, we shall use the concept of fiscal neutrality. In the earlier editions of this book, we described this concept as 'a distinctly unfamiliar idea in the UK'; since then, it has become a political cliché, particularly among those whose conception of what it means, or what might be involved in achieving it, is somewhat hazy. A neutral tax system is one which seeks to raise revenue in ways that avoid the distortionary substitution effects we have described; it is designed to minimize as far as possible the impact of the tax structure on the economic behaviour of agents in the economy.

Although the need for fiscal neutrality is now a popular rallying cry, there are also many who take the view that a major function of the tax system is to encourage good things and to discourage bad things. Even if one takes this view, there is much to be said for understanding the notion of neutrality and what a tax system which generally sought to achieve it would be like. Even if you know where you are going, it is generally valuable to know where you are starting out from, and if you are aiming to influence people in certain directions, it is useful to have an idea of what things would be like if you were not trying to do so. The neutral tax system, in effect, provides a bench-mark against which non-neutralities, intentional or otherwise, can be judged.

We have described one argument for neutrality—minimization of the excess burden of tax disincentives. But there is a more basic argument. The effects of taxation are generally not obvious, and are very often not what they seem. We shall describe in subsequent chapters the ways in which behaviour and institutions have been moulded by the British tax system—and while there is room for argument about the desirability or undesirability of these effects, it is really very difficult to argue that many of them have ever been explicitly intended by any one. The present state of the British tax system is the product of a series of unsystematic and *ad hoc* measures, many undertaken for excellent reasons—for administrative convenience or to encourage deserving groups and worthy activities—but whose over-all effect has been to deprive the system of any consistent rationale or coherent structure. We should be rather content if a tax system can achieve its basic functions of raising revenue and relieving inequalities of income and wealth without doing too much damage in the process. Clearly, this is a good deal less than an ideal tax system, but it is a good deal better than what we have at the moment. We now turn to some description and analysis of what that is.

2

The UK income tax

Income tax was first introduced to Britain during the Napoleonic Wars, but it only became a permanent feature of the tax system in 1842. As part of Peel's economic reforms it was reintroduced to replace in large part the revenue previously derived from tariffs and from various archaic taxes. It was imposed at the single low rate of 7*d.* in the £ (3 per cent) and, although this varied from time to time and ministry to ministry in the course of the nineteenth century, these essential elements never changed. The highest rates were reached during the Crimean War, when the tax threshold was an annual income of £100 and the rate 1*s.* 4*d.* (7 per cent); but even at this time there were less than half a million taxpayers. Thus income tax was then an impost of no interest or relevance to the great majority of the population.

The numbers of taxpayers did not exceed a million until the early years of the twentieth century. In 1909 effective progressivity came to the income tax with Lloyd George's 'people's budget' in which he proposed a 'supertax' on incomes over £5,000 per annum (equivalent to over £150,000 at current prices). This took the maximum rate to the unprecedented level of 1*s.* 8*d.* (8 per cent). These proposals generated a constitutional crisis (the supertax was not the most bitterly resisted element, although it was the most quantitatively significant) and they were implemented only in association with a fundamental reform of the House of Lords. During the First World War enormously increased revenue requirements led to top rates of tax at over 50 per cent. Although there were reductions thereafter, rates and revenue remained well in excess of pre-war levels while the supertax, renamed surtax, became a permanent and accepted feature.

Even then, however, liability to income tax was still confined to a small and affluent minority. Average wages in 1939 were around £180 per annum; there was no possible liability to tax for a married couple with earnings below £225 at that time, and there were less than four million taxpayers in a working population that exceeded twenty million. The decision that Second World War expenditure should be substantially financed from taxes changed this situation radically. Tax rates were increased and thresholds lowered at a time when money wages were rising rapidly. This brought about not only a quantitative change in the significance of income tax, but also a qualitative change in its method of operation. The number of tax-payers soon exceeded twelve million, so that the majority of working people now came within the ambit of the tax. These included large numbers of households lacking significant capital resources and ac-customed to budgeting on a weekly basis; so the only practical method of enforcing tax liabilities was by deduction from wages before they were received. The Inland Revenue concluded that this was impracticable, and published a White Paper (Cmd. 6348) ex-plaining that view; simultaneously, however, it was instructed to devise a scheme for doing so. PAYE (Pay-As-You-Earn) was in-troduced and has remained the principal means of collecting income tax since then. By 1960 essentially the whole of the working popu-lation was covered by income tax.

Some caution is required in interpreting historical information on the rate structure and tax thresholds, since from 1920 to 1973 there operated a system of 'earned income relief', by which in addition to the basic personal allowance (the tax threshold) a fraction of earned income (lately two-ninths) was deducted in the computation of tax-able income. This means that in measuring their effect on earned income, the nominal tax rates which applied during this period should be reduced by two-ninths: the rate of 8*s*. 3*d*. which applied from 1965 to 1971 was in fact equivalent to 32 per cent on earned income. It also means that the real value of tax thresholds was actually nine-sevenths of their nominal value, since they were cre-dited in full against only seven-ninths of earned income. Thus the indicated tax threshold of £325 in 1970 is equivalent to an effective tax threshold on earnings of £418. This mumbo jumbo was swept away in 1973, and at the same time the separately assessed and administered surtax was integrated into a single system of unified income tax. In consequence, the essentials of the current structure of UK income tax are relatively easy to explain, and to this we now turn.

The taxation of individuals

First we set out the position for a single individual, later considering explicitly the relationship between the tax treatment of individuals and households. Everyone is entitled to a 'personal allowance', a fixed amount of income that can be received free of tax. This allowance is £2,205 per annum (1985/6). It is virtually inconceivable that any adult in full-time work could have earned less than this figure, and most long-term recipients of social security benefits would receive more than this. It follows that any one who does not pay income tax is likely to be dependent on someone who does, or is a pensioner (although the old age pension is taxable, a specially enhanced personal allowance for the elderly ensures that the national insurance pension is not in fact taxed in the hands of those with no other source of income). All income in excess of this personal allowance is subject to tax at the *basic rate* of 30 per cent. When taxable income exceeds £16,200 higher rates apply, commencing at 40 per cent and rising to 60 per cent on taxable income above £40,200 (i.e. this rate applies when the total income of a single person exceeds £42,405). These rates are graphed against income in Figure 2.1, as is the corresponding schedule of average rates of tax. The average rate of income tax rises continuously, but is always below the marginal rate of tax (it is easy to check that each of these characteristics implies the other).

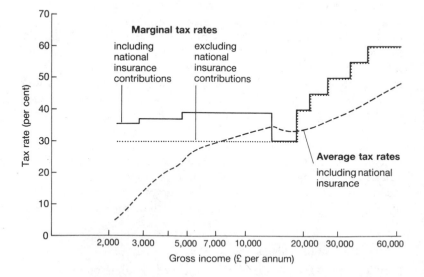

Fig. 2.1. Average and marginal rates of tax in the UK

In Figure 2.2 we show the average and marginal tax rates implied by the tax schedules of the UK, USA, and West Germany. The diagrams illustrate the rates that apply to a single man with a given proportion of average earnings (which are much higher in the other two countries). The long basic rate band in Britain is unusual. In the other countries, the starting rate is lower but it rises more or less continuously. Before 1979/80, the marginal rates on high incomes and the average rates charged on very high incomes were much higher in the UK than in these other countries. This is not now true, and the top marginal rate of tax on earned income of 60 per cent is no longer out of line with 50 per cent in the USA and 56 per cent in West Germany.

There is a second tax on earnings, however—national insurance contributions. These have a rate schedule of their own which since 1985 has included several rate bands. Someone with an income between £35·50 and £55 per week is taxed at 5 per cent, with a 7 per cent rate applying up to £90 and the full 9 per cent rate operating only on incomes over £90 per week. However, these bands operate differently from those of income tax. If your income is above the personal allowance for income tax, you pay only on the income that is above the threshold; but as soon as you reach a higher rate of national insurance contribution you pay tax at the higher rate on the whole of your income. It follows that someone who earns only £89 pays £6·23 (7 per cent of £89); someone who earns £91 pays £8·19 (9 per cent of £91). Since he also has to pay 60p in income tax on his additional £2 of earnings, he is likely to be worse off. Lower rates of contribution are payable by those who are contracted out of the State Earnings-Related Pension Scheme (SERPS; see Chapter 7). Investment income and pensions are not subject to national insurance contributions; the self-employed are required to meet a weekly poll tax of £3·50 and a surcharge of 6·3 per cent of earnings between £4,150 and £13,780.

Before we leave this issue, there is one further complication we should note. In the vast majority of pension schemes—public or private—benefits are based on final salary and are independent of contributions. In these cases, the contributions payable by an individual are simply a tax, albeit one paid to a pension fund rather than to the government. Since contributions to many pension schemes are 5 or 6 per cent of salary, this addition to the effective marginal rate of tax is far from negligible.

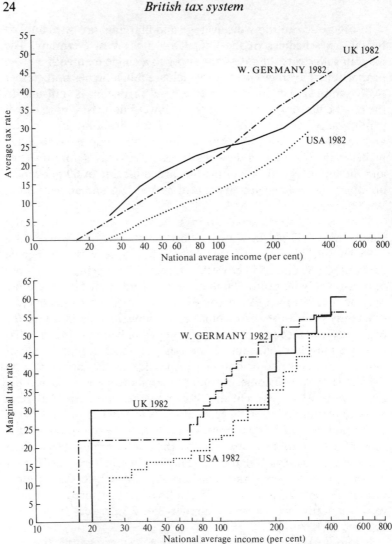

Fig. 2.2. Average and marginal rates of tax in different countries
Source: Inland Revenue, evidence to Treasury and Civil Service Committee, The Structure of Personal Income Taxation and Income Support, 1983.

In Figure 2.1, we show how the income tax schedule is modified by the existence of national insurance contributions. With this schedule, there is actually a range in which the average rate of tax falls. Someone who earns £13,000 per annum pays an average rate of tax of 34 per cent and a marginal rate of 39 per cent. Thereafter, the marginal rate falls to 30 per cent and because it is below the average rate, the average rate falls, until at an income of £18,000 it is 33 per cent. On higher incomes, the marginal rate of tax is 40 per cent or more and so the average rate rises once more. It is surprising that the lowest marginal rate of tax should be paid by someone who is within the top 5 per cent of the income distribution.

Employers as well as employees are required to pay national insurance contributions. These are progressive on individual earnings, with four rate bands: 5 per cent on earnings between £35·50 and £55; 7 per cent from £55 to £90; 9 per cent from £90 to £130, and 10·45 per cent thereafter. As with employee contributions your income determines the rate that applies to the whole of your earnings. This adds to the effective burden of income tax since, as we noted in Chapter 1, there is no substantive difference between employer and employee contributions in the long run. In Table 2.1 we show the total direct tax burden. The average tax rate at each level of income is the proportion of earnings taken in income tax and national insurance contributions. The marginal tax rate is calculated as the fraction of total employee remuneration (including national insurance contributions) that is taken in tax; it therefore measures the size of the wedge between what an employer has to pay and what his employee ultimately receives.

Table 2.1: *Average and marginal direct tax rates at various income levels*
(single person, no other allowances)

Income (£ per week)	Average tax rate (%)	Marginal tax rate (%)
50	16	39
75	27	41
100	35	44
150	41	45
200	43	45
300	44	37
500	47	49
750	52	59
1,000	56	64

The average tax rate rises steadily up to average earnings (around £180 per week). It is more or less flat until twice average earnings are reached, and climbs steadily thereafter. The marginal tax rate is generally between 40 and 50 per cent, and this is constant over a relatively broad range of incomes, with an extraordinary drop after the national insurance ceiling is reached but before higher rates begin. Most people, then, face a marginal direct tax rate of between 40 and 50 per cent; and this is increased still further by the effect of indirect taxes on the goods and services which income is used to buy. In Chapter 14 we consider the distributional impact of the tax system taken as a whole.

Families and children

So far, we have described the system simply as it relates to a single individual. We should now consider how it is modified in its application to households. In general, the British tax system starts from the premiss that a wife is a dependant of her husband. Thus the husband is responsible for submitting a return of their joint income and is liable for their joint tax. Any income of the wife's is aggregated with his, and in recognition of these obligations he is given an addition (£1,250 in 1985/6) to his personal allowance. There are two modifications to this general principle. One is 'wife's earned income relief'. A working wife receives a personal allowance of her own, equal to the personal allowance of the single individual, and this is available against her earnings (but not her investment income). There is no consequential reduction in the additional personal allowance given to the husband. The second modification is the availability of an option for separate taxation of the earned income of the two partners. Investment income continues to be added to the income of the husband, who receives only the personal allowance of the single man. Since this option implies the loss of the increment to the married man's personal allowance, it is only advantageous to a couple who would otherwise pay substantial amounts of higher rate tax: i.e. if their joint income exceeds about £25,000. We consider further in Chapter 14 the appropriate treatment of the tax unit.

The household may also include children. Their dependent status was traditionally recognized by conceding an additional allowance to a taxpayer who was responsible for the maintenance of a child. These allowances interacted somewhat uneasily with the system of family allowances, a weekly cash payment made to the mother through the Post Office. In 1979, these two allowances were integrated into a single child benefit, now £7 per week, payable in the same manner as family allowances.

The head of a single-parent family receives the additional personal allowance of £1,250 payable to a married man, but with unimportant exceptions this is the only allowance for dependent children that is now provided via the tax system. A single-parent family also receives an additional child benefit of £4·55 a week for the first child.

Children are taxed on their own income, as separate individuals. Obviously few children have amounts of income that exceed the exemption limits. To prevent avoidance of too blatant a kind, the investment income of children is taxed as if it had been received by the parents if it is derived from money that the child has been given by the parents. For a brief period, all investment income of children was taxed in this way, but this provision has now been repealed.

The tax base

For earned income, the definition of the income that is potentially subject to tax poses no particular problems. For investment income, the tax base primarily relates to interest, dividends, and net rents received. Capital gains are not subject to income tax; thus the dividend received from a share is subject to income tax, but any profit made on selling the share is not. Until 1965 such capital gains were generally exempt from tax; since then there has been a distinct capital gains tax. From 1982 gains are calculated after deduction of an 'indexation allowance' designed to reflect the impact of recent inflation on the value of the asset. The first £5,900 of the remaining gain is tax-free and the rest is charged to tax at 30 per cent. The distinction between income and capital gains is blurred, and someone who generates capital gains in a regular way of business may be deemed a trader and find his profits subjected to income tax. Regularity is broadly a sufficient definition of trading, but not a necessary one: the classic case in English law is of a man who made a shrewd purchase of toilet-paper in Germany—once—and whom the Revenue successfully charged with income tax on the resulting profit (*Rutledge* v. *CIR*, 1929).

The tax base is also modified by the existence of a number of minor allowances. In the USA, where such allowances are much more extensive—taxpayers there can, for example, deduct the amount of their medical expenses and their losses from theft—they have become known as 'tax expenditures'. The implicit or explicit suggestion is that such exemptions require justification of much the same kind as is given to positive items of government expenditure. Such allowances are available to the blind, for single-parent families, and to those who need and use the services of a housekeeper. Apart from the basic single and married personal allowances, the items of most significance, in both the amount of the tax expenditure involved and the number of taxpayers affected, are the allowances for mortgage interest and pension contributions. Historically, tax relief was available on all interest payments; and since interest receipts are taxable the logical case for permitting interest payments to be deductible is quite persuasive. In recent years, however, this relief has been systematically restricted, and it is now generally confined to interest on loans of up to £30,000 whose purpose is stated to be for the purchase or improvement of the taxpayer's main residence. An employee who contributes to a pension scheme approved by the Inland Revenue can deduct the whole of what he pays from his taxable income. Nor is he liable for tax on contributions that his employer makes on his behalf.

How tax is collected

For the vast majority of taxpayers, all or virtually all their earnings are from employment and tax is deducted by their employers under PAYE procedures. People in this category, with simple incomes and modest earnings, are normally required to make a return of income only every five years. When they first become potentially subject to tax, they will be asked to file a tax return. This is in general somewhat confusing, since the form appears to be principally concerned with their past income when in fact its actual purpose is to elicit their present circumstances with a view to establishing their future allowances. On the basis of this information the Revenue issues a 'notice of coding' to the taxpayer and to his employer. The notice of coding is a cryptic document, which concludes with a code number of the form 282H. The numerical part of this code is one-tenth of the taxpayer's total allowances for the year; the letter indicates marital status (H, higher for married men; L, lower for single persons or married women). But no action is required from the taxpayer: his employer will now deduct tax in the light of this coding using the tax tables with which he is supplied.

Before describing the basis of these tables, we should notice an important administrative difference between the ways in which the two taxes on earnings—income tax and national insurance contribution—are levied. Income tax is levied on a cumulative basis, so that the whole year's income is taken into account. So in computing liability, low earnings in one week will be offset against high earnings in the next, and vice versa. National insurance contributions are charged non-cumulatively, so that liability in each week depends only on earnings in that week, and is not affected by the amounts that are earned in earlier or later weeks. This is why students, who may have earnings that exceed the exemption limits for only a small number of weeks in the year, pay national insurance contributions but do not usually pay income tax; and why people who start work midway through a tax year pay less in the first months of employment than they do subsequently. An unusual feature of the British tax system is that income tax is not only levied on a cumulative basis, but also collected on a cumulative basis. In other countries it is common to levy tax cumulatively, but to collect it non-cumulatively: tax is paid each week on the basis of earnings in that week and if an adjustment is necessary when the whole year's income is assessed (as is often the case for those with fluctuating earnings) this is done at the end of the year.

The British tax system, by contrast, tries to ensure that at each point in the tax year an appropriate proportion of the whole year's liability has been paid. A non-cumulative system credits the taxpayer each week with $\frac{1}{52}$ of his annual allowances. The cumulative system does this also; but if income in any week is less than the allowance for the week then the excess is credited against tax that has previously been paid in the year, and a tax refund becomes due. If all the tax previously paid has been refunded, or at the beginning of the tax year when little or no tax has been paid, these unused allowances cannot be credited against earlier tax payments and are carried forward to be offset against taxable income in future weeks. It is therefore necessary to maintain throughout the year for each taxpayer a record of the total tax he has paid so far and the total allowances ('free pay') for which he has already been given credit. If these procedures work well, they ensure that by the end of the year the taxpayer will have paid the right amount of tax and no significant adjustment to his liability will be required. The advantages of a system that reaches the right answer in this automatic way are obvious. So are the problems: each taxpayer must carry with him from week to week and employment to employment records of his tax position for the year so far, and this is an expensive administrative operation.

The system works less smoothly when an individual's allowances change during the year (perhaps a male taxpayer marries). He must then inform the Inland Revenue which will revise his coding. He receives an immediate refund which reflects the tax he has overpaid in each week of the tax year so far. This system cannot operate in reverse for someone whose allowances go down (because he gets divorced, for example); if it did the taxpayer might have no net income for several weeks as previously underpaid tax was recouped. Broadly, he will be credited with the tax he *should* have paid so far, and the deficiency collected by a reduction in his allowances in future tax years. Fortunately, allowances rise in practice much more often than they fall.

Earnings from employment are taxed under what is known as schedule E. Earnings from business are taxed under schedule D. (The authors' salaries are taxed on schedule E but any royalties from this book fall under schedule D.) These terms, which derive from the income tax legislation of 1803, are not referred to in the forms or guidance supplied to the taxpayer, but are of some practical importance to him. A much wider range of expenses can be deducted under schedule D than E: under D the test is broadly that the expenditure was incurred for the purpose of earning the income, while under E it is necessary to suggest that one would be dismissed if one did not spend the money in that way; and in the case of expenditure on travel to work even that is not sufficient justification. Schedule D earnings are subject to a surcharge, described as national insurance contributions, of a flat weekly sum of £3·50 plus 6·3 per cent of earnings between £4,150 and £13,780. The administrative procedures for collection are quite different. Tax under schedule D is paid in two lump sums—for the tax year 1985/6 these would be due on 1 January 1986 and 1 July 1986. Liability is calculated on a 'preceding year' basis; thus these assessments would be based on earnings in the year 1984/5. Since business accounts take time to compile there is some reason for this. The tax therefore appears to be paid a year in arrears, which sounds a rather favourable option.

However, the system is in fact much more complicated and less advantageous to the self-employed than this would suggest. It is impossible to provide a brief and intelligible—or indeed lengthy and intelligible—description of the rules but a consequence is that in the early years of a business some components of income may be taxed two or even three times while others will not be taxed at all. This is obviously a licence for abuse.

The scope for abuse is much increased where partnership taxation is involved. The reason is that tax is in theory levied on the partnership rather than on the individual partners. Of course it is not really possible to do this in a system where there are personal allowances and progressive rates on individual income but the appearance is maintained by an elaborate apparatus which first disaggregates the calculation to the level of the individual partner and then adds up the answers. But a consequence is that the partnership may be deemed to have closed down and restarted when partners are added or leave (which in the case of a large partnership happens all the time). By a suitable choice of closing and restarting dates, a partnership with fluctuating profits—stockbrokers are particularly well placed—can arrange to pay tax twice on their poor years and not at all on their good years. A sample of partnership accounts examined by the comptroller and auditor-general showed that these partnerships had paid tax on 77 per cent of the profits that they had actually earned in the period in question (Public Accounts Committee, 1977). The 1985 Finance Act reduced opportunities for this kind of abuse without altering the underlying problem.

The principle of getting hold of the money before the taxpayer has a chance to spend it is applied as far as possible to investment income also. Most payers of interest (except that on certain kinds of National Savings) are required to deduct and transmit to the Revenue the basic rate tax due before sending the balance to the lender. It is interesting to note that one security—War Loan—is exempt from this requirement and stands at a premium in consequence. This tax can be reclaimed by any one not liable to tax; higher-rate taxpayers will be assessed for an additional charge. The treatment of company dividends is more complicated (see pp. 164–6 below) but the effect is the same. A different arrangement is applied to bank and building society interest. In return for a negotiated payment by banks and building societies (the so-called composite rate) their interest is exempted from basic rate tax. No refund is available to

those who are not liable to tax, who would therefore be well advised
to deposit their money elsewhere (but are often not well advised).
Investment income is also taxed on a preceding year basis, though
there are some minor differences between the methods used here and
those for schedule D income.

Administrative problems

The administration of any tax system is an inevitable butt for criticism, but there are two characteristics of British tax administration
that can be given objective description. Few people understand how
it works, and it is very expensive. The first of these propositions is
easily documented.

In the 1950s the Government Social Survey concluded that 'our
evidence suggests that if productivity is related to income tax in any
way it can only be related to misconceptions about the system. It
cannot be related to the system because only 3 or 4 per cent are
sufficiently informed of the system' (Radcliffe Report, 1954, App. 1,
para. 129). Brown (1968) also found almost total ignorance of the
rates or operation of the tax structure; though Lewis (1978) indicates
that the administrative changes of 1973 (the unified tax system)
may have increased understanding. And in spite of the apparent
advantages to him of a wholly automatic system of tax deduction,
the bewildered British taxpayer is in contact with the Inland Revenue
more frequently than his American counterpart (four times as often,
according to the estimates of Barr *et al.*, 1977). The American taxpayer must complete a return every year, but normally that is the
only correspondence with the Internal Revenue Service that he has.

Why is British tax administration so complicated? It is easy to
reply that this is because of the extensive demands made on it, and
this is a continuing theme of annual Inland Revenue reports. But
we do not agree that the system is so complex because it is so fair;
indeed it is complexity which is a principal source of inequity. (The
taxation of partnerships is a good example—the opportunities for
abuse are entirely the product of an unnecessarily tortuous administrative mechanism.) And in its central elements, the British tax
system is actually rather simpler than that of most countries. The
range of allowances available is very limited and the rate structure
straightforward. It is peripheral elements which are the obstacle to
understanding. Although the system of cumulative PAYE has some

advantages, it has the effect that the weekly deductions made from wages are computed on a basis which is not explained or in practice explicable to the average worker. The interaction of cumulative income tax deductions with non-cumulative national insurance contributions computed on different principles aggravates this. The schedular system and the preceding year basis require professional tax expertise for adequate comprehension, and indeed description of them is to be found only in technical literature. The representative taxpayer rarely makes a tax return, and as a rule does not see any statement of how his liabilities have been computed. Filling in such a return is not a purposive activity: it does not enable the recipient to check how much tax he owes or is owed, or indeed to do anything except post the form back to the tax inspector, and it is therefore not surprising that this generates irritation rather than understanding. It is extraordinary that the design of tax forms that do allow the respondent to check his liabilities is left to commercial organizations such as the magazine *Money Which*. The appearance of both the tax return and the accompanying instructions compare very unfavourably with similar documents in other countries (though there have been recent improvements). But it remains difficult to resist the conclusion that the Inland Revenue does not feel that its work could be helped if the taxpayer had a better understanding of the basis or methods of collection of the taxes involved.

Collection costs absorb about 2 per cent of income tax receipts. While this proportion may not seem high, judged by either international or historical standards it is a substantial figure. It is twice as great as in Sweden or Canada and four times as great as in the USA; and the US Internal Revenue Service and the UK Inland Revenue employ similar numbers of staff although there are four times as many taxpayers in America. These calculations leave out administrative costs imposed on taxpayers (which are certainly higher in the USA) and on employers (which are probably higher in the UK). Sandford (1973) suggests that the total administrative costs of UK income tax are in the range of 4 to 6 per cent of revenue.

Why are costs so much higher in the UK than in the USA? One reason that is often given is that the USA employs 'self-assessment'. It is not clear to us exactly what people have in mind when they talk about 'self-assessment', but the American system is, at least at first sight, very different from the one that operates here. At the end of year, every taxpayer is responsible for completing a tax return, calculating the tax due, and posting a cheque, or more frequently claiming a refund, from the Internal Revenue Service (IRS). But it is wrong to suppose that costs are lower in the USA because the taxpayer does the calculations instead of the taxman. In a world of microcircuitry, arithmetic is cheap, and indeed the IRS checks the calculations on every return before it accepts them. To see what the significant differences between the two administrative mechanisms are we need to probe more deeply.

One reason that costs are so much lower in the USA than in the UK is that the IRS makes extensive use of computers while its British counterpart does not. Plans to computerize the operation of PAYE have been under discussion since the early 1960s. It seems likely that they will actually come into effect by the end of the 1980s, at the end of an extraordinary saga of delay, disaster, and policy reversal. This is not the only area in which the British government has found large-scale computerization projects difficult to implement—computerization of social security has also encountered substantial problems, and the history of vehicle and driver registration is already legendary, although VAT, which has been efficiently computerized from inception, is a conspicuous exception to a generally unhappy tale. The reasons would deserve a book in themselves but two inter-related problems seem paramount. The first is that the organization and training of the British civil service yields almost no one who combines understanding of policy with experience of computer system design. The second is a tendency to pursue solutions that are over-centralized and over-sophisticated.

Both characteristics are evident in Inland Revenue computerization. The delay in implementing a strategy has not been used as an opportunity to consider new administrative or policy options, but rather as an excuse for postponing them. The scheme to be used involves a small network of very large computers with sophisticated communications between them and to local offices. Something of this kind was necessary when the sheer volume of computation involved in tax assessment was beyond the capacity of any but the largest of computers, but this is no longer the case. We believe a more flexible system, and one better adapted to the greater integration with social security, which we discuss in Chapter 7, would be achieved by the provision of intelligent terminals in local offices.

The second major reason that American administrative costs are lower than British is derived from a major difference of overall approach. In the USA, the primary source of information is the taxpayer's annual return, and although there is an extensive network of reporting of income paid and of deducting tax at source this is for the purposes of detecting fraud and facilitating collection. In the UK, payers of income are the primary information source, the system seeks to extract the exact amount of tax due at this stage, and the annual return of income is subsidiary (which is why many taxpayers are not required to make one). The origins of this difference are historical. Britain was the first country in the world to adopt an income tax, and it was then a flat-rate tax on certain kinds of income. Because there was considerable resistance to the disclosure of personal affairs involved in making a return of income it was natural to collect it from those who paid the income rather than those who received it—and this indirect method of collection was how all taxes had previously been administered.

By contrast, the American federal income tax was introduced in 1913 and was conceived from the beginning as a progressive tax on the total income of individuals. It was therefore an obvious procedure to require an annual return of that income from the individuals concerned. The British income tax was in the process of acquiring a similar character. But there had never been a fundamental review of the suitability of the whole administrative structure for the purposes of a modern fiscal system, and there has still never been one. The framework of tax legislation and administration is still based on Addington's construction of 1803.

Thus Britain imposes extensive responsibilities on those who pay income, and the administrative mechanisms seek to ensure that as far as possible the exact amount of tax due is deducted at that stage. Most other countries impose some reporting obligations on payers of income and require some 'withholding' of tax to ensure that the tax is collected before the associated income has been spent. But since they ultimately rely on the taxpayer's own returns of income, they are not too concerned if the reporting mechanisms are occasionally imperfect or the amounts withheld are inaccurate. The major contrast is between exact withholding without general end-of-year assessment—the British system—and approximate withholding with universal end-of-year assessment—the American system, which is usually favoured elsewhere.

The principal merit of the British system is that it imposes minimal demands on the taxpayer. He does not know how it is that he pays what he does, but he does not need to know. But there are a range of substantial disadvantages. If withholding is to work, it is necessary to have a single basic rate for the vast majority of taxpayers—a company cannot be notified of the different marginal rates of tax of all of its shareholders. We shall argue in subsequent chapters that this is not an unduly serious restriction. More seriously, the absence of any general end-of-year assessment constrains the solution to a whole series of problems. How can we reform local authority finance? How can we achieve a sensible relationship between the tax and social security systems? How can we establish independent sources of finance for devolved assemblies? And the experience of other countries suggests very clearly that it is more expensive to maintain the apparatus required to achieve exact withholding than to accept lower standards of withholding and process an annual return from every taxpayer. For these reasons, Eire is the only other country to have followed the British model.

We believe Britain should bring its procedures into line with the rest of the world. That requires, as a first stage, the abolition of the schedular system, by which different rules are applied to different kinds of income, and liability is based on the sum of incomes which were received in a hotchpotch of different years. We propose instead that tax due in any year should be based on income in that year, with an annual assessment of an individual's total income. Many people will find it incredible that this does not already happen. If the present system did not exist, it is inconceivable that any one would propose it should be introduced.

The second step is the abolition of the cumulative PAYE system. Under a non-cumulative PAYE system, an individual would be credited each week with $\frac{1}{52}$ of his annual allowances, so that a person with a single personal allowance of £2,205 would be allowed up to £42·40 per week tax-free. He would pay tax at the 30 per cent basic rate on the excess, so that with earnings of £50 in a week the tax due would be £2·28. If income accrues evenly throughout the year, he will pay just the right amount of tax. With a progressive tax system, however, a worker whose earnings fluctuate from week to week may pay too much tax. If his 'good' weeks push him into a higher tax bracket, the rate at which he pays extra tax on his extra earnings will be greater than the rate at which his liability falls in the 'bad' weeks, and hence he would be due a refund of overpaid tax at the end of the year. Surprisingly, in countries where this operates this 'over-withholding' and consequential refund is generally rather popular with taxpayers (Barr *et al.*, 1977, p. 143). But we have already seen that to make the British withholding system work it is necessary that most taxpayers should pay the same basic rate of tax—which means that over-withholding would rarely arise. We can only operate a cumulative PAYE system, it seems, if we do not need one.

We believe these reforms are necessary and desirable within the context of the present income tax system. We also think it essential that computerization be introduced as fast as possible. These administrative changes are prerequisites for the more fundamental structural reforms that we discuss in subsequent chapters. The Inland Revenue's principal administrative objection to our proposals for an expenditure tax is apparently that it would require annual returns from all taxpayers (Commissioners of Inland Revenue, 1979). We cannot imagine that they are unaware that this is currently the general practice in every other major country in the western world.

The black economy

There is evidence of increasing concern about the growth of the 'black economy'. The black economy includes the moonlighting plumber who expects to be paid in cash, the waiter who fails to declare his tips, the barmaid who is paid from the till at the end of the evening; all those areas of legal activity from which tax is properly due but from which it is not collected because the income in question is not declared. By the nature of the phenomenon itself, it is hard to find evidence on the extent of the black economy. But in research, as elsewhere, fools rush in where angels fear to tread. In order to protect ourselves from possible libel actions, we leave it to the reader to distinguish one from the other in the following account of evidence on the subject.

It is sometimes suggested that trends in the black economy can be inferred from movements in the use of notes and coin in payments. The most obvious point to be made is that for a long period the volume of transactions has increased more rapidly than the use of notes and coin. Thus the prima-facie case to be made from these data is that the black economy has been steadily declining. A much more likely explanation is that changes in money transmission habits in the legitimate economy, particularly the increased use of cheques and credit cards, have reduced people's needs for cash. With some strain on credulity, writers such as Feige (1979) have reinterpreted this information to assert that the black economy is large and growing. While that might be true, the problem of estimating demand for money functions has already produced one of the largest and least conclusive literatures in economics, and the notion that this can be done with sufficient accuracy to enable trends in the black economy to be inferred from the residual is absurd.

The Central Statistical Office has claimed to have detected 'a glimpse of the hidden economy in the national accounts' by comparing income- and expenditure-based estimates of national product (MacAfee, 1980). While at first sight this sounds promising, more careful consideration of how black economy transactions are recorded, if at all, suggests that some would be recorded as income only, others as expenditure only, and some as neither, depending on the precise measurement techniques employed. It is also unfortunate, if not surprising, that statistical revisions subsequent to the publication of the article have largely eliminated the discrepancies on which its findings were based. The article's title, though modest, is perhaps not modest enough. The chairman of the Board of Inland Revenue suggested in 1979 that the black economy might be 7½ per cent of national income, a figure subsequently modified to a 6 to 8 per cent range. This figure, although often repeated, does not appear to be based on any survey or on other evidence and in the absence of any substantiation no real weight can be given to it.

A different approach was adopted by Dilnot and Morris (1981) who examined the income and expenditure records of households that spent significantly more than they claimed to earn. Discrepancies of this sort for which there was no other apparent justification were sufficient to account for between 2 and 3 per cent of recorded income. This painstaking micro-economic research seems to us much more likely to identify the black economy than generalizations based on broad aggregates or anecdotes, but it suffers from the difficulty that people engaged in large-scale tax fraud are unlikely to participate voluntarily in surveys of their income and expenditure, whatever guarantees of confidentiality they may be given.

Tax authorities have the great advantage that, unlike academic researchers, they can compel people to have their income surveyed.

By far the most substantial study of the black economy is the American Taxpayer Compliance Measurement Programme (IRS, 1979). This computes the additional income recorded, and tax assessed, when households are subject to detailed audit of their affairs, and uses statistical techniques to estimate the total income and revenue which would be obtained if the whole population could be subjected to infinitely detailed scrutiny. The Internal Revenue Service concludes that between 91 and 94 per cent of income from legal sources is reported to it.

These indications that the black economy may be quite small may come as a surprise to the many people who bore their friends, and the authors of this book, with endless stories about people who demand payment in cash, although the view that all cash transactions are outside the formal economy is as fallacious as the belief that all cheque transactions are reported to the Inland Revenue. It is a fact that most economic activity in the UK is in the hands of large organizations which as a matter of course comply with legal requirements to report income and output and to withhold tax. This concentration is not wholly a desirable fact; and the black economy, if kept within very limited bounds, is not necessarily to be regretted. The existence of small amounts of economic activity on which the marginal rate of tax is zero, much of which would simply not be undertaken at all if it were confined to the formal economy, may reduce the disincentive effects of taxation. When this achieves proportions that encourage large-scale fraud or lead to a cumulative collapse of the moral force of the tax system, our reactions should be rather different; what is the honest taxpayer in Italy to do? But there is nothing more likely to encourage such fraud and such collapse than the wide circulation of exaggerated, and unfounded, reports of the extent of 'black' activities.

Nor, it should be stressed, is it worth spending £1 to collect £1 in tax. The money paid in salary to the revenue investigator, or the social security snooper, represents resources diverted from productive activity; the money they retrieve from the illicit window-cleaner is simply a transfer from his pocket to the wallets of better-disciplined taxpayers. The proper measure of the product of such expenditure is the cost—in administrative costs, in compliance costs, and in the resulting distortion of economic activity—of collecting that same revenue by other means.

Tax avoidance

Poor people who engage in the black economy are illegally evading
tax. Richer people diminish their tax liabilities by legal tax avoidance. Like the black economy, tax avoidance has come under increasing scrutiny. The mechanisms by which Lord Vestey, the
'master butcher' and one of Britain's richest men, has avoided paying
any significant amounts of tax over an extended period have been
given much publicity. So too have the activities of Roy Tucker and
his Rossminster Group, who were leaders in the construction of
elaborate avoidance schemes in which convoluted series of artificial
transactions were devised with no ultimate consequence other than
the creation of a tax deduction for the customer, a profit to the
inventor of the schemes, and a loss to other taxpayers. Extreme cases
of this kind have now come to an end, under the twin blows of a—
literal—frontal assault on Tucker's premises by representatives of
the Inland Revenue and rulings by the House of Lords that transactions that have no shred of commercial motive are not effective
for tax purposes.

We shall stress at other points in this book the importance of
looking at how the tax system actually works, and that this is particularly important in examining its effects at the upper end of the
income distribution. But we should make the general observation
that, as Kaldor put it, 'the existence of widespread tax avoidance is
evidence that the system, not the taxpayer, stands in need of radical
reform' (Kaldor, 1980, p. 18). Tax avoidance cannot be defeated by
appeals to the conscience of taxpayers—nor should it. The annual
accretion of new provisions to deal with recently discovered avoidance devices is inevitably ineffective also; the Revenue puts itself in
the position of men who go to shut the stable door every time they
see a horse bolting.

The taxation of earnings

Some of the most important changes to have occurred in the structure of income taxation in the UK in the last ten years are the reductions in the highest rates of tax. In 1979, the rate of tax on earnings rose to 83 per cent; since investment income was subject to a 15 per cent surcharge the maximum rate of income tax was 98 per cent. The highest rate of tax on any form of income is now 60 per cent. This seems a rather inegalitarian move, and this was certainly part of its intention. But it should also be seen as a move towards realism in taxation.

We think it should be obvious to any one who stops to think about the matter for a few minutes that it is entirely impracticable to tax things at 98 per cent. The pressure to avoid tax becomes so strong that virtually any avoidance scheme becomes worth while, and no aspect of the activity is of any importance other than its tax implications. Even if as a result of measures for avoidance four-fifths of the receipts disappear, the after-tax returns have been multiplied tenfold; and if finding loopholes is so profitable it will prove impossible to stop them up.

We hope that these new moderate levels of maximum rates persist. But we doubt it, and suspect that further political changes will bring further changes in this part of the tax schedule. The reason is that this debate is conducted in a political fantasy world, in which one side professes to believe that these high rates have massive disincentive effects on economic behaviour and on innovation and enterprise in the UK economy, while the other asserts that they are a necessary mechanism for achieving redistribution and a fair distribution of the overall tax burden. There is very little evidence to support either of these propositions. They ignore the central fact about these apparently punitive rates; they are unenforced and unenforceable. They have principally been paid by senior managers in large corporations, and it is doubtful whether these people are primarily motivated by the likely effects of their additional effort on their after-tax earnings. Thus the disincentive effects are much less than often suggested. On the other hand, if one identified the wealthiest individuals in the UK one would find rather few senior managers among them. In consequence, these very high tax rates have had, and are capable of having, very little effect on inequalities in living standards. We argue these points in more detail in Chapters 3 and 4, and return in Chapter 5 to assess the consequences and point to needed reforms.

A more technical change in income tax rules has proved to be almost as important for senior managers as these reductions in the higher rates of tax. Suppose a company's shares stand at 120p. A company may give its executives an option on these shares. Suppose it gives them an option to buy 100,000 shares at 100p in five years' time. This means that the executives may, if they wish, buy the shares at that date at that price. Suppose the company has done well and the shares are worth 200p. Then the managers can exercise their options, and realize an immediate profit of £100,000. If, on the other hand, the company has performed badly and the share price is only 50p, then they do not have to exercise the option. They may, and should, choose to throw it away, in which case they gain nothing and lose nothing.

It is apparent that an option is a valuable asset, and indeed there are options markets in which rights of this kind are bought and sold. Prior to 1980, anyone receiving such an option would have to pay tax on its value. Now, however, you pay tax only on the gain you make if you eventually exercise the option, and if the scheme meets certain Inland Revenue rules you need pay only capital gains tax, at 30 per cent, on the profit. These concessions have made such options very attractive to managers, and most large companies now have option schemes. The result is that managers have made profits very substantially larger than anything they might have received in salary. Sir Michael Edwardes, for example, was offered 21·9 million options at 14p per share on becoming chairman of Dunlop. Within weeks a bid was made for the company at a much higher price, and Sir Michael had made a paper profit of over £3 million. Under pressure from other shareholders, he agreed to relinquish the options.

The option is only valuable if the company's share price rises, so that the manager has an incentive to see the company do well; and indeed this is often used as justification for such schemes. The incentive would, however, be greater if the manager lost money if the shares went down, as well as making money if the shares went up—as he would if he were in the same position as other share-holders. Moreover, a firm that paid its executives a substantial salary, or a profit-related bonus, would be able to deduct the sum against corporation tax; whereas no such deduction is available for the cost of share options. Thus for a corporation tax-paying company the tax advantage to the manager may be offset by an additional cost to the company. It is possible that the popularity of such schemes reflects as much the opportunity to pay large sums to managers in politically inconspicuous ways as any other advantages they may have.

Taxation and effort

The effects of income taxation on work effort are a continuing subject of concern and discussion. This is not surprising—'reduce my taxes so that I can work harder' is generally a more winning argument than 'reduce my taxes so that I can be better off'. Unfortunately, this makes this an area in which it is hard to disentangle rhetoric from evidence.

In Chapter 1 we described how an income tax would affect work effort in two ways. The income effect describes the way in which tax reduces the taxpayer's real income. It leads him to take less leisure and to do more work, in order to maintain his standard of living, and is a function of the average rate of tax. The substitution effect depends on the way in which tax makes additional work less attractive than additional leisure and is related to the marginal tax rate. This analysis suggests that if we wish to identify those people on whom the effects of taxation on effort are likely to be greatest, we should look at cases where the substitution effect dominates the income effect—typically, where the marginal tax rate substantially exceeds the average rate. It is not necessarily there, however, that most economic damage is likely to be done by taxation. This will occur at the points where the marginal rate of tax is highest and hence the substitution effects are greatest. The total damage done will depend on the numbers of people falling into such categories as well as the size of the effect.

We now turn to the actual British tax structure. High marginal rates are encountered in Britain at income levels where higher rate tax begins to bite effectively—at incomes of £20,000 and above at 1985/6 rates—and increasingly at higher incomes. But they arise also at below-average income levels (those below £6,000 per annum). The reason that this latter group may pose a problem is not due solely to the operation of the income tax—the rate faced by people in this category is much the same as that for those on somewhat higher incomes—but to its interaction with the wide range of *ad hoc* means-tested benefits that exists in the UK. Since these benefits are gradually (or in some cases suddenly) withdrawn as income increases, there is an 'implicit tax rate' applicable to each benefit. This 'implicit tax rate' is the proportion of any rise in income which is lost as a result of an offsetting reduction in benefit. These rates vary from item to item. They include 50 per cent for family income supplement (FIS), and may be as high as 42 per cent for housing benefit, and it is quite possible for several to be operating simultaneously. Each of these involves a different means test, with somewhat different criteria, so that the actual marginal tax rate faced by a low-paid worker may be anything between zero and a figure above 100 per cent depending in an arbitrary way on his particular combination of income and family and other circumstances. (This is the so-called 'poverty trap', discussed in Chapter 7.) But the typical rate is clearly in excess of those applicable at higher incomes. So the function that relates the marginal tax rate to the income of a UK employee is U-shaped: the rate of tax he pays on additional earnings is high at low incomes, falls as income grows towards average income, where it stabilizes at around 39 per cent, before rising again with higher rates of tax.

Disincentive effects will therefore be most marked at the lowest and the highest levels of income. It is to these—especially the former—that most attention has been given in empirical work. Most people in full-time employment work just under forty hours a week, and variations in hours of work over the year come more from differences in lengths of holiday or periods of sickness than from changes of hours worked per week. Individuals may not be completely free to choose their hours of work. Hence it seems likely that hours worked will be relatively unresponsive to changes in wages and hence taxes. This does not mean, however, that a progressive tax system has few disincentive effects. A change in wages leads to both an income and a substitution effect. It is the substitution effect that matters when assessing the welfare consequences of progressive taxation. Only by estimating the sizes of these two effects separately can we judge the likely impact of the various tax systems. Even if hours worked remained approximately constant, if this results from offsetting income and substitution effects then the efficiency costs (dead-weight loss) imposed by taxation can be substantial.

To examine this issue requires an econometric study of the effects of changes in wages on the number of hours worked. Such investigations raise rather difficult technical issues of estimation and there is, as yet, no consensus as to the likely size of the substitution effects. There are three main problems with these econometric studies. The first is that the budget constraint that a household faces is likely in practice to be highly non-linear. This may result from a progressive marginal rate structure of the income tax but can also result from the existence of means-tested benefits. As a result the marginal wage of an individual is determined at the same time as his hours of work. Techniques to deal with this problem have been developed by Hausman (1981) and he finds substantial substitution effects which roughly offset the income effect. The second problem is that households are choosing to supply labour not just in the current period but throughout their life-cycle. The effect of a change in wages on labour supply may depend upon whether that change is perceived as a permanent or a temporary change. The temporary change may induce a much larger increase in labour supply while the earner takes advantage of a transitorily high earnings opportunity. A permanent change may have much less effect and might even induce the individual to consume more leisure over his lifetime. Although it is sometimes possible to obtain data on an individual for several years in succession (known as 'panel data') it is difficult to infer from a small number of observations the likely response of labour supply over the whole lifetime. The final problem is that very few surveys actually contain observations on the wage rate. The typical survey contains an estimate of earnings and hours worked, and the wage rate is obtained by dividing one by the other. Any errors in the measurement of hours worked—the variable we are trying to explain—will lead to corresponding errors in the estimated wage rate— the explanatory variable—which can lead to serious biases in the estimated effect of wages on hours worked.

It is difficult to believe that econometric study has yet arrived at a definitive conclusion as to the effect of taxes on labour supply. Much interesting research is being carried out (see Hausman, 1981, and Blundell *et al.*, 1984) but much remains to be done.

Although this econometric evidence is suggestive, it cannot be regarded as decisive. We have noted that there are technical problems involved in statistical studies of this kind and these may bias the conclusions towards insignificant results. Moreover, the studies are necessarily concerned with easily measurable dimensions of performance at work, such as hours of work or earnings in a particular occupation. If workers are deterred from seeking or accepting promotion by the effects of taxation, then this will not be adequately measured by these methods (though it seems improbable that incentive effects, if large, would be confined to those items that cannot easily be appraised). Further, the hours and the effort that people put in at work are closely related to group norms; if these norms are influenced by the existence of taxation, as seems quite likely, then there may be effects on group behaviour which are not fully observable in the actions of individual workers. Although an individual may not be able to choose to work a seven- or a nine-hour shift rather than one that lasts for eight hours, the reason for adopting some particular shift length will be related to the wishes of workers generally; if taxes were different, it is very possible that most people would want to work for longer or shorter periods and that the normal shift length would be changed.

A final, but very important, reservation is that much of our discussion so far—theoretical and empirical—relates to what we might describe as 'primary' workers: people who may decide to work more or less but for whom the question of whether or not they enter the labour force is not in doubt. But there are also 'secondary' workers— married women are the most important group in this category— who may choose to work or not according to a range of considerations which will clearly include financial ones. For such workers, what affects their decision to enter the labour force is not any marginal rate of tax but the average rate of tax on the whole of their earnings. This may, depending on the treatment of the tax unit, be affected by the earnings of the husband (in the UK it is). The influences on these work/leisure decisions are rather different, although the operation of income and substitution effects may be similar in its end result—taxation by reducing the net earnings of the husband encourages the wife to work but by reducing the net earnings of the wife has a disincentive effect also. The empirical evidence suggests that this aspect of labour supply is much more sensitive to changes in wage rates or taxes than the hours or effort of primary workers: these are determined mainly by conventional expectations and fixed commitments of the family, while it is the wife's labour supply that provides the margin at which adjustments are made and where the main effects of changes in incentives are likely to be observed.

Somewhat different considerations arise in evaluating incentive effects at the other point in the income distribution at which they may potentially be important—near the top. Here we are primarily concerned with managers. We are also more concerned with the quality of effort than with its quantity. The performance of a senior manager may often depend less on how long he spends in the office than on how well he works when he is there—though there may, but need not, be some correlation between the two. His incentive to do better lies not in overtime payments for extra hours but in the hope of promotion and, to a much greater extent than for lower-paid workers, in the intrinsic satisfaction of the job itself. These factors mean that it is much harder, and more subjective, to assess the effects of taxation on managerial effort. Experimental studies are excluded, and there is no body of data that is even potentially available for econometric assessment. Such evidence as exists is derived from interview surveys, which are not (here as in many other economic contexts) a very satisfactory method of investigation: they can reveal attitudes to taxation, but these are not necessarily good indicators of what people actually do. Thus a recent survey (Opinion Research Centre, 1977) established that those with high incomes were more likely to consider the present income tax 'not sensible' but that is neither surprising nor very helpful.

The most carefully designed surveys of the impact of taxation on the higher-paid are those of Break (1957) and Fields and Stanbury (1971). Both these are studies of British solicitors and accountants. These groups are likely to be relatively well-informed about the tax system, and are also in a better position than most to vary their effort and hours of work. Break found that only 13 per cent of his sample made plausible reports of disincentive effects of taxation and that the proportion credibly describing incentive effects was almost as great. However, the former (though not the latter) proportion rose substantially with income, as the theoretical analysis would suggest it should, and reached 30 per cent for those with incomes over £5,000 a year. (This is equivalent to around £40,000 at 1985 prices. In 1956 it implied a marginal tax rate of about 70 per cent;

the effective rate on such an income would now be 55 per cent.) Fields and Stanbury replicated Break's work in 1968, and found that disincentive effects had significantly increased: the proportion of their sample reporting these was 19 per cent, and this increase occurred primarily among those on moderate incomes; the fraction among the highest income group remained at 30 per cent. These figures tell us the number of people who plausibly claim that taxation affects their work effort. They do not, however, tell us the magnitude of the effect on those who are influenced; and they are difficult to interpret adequately because they fail to distinguish income and substitution effects. Nevertheless, they are consistent with the hypothesis that was supported for low-income earners: disincentive effects exist, but they are not substantial. A further indication is provided by the observations both of Break and of Fields and Stanbury that the hours of work of those reporting disincentives differed little from the rest of their sample. They interpreted this as implying that those most affected were by nature more hard-working; there are alternative, and less disturbing, explanations.

A somewhat different kind of interview study is that of Fiegehen and Reddaway (1981). A selection of companies were approached to ask what difficulties they had experienced as a result of the impact of taxation on their senior executives. They were particularly concerned with cases where managers emigrated, or refused to return from overseas postings, or where suitable candidates were reluctant to accept senior positions. They discovered that the incidence of such problems was negligible. This will surprise only those politicians and industrialists who have repeatedly asserted the opposite. It would be surprising if large numbers of men aged 45–55 were willing to tear up their roots and transfer their families to another country in order to earn larger salaries unless under very acute financial pressure; and even more surprising if people with successful careers in industry declined to join the board because they thought the additional after-tax remuneration inadequate.

This does not demonstrate that high rates of tax on senior managers have no adverse effects. It is evident from Britain's economic performance that the quality of industrial management in the UK has been relatively poor, while Britain's international reputation in the professions, the provision of financial services, and in academic studies is comparatively high. It is possible to argue that industrial management is intrinsically less attractive than these alternative careers, and that the British tax system has made it difficult to offer the material rewards which are used in other countries to offset this.

Our discussion of disincentive effects so far relates to the amount of work that people do, given that they choose some particular occupation. But the effects of taxation on whether they choose that occupation at all may be of as much or more practical importance. There are three levels of choice in this decision. First, there is the issue of whether people choose to live in the UK rather than in some more lightly taxed jurisdiction—the effects of taxation on the decision to emigrate. Second, given that people live in the UK there is the question of whether they choose to work at all or not; we have already noted this possibility for 'secondary' workers, but retirement is also a decision that may be postponed or brought forward in the light of financial considerations influenced by taxation, and this was one of the effects noted by Break. There is a growing body of evidence to suggest that the retirement decision is sensitive both to tax rates and to the relationship between pension entitlement and earnings from work done after the official retirement age (the 'earnings rule' and similar provisions) (Zabalza *et al.*, 1979). Unlike most disincentive effects, which depend on marginal rates of tax, 'all-or-nothing' decisions to emigrate or to retire are principally determined by average rates of tax on the whole of earnings—it is difficult for most people to retire a little more or a little less and impossible to emigrate a little more or a little less.

A further issue is the way in which taxation affects choices between jobs. It is well known (for example, Goldthorpe *et al.*, 1970) that car factories, as one example, tend to recruit workers who attach especially great importance to financial rewards and give low priority to a satisfying work environment. Income taxes substantially reduce the differential between jobs like these and others which are less well paid but more congenial. Some friends of the authors are badly paid academics rather than well-paid tax inspectors because they do not feel that the net addition to their income would compensate them for the loss of their friends and fulfilment in their work. High marginal tax rates will make it more difficult to recruit people to these less attractive occupations, though it is important to note that a society that feels it needs to recruit a certain number of tax inspectors will therefore be forced to raise their pre-tax salaries and thus part of the incidence of the income tax will fall on the employer rather than the employee.

Fringe benefits

If cash income is taxed, then employers have an incentive to pay in kind rather than in money. Tax law has come to recognize this, and if a firm pays for its employees' groceries they will find that they have to pay tax just as they would if they had been given cash to settle the supermarket bill. But a plethora of fringe benefits still exist. There are a range of items that are necessary for work but that also yield personal utility. This boundary was explored in a celebrated case by a female barrister who argued that the dowdy clothes she was required to wear in court should not be treated as part of her personal wardrobe; but the House of Lords ruled that even if they failed to provide the benefits of *haute couture* she derived warmth and decency from them, and hence they should be seen as items of consumption rather than tools of her trade.

But a rigid boundary cannot be defined. The light and heat provided in an office or a factory substitute for the light and heat you would otherwise need to pay for at home, but no one would seriously propose you be taxed on the benefit you derive from them. But what about the space where you park your car, or the meals that you eat while at work, or the nursery that looks after your children—all areas of contention?

The most important of these kinds of fringe benefit are company cars. There are some employees—such as travelling salesmen—for whom a car is a tool of the trade. But cars are now provided by companies for the majority of executives (Table 3.1) in the private sector. Such provision is subject to tax based on a scale charge related to the size or cost of the car, and the tax saving from company car provision, though real, is now modest (Ashworth and Dilnot, 1986). It may, moreover, be dissipated in the two kinds of inefficiency generated by fringe benefit provision. Because the tax advantage makes the good that is the subject of the fringe benefit relatively cheap, too much of it will be consumed relative to other commodities. Companies will be expected to buy more expensive cars for their employees than the employees would buy for themselves from taxed income, and there is clear evidence that this is what they do. At the same time, the type and perhaps even the make of cars individuals have will be determined by their status in the company rather than by their—variable—personal preferences for cars. It is because it both distorts and diminishes choice that payment through fringe benefits is an inefficient method of employee remuneration.

Table 3.1: *Fringe benefits for company directors, 1984*

Benefits at least as great as:	Provided by per cent of companies
6 months' salary if ill	97
½ director's pension for widow	97
Free petrol for private use	82
Free medical checks	74
Life cover of 4×salary	73
Car worth £14,000	72
½ salary permanently if ill	64
Medical insurance for self and spouse	64
Pension of ⅔ salary after 20 years	63
Pension contributions at least 20% of earnings	57
Free advice on personal finance	47

Source: T. Vernon Harcourt, *Top Management Remuneration 1984–5*, Charterhouse J. Rothschild, 1984.

Some fringe benefits are job-related—concessionary coal for miners, or air travel for airline employees, or discounts for shop workers— and the tax system tends to take a benign view of these. Others are legitimated by explicit concession, such as pensions, life insurance, and other dependants' benefits. The incentive to provide fringe benefits increases with the marginal rate of tax, and so we would expect fringe benefits to increase as a proportion of total salary as incomes increase.

Table 3.1, which shows the range and generosity of benefits provided for company directors, demonstrates that this does indeed appear to be true, and it is common for those recruiting for high-level appointments to talk about a 'remuneration package' rather than a salary. But we should also expect a reduction in top marginal rates of tax to reduce the incidence of fringe benefits, and this does not seem to have occurred (Table 3.2). Possibly benefit provision has come to reflect status rather than the pursuit of economically rational payment systems. By diverting money that might otherwise be paid as salary into conspicuous items of consumption—company cars, longer holidays, and lavish expenditure on offices, travel, and accommodation for senior executives—fringe benefits may well serve to increase the visibility of differentials and the extent to which they are resented. Many people would find it easier to see why their employer should pay more to those with greater responsibilities than why he should offer them larger desks and plusher carpets, and it is difficult to disagree.

Table 3.2: *The incidence of fringe benefits, 1975–81*

Percentage of companies providing:	1975	1981
Company car	60.0	74.2
Subsidized lunches	63.6	72.0
Medical insurance	37.9	60.4
Share options	4.3	10.6
Share purchase schemes	3.5	6.5

Source: Inbucon Report for Inquiry into Civil Service Pay, Cmnd. 8590-I, HMSO, 1982.

4

The taxation of investment income and savings

Over the last six years the maximum rate of tax on investment income has been reduced from 98 per cent in 1978/9 to 60 per cent in 1984/5. This was achieved by the reduction in the higher rates of tax in the 1979 Budget and the abolition of investment income surcharge in the 1984 Budget. In part this reduction reflected an acknowledgement that tax rates of 98 per cent were wholly ineffective. As we explained in earlier editions, the system of taxing investment income contained so many loopholes that any one potentially liable to a tax rate of 98 per cent was able to drive a coach and horses, or perhaps a large Rolls-Royce, through this apparently penal tax. A strategy of investing in securities that offered primarily capital gains rather than income, including some government securities, was sufficient to reduce the effective tax rate to somewhere between 40 and 50 per cent.

It is clear that the incentive to invest in schemes designed solely for their tax avoidance properties has been sharply reduced. At a tax rate of 98 per cent, for every £1 received net of tax by the taxpayer the Inland Revenue receives £49. At a tax rate of 60 per cent the amount received by the Inland Revenue is only £1·50 for each £1 received by the taxpayer. Nevertheless, opportunities for tax avoidance still exist, and these arise when one form of investment income can be converted into another legal form that is taxed at a lower rate.

Opportunities for tax avoidance, and the diversion of resources that these entail, would not exist if all forms of investment income were taxed in the same way. But they are not, and the principal difference is between returns that are taxed as investment income and those that are taxed as capital gains. Although, as we have seen, the top rates of tax on investment income have fallen to 60 per cent (the same as on earned income) the tax rate on capital gains is 30 per cent. Moreover, capital gains tax is levied only on the value of the gain after inflation has been taken into account. Suppose that you buy a security for £100 and sell it five years later for £200, the inflation in the interim being 50 per cent. Instead of being taxed on the nominal capital gain of £100 you are allowed to compute the taxable gain taking inflation into account. From the sale price of £200 you are allowed to deduct an adjusted acquisition cost of £150 (which is the actual acquisition cost of £100 grossed up by the 50 per cent inflation rate), and the taxable gain is therefore only £50. Suppose instead that the money had been invested in a bank account and the accrued interest had been reinvested. The investment income arising from the bank account would have been fully taxed with no allowance for inflation. Tax would also have been collected as the interest accrued rather than collected at the end of the investment period. In addition to the advantages of being taxed at lower rates and adjusted for inflation, capital gains are also only taxed if their realized value in any year exceeds a rather high threshold. At present this is £5,900 per annum. Only if realized capital gains after the allowance for inflation exceed this are they taxed at all.

It can be seen, therefore, that despite the reduction of tax rates on investment income the attraction of converting such income into capital gains remains. There are several methods for doing this. One is to invest in companies that pay a low dividend yield and plough back their earnings into internally financed investment. Another, and safer, investment is to purchase index-linked government securities. If held to maturity these offer a guaranteed real rate of return (in terms of the retail price index) and offer a low interest rate so that most of the return is received in the form of a capital gain.

It is evident that tax avoidance opportunities not only reduce effective tax rates but also lead taxpayers to invest in schemes chosen primarily for their tax-minimizing properties. A glance at the personal investment columns of any leading newspaper will suffice to demonstrate the importance of tax considerations in selecting a portfolio.

The 1984 Budget attempted to tackle some of these issues, and adopted as its theme 'fiscal neutrality'. Concern over the widely varying tax treatment of different types of saving and investment led to a number of measures designed to promote more uniform taxation of income from capital. Many of these measures were concerned with the structure of corporation tax and these are discussed in Chapter 11. Others were concerned directly with income tax and included changes in the tax treatment of life insurance premiums and the abolition of investment income surcharge. To see these measures in their proper context we need to understand the way in which income tax has affected the pattern of personal savings in the UK.

Taxation and savings

A major effect of the British tax system has been its impact on savings behaviour. Mill's dictum that 'no income tax is really just, from which savings are not exempted' (1865, p. 404)—i.e. no income tax is just unless it is an expenditure tax—has not been generally accepted. But there are three forms of savings that have received exemption or highly favourable tax treatment: investment in owner-occupied housing, pension funds, and, until 1984, life insurance. In consequence, these means of saving now account, in aggregate, for almost the *whole* of net personal saving in the UK. We consider each of them in turn.

Owner-occupied housing is given favourable tax treatment in several different ways. The income that is derived from it is not subject to tax. This concept of income from owner-occupation puzzles many people, who see their houses as items of expenditure, not of income. If individual X rents a house from individual Y, the rent that is paid is taxable income in the hands of Y. But if X and Y happen to be the same person—i.e. if the owner of the house is also the occupier— no money actually changes hands and so the tax liability disappears. There is therefore a strong tax incentive for them to be the same person—a bias in favour of owner-occupation as against renting. At one time, tax was imposed on the notional 'income' from an owner-occupied house, under schedule A of income tax legislation. This tax was based on the rateable value of the house, a sum which was computed primarily for the purpose of levying local rates and which purported to be the amount for which the property could have been rented in 1939. These figures became increasingly ludicrous, and when rateable values were revised in 1963 the government was confronted with the option of either facing angry reactions to enormous increases in the amount of tax payable under schedule A or abolishing it altogether; it adopted the latter course. In addition to the exemption of this schedule A income the interest paid on loans of up to £30,000 for house purchase attracts tax relief. As we have noted, the anomaly here is not so much that this interest is deductible but that other interest payments are not. And finally, while capital gains in general are taxed those that are obtained on the taxpayer's principal residence are exempt.

It is the experience of most commentators on taxation that there is nothing more calculated to provoke a flood of apoplectic letters to the newspapers than the suggestion that the tax system is unduly favourable to owner-occupiers. Although the existence of the tax privileges we have described is incontrovertible, the writers of these letters have a point. What the tax system favours is owner-occupation, not owner-occupiers, and this distinction is not always made clear. It is not simply taxation which has led to the disappearance of private rented housing in this country—the existence of rent control and other legislation to protect tenants has probably been more important—but this has undoubtedly been a contributory factor. The result is that the only widely available forms of tenure in this country are now local authority housing and owner-occupation, and people who are not interested in or not eligible for the former have little alternative to the latter.

They are then faced with buying houses at prices which have been forced up by the tax-stimulated demand for them: prices which reflect the capitalized value of the tax concessions, as described in Chapter 1. Thus current house-buyers obtain relatively little benefit from the concessions. Indeed they may be worse off, since young married couples are forced to save for deposits towards house purchase or to repay associated mortgages at a time in their lives when incomes are low, outgoings high, and large compulsory savings of this kind inappropriate. In a better-organized world, many people in this category would rent property, at least for a time, and that is what they do in many other countries.

The principal losers from these features of the tax system have been people who might have preferred to rent property—people who find mortgage repayments a very serious burden, people who have or would like to have jobs that involve frequent movement around the country. The principal gainers have been those who have owned houses in the past—or rather their descendants, since capital gains on the house you are living in are virtually unrealizable. Perhaps if it had been understood that the main beneficiaries of the policy of tax concessions to owner-occupation were the dead, the policy might have been adopted somewhat less enthusiastically. But this account demonstrates why tax capitalization is such a dangerous trap: although we believe it would be better if the system had never incorporated these concessions, it does not seem that it would now be either equitable or desirable to withdraw them. The losses from so doing would be principally borne by those who are currently struggling to meet the initial mortgage repayments on a house—people who have derived little benefit from the concessions and who may actually have suffered from them.

The second form of privileged saving is through pension funds. Provided that the fund meets a series of Inland Revenue criteria, pension contributions (whether made by the employer or by the employee) are excluded from taxable income, and in addition no taxes are levied on the investment income of pension funds themselves. But payments made out of a fund are taxable in full as earned income (except for that portion that may be commuted as a lump sum). In effect, savings made through a pension fund are a means of accumulating free of tax, and their treatment is the same as that which would be applied to all savings under an expenditure tax which we discuss in Chapters 5 and 6. Not surprisingly, pension schemes have been growing very rapidly. Similar opportunities are available for the self-employed. The establishment of a pension fund enables both the employer and the employee to save free of tax in order to provide for future pensions, and unless an individual has access to investment opportunities not available to the pension fund the most efficient means of providing for retirement is to invest in a pension fund.

Until recently, the other form of saving that attracted tax relief was life insurance. Before 1984 the Inland Revenue subsidized (at a rate of 15 per cent) premiums paid on a 'qualifying policy' subject to an upper limit on the total of premiums paid. In addition, the funds of life insurance companies themselves were taxed more favourably than those of other companies. The result was that an attractive way to save over a longer period was to purchase a life insurance policy. This form of investment had a number of disadvantages because the money could not be withdrawn before the policy matured without suffering a significant penalty. Moreover, as Kay (1982) showed, such policies were attractive only because of the tax relief. Examining the results for 61 companies Kay found that, disregarding tax relief, investing in a building society account would have yielded a higher rate of return than most of the life insurance policies. But when tax relief was taken into account the number of insurance companies that 'beat' the building society account increased from 19 out of 61 to 59 out of 61. It was never clear why incentives to contractual savings should be tied to life insurance, and in 1984 the chancellor abolished the tax relief for premiums on such policies.

As a result of these tax privileges, there have been dramatic changes in the structure and composition of personal wealth in the UK. Table 4.1 documents this. Over a 25-year period, the proportion of personal wealth accounted for by the three forms of privileged assets—houses, life insurance policies, and pension funds—has risen from 29 per cent to 49 per cent. In the same period personal holdings of equities and other marketable securities fell, as a proportion of wealth, by about two-thirds. In 1984 the chancellor tackled some of these problems when he reformed corporation tax (see Chapter 11) and removed the tax privileges of life insurance policies. The logic of the argument was clear. The next step would be to attack the privileges afforded to saving through pension funds and investment in owner-occupied housing. But in the 1985 Budget not only did he fail to take such measures, he actually promised not to remove these tax privileges during the lifetime of the current Parliament. The net effect of the changes over the last few years has been to reinforce the special and privileged position of housing and pension funds as vehicles for personal saving. Individuals in jobs that provide an occupational pension and offer the prospect of home-ownership receive tax privileges for their savings that are not open to others. Since it is evidently very difficult to withdraw the tax privileges afforded these two assets, we ask in later chapters whether there are other methods of removing their advantages by extending tax privileges to all forms of saving.

Taxation and small business

Although fiscal neutrality was the theme of the 1984 Budget, one type of investment has been singled out in recent years for deliberately favourable treatment—investment in new small businesses. There are two reasons for this. First, the rate at which new businesses are created is lower in Britain than in the United States. Secondly, existing privileged assets have certain characteristics in common. They are all what one might loosely describe as civil servants' assets rather than entrepreneurs' assets. As such they are well suited to people who have conventional intentions and predictable career prospects, but not to those who have no settled plans, who wish to take risks, or who have uncertain incomes. They are all highly illiquid: none of them can readily be realized in an emergency, to tide over in the period between jobs, to start a business, or to buy or expand one. Two of them significantly reduce mobility between locations and between occupations. Indeed it is a notable feature that while it is normally part of the function of wealth to enhance economic freedom and personal security, these assets contribute very little to them. Each imposes contractual commitments which must be met even in adverse circumstances. Money in the bank increases an individual's ability to disagree with his employer; wealth that principally takes the form of accrued pension rights reduces it. (Although transferability of pension rights has been increased substantially, such rights are in almost all cases more valuable to those who remain with their present employer, and this is particularly true in the private sector.)

Table 4.1:   *The composition of personal wealth in the UK*

	1957 (%)	1981 (%)
Housing (less mortgages)	16.9	32.3
Life insurance	7.8	7.3
Pension funds	4.3	8.7
Equities[a]	16.7	6.8
Bonds and government securities	20.6	4.6
Deposits	18.4	17.3
Other	15.3	23.0
Total net worth	100.0	100.0

[a] Equities include unit and investment trusts.
Source: J. Hills, *Savings and Fiscal Privilege*, IFS Report Series No. 9, 1984, Table 3.1.

One result of this is that Britain now has the most attenuated small business sector of any country in the industrialized world. The Bolton Committee (1971) found that, of thirteen countries it examined, the proportion of manufacturing employment in small establishments (less than 200 employees) was lowest in the UK and was not much more than half that of the average of the other countries surveyed; and for very small firms the contrast is even more marked (Prais, 1976, p. 160). Technological factors are of course an element in the decline of small firms but they can hardly account for the fact that while the number of small firms in the UK has halved in the last forty years it has almost doubled in the USA (Bolton, 1971, para. 6.9). Nor does such evidence as is available suggest that these trends result from the peculiar preferences of the British for large-scale organization. A recent international survey (*Vision*, 1977) showed that 61 per cent of workers in Britain would prefer to work in firms with less than 500 employees. More significantly, Britain emerged as having much the highest proportion of the population who had thought about setting up their own business, and the lowest percentage (after Holland) who had actually done so. And the finding that the median age of small firms in the UK is (at 22 years) three times what it is now in the US and four times what it was in the late nineteenth century (Bolton, 1971, paras. 6.14–15) does not suggest that youthful vigour is characteristic of what remains.

The other side of this coin is the rapid growth in the size and significance of institutional investors. In the stock-market, personal shareholders have been persistent sellers of equities and financial institutions persistent buyers. In consequence, the distribution of holdings has been transformed as shown in Table 4.2. Not only are these institutional holdings large, but they are held in large units. Individual shareholdings of £100,000 or above represent almost 90 per cent of the value of equities held by insurance companies (Erritt and Alexander, 1977). It is impossible to deal in quantities approaching this volume in the shares of any but a small number of large companies, and so the horizons of institutional investors are necessarily limited. Thus the growth of the institutional investor has not only channelled funds away from the smallest companies—in 1971 it was estimated that the total made available from these sources to companies with under 200 employees was about £7 million (Merrett-Cyriax, 1971). It has also promoted concentration among very large companies, a process which has also gone beyond levels that have been achieved in other comparable countries or that are easy to justify on economic grounds (Hannah and Kay, 1977, Table 8.4 and *passim*).

In order to encourage the creation of small businesses a number of tax incentives have been expanded in recent years. Small companies pay a lower rate of corporation tax, the first £100,000 of capital gains made by the owner or director of a business who is over sixty (and has worked for the firm for ten years) is completely tax-free, and transfers of certain business property can be reduced in value by 50 per cent for the purposes of computing a capital transfer tax liability. But perhaps the incentive on which most attention has been concentrated is the Business Expansion Scheme (BES) introduced in the 1983 Budget (as a successor to the 1981 Business Start-Up Scheme). Under this scheme an investor may contribute up to £40,000 in shares of unquoted UK companies (provided that he does not work in the business) and deduct the sum so subscribed against his taxable income. As such the BES provides tax relief at the individual's marginal tax rate and hence is equivalent to the treatment of savings under an expenditure tax as described in Chapters 5 and 6. But since the returns may be received in the form of capital gains, which may either pay little tax or be free of tax altogether, this treatment is in fact more favourable than that which would obtain with an expenditure tax. Moreover, the risks entailed in investing in unquoted companies may be spread by investing through one of the many intermediaries ('approved investment funds') that have sprung up.

Table 4.2:   *Ownership of shares by category of beneficial holder*

Holder	1963 (%)	1969 (%)	1975 (%)	1981 (%)
Personal sector	56	50	40	28
Financial companies and institutions	30	36	48	58
Other	14	14	12	14

Source: Erritt and Alexander, 1977; *Economic Trends,* July 1982; J. Hills, *Savings and Fiscal Privilege,* IFS Report Series No. 9, 1984.

The significance of the BES may be seen from Table 4.3. This shows the effective tax rates for different types of investor on income received from an investment in machinery in a typical manufacturing project. The effective tax rate includes taxes levied at both the corporate and personal levels, and shows clearly how the degree of fiscal privilege varies from one investor to another. For this particular type of investment, pension funds are actually subsidized by the rest of the community. Insurance companies pay a small positive tax rate which is somewhat below that of a household paying the basic rate of income tax. Higher rate taxpayers pay a much higher rate, but if they invest via the medium of the BES not only is the tax rate reduced, it becomes very substantially negative. A large tax has been transformed to an even larger subsidy. One consequence of this was that many of the early BES companies were set up to obtain the tax advantages without incurring the risk that the chancellor was trying to encourage. Schemes to invest money in farming, property development, antique furniture, and other 'asset-backed' schemes were eventually outlawed. But the experience of the BES demonstrates the difficulty of trying to encourage enterprise without at the same time stimulating tax avoidance whenever special privileges are available. There is little doubt that the aim of providing help to new businesses at the beginning of their lives rather than at the end of the life of the founder of the business (as with special concessions under capital transfer tax) is to give help when it is most needed. But it raises the question of whether more general savings incentives all round would be more efficient than attempts to single out particular types of investment for special treatment.

Table 4.3: *Effective tax rates on income from capital in the UK*

Investor	Tax rate (%)
Pension fund	−42.0
Insurance company	9.9
Household—30% tax rate	12.3
Household—60% tax rate	68.5
BES—household with 60% tax rate	−176.2

Note: The effective tax rate is calculated for a project earning a pre-tax real rate of return of 10% p.a. invested in manufacturing plant and machinery and when the proceeds are distributed as dividends. For the BES investment the profit is paid out via a repurchase of the investor's shares. The inflation rate assumed is 5% p.a.

Source: Own calculations.

Taxation and distribution

Consider the career of someone now retiring from a senior position
on the board of one of Britain's largest 100 corporations. Such a
person would probably have begun his managerial career just after
the Second World War and might in the late 1940s have been earning
£200 per year. Moving rapidly ahead of his contemporaries he might
twenty years later have expected to earn £15,000 per year; with
promotion to the board and inflation in the 1970s this figure increases rapidly and he earns £40,000 or more for six or seven years
before retiring with a peak salary of perhaps £80,000. Few people
are as successful as this: there are perhaps twenty people starting
work this year who can aspire to these heights.

Our hypothetical manager has fairly frugal tastes, and throughout
his lifetime has reckoned to save around a quarter of his after-tax
income. On retirement, the accumulated wealth of such a man would
approach £200,000. Feeling, with some justice, that he has been
unusually fortunate in his career and unusually thrifty in his actions,
he may be somewhat surprised to discover that there are in Britain
at least 100,000 people richer than he is, and that they control almost
20 per cent of all personal wealth. The example illustrates a central,
but poorly realized, effect of the British tax system—but one which
is an inevitable consequence of a system in which high rates of tax
on earned income are seen as the major redistributive device. There
is a large number of very rich people in Britain, but the proportion
of them who became rich as a result of personal savings from their
own earnings is negligible.

If the much lower maximum rates of tax introduced in 1979 persist
for the next thirty years then the results of the sort of calculation we
have presented will look very different. But the picture we have
painted is historically accurate—it is possible that in future senior
managers will be able to accumulate really substantial wealth from
their salaries but that has certainly not been true in the past. Where
then does the wealth of the rich come from? It is likely that some
are in fact professional managers since, as we have noted above, the
impact of taxation on high earnings is not quite what it seems—
but it is nearly what it seems, and it is not likely that many top
wealth-holders are in this category. There are not many employees
in other sectors who are as well paid as such a manager—a handful
of lawyers, accountants, actors, and sportsmen. The main sources

of wealth are necessarily inheritance and capital gains, and most fortunes are the product of some combination of the two. Thus Harbury and Hitchens (1979) found that 60 per cent of their sample of top wealth-leavers had fathers who were themselves in the top 1 per cent of the wealth distribution, and over 80 per cent had fathers who were in the top 10 per cent. Industrial occupational categories do not, unfortunately, distinguish proprietors from professional managers; but the industrial breakdown given by Rubenstein (1974) suggests strongly that it is primarily the former who are the business men represented among the top wealth-leavers.

Of course, to say that inheritance is close to being a necessary condition for wealth and that capital gains are the main route to increasing it is not to suggest that there is no relationship between wealth and personal exertion. Small business men are generally in the position of being able to turn part of the earnings of setting up or expanding their firms into lightly taxed capital gains, although it is important to recognize that it is difficult to realize these gains without relinquishing partial or complete control of their operations. In the study by Harbury and McMahon (1973) the two sectors in which the influence of parental wealth on the fortunes of the son is smallest are engineering and finance: the former is the area of the industrial economy where small firms remain most prominent, while finance embraces those sectors in which earnings can be most readily and conveniently taken in the form of capital gains. That the expansion of a small engineering firm is a major route to self-made wealth is not something that causes us concern. The prominence of the financial sector here is rather more disturbing, since one does not have to take a wholly unsympathetic view of the activities of the City to believe that the correlation between private gain and social benefit is probably less strong in this area than it is in manufacturing industry, and within the sector itself it is generally easier to defend the utility of those actions that generate high earnings than those that generate major capital profits.

The normal justification of inequalities of wealth derives from the need to sustain enterprise and effort. But it is difficult to survey the kind of evidence we have been describing without feeling that only a rather small proportion of major wealth inequality in the UK actually serves this function. Under the present UK tax system it is not too difficult to stay rich, but it is distinctly difficult to become

rich—though these difficulties operate haphazardly, and with a degree of differentiation between sectors which seems, if anything, the
opposite of that which consciously determined social priorities might
dictate. It is not surprising to discover that the degree of concentration of wealth in Britain has been declining, though slowly
(Table 4.4).

Table 4.4: *Trends in the distribution of personal wealth in the UK*

	Share of different percentile groups in total wealth (%)						
	England and Wales, adult population[a]			UK over 18			
	1911–13	1938	1966	1971	1976	1979	1983
Top 1%	69	55	31	31	25	24	20
Top 5%	87	77	56	52	46	45	40
Top 10%	92	85	69	65	61	59	54

[a] Taken as over 25 in 1911–13, 23 in 1938, 19 in 1966. Figures for 1938 and 1966
(England and Wales) not strictly comparable.
Sources: Revell, 1965; Atkinson and Harrison, 1978; *Inland Revenue Statistics 1985*,
Table 4.7.

But we attach importance not only to the concentration of wealth
but to the mobility that underlies it. A concentrated structure is
more acceptable if it is held by a changing group of people who are
enjoying in their own generation the rewards of their own achieve-
ment than if it is owned by those whose families have always owned
it—both because such a distribution should arouse less resentment
and because such inequality is more likely to serve a function that is
of benefit to the population as a whole. There is justice both in
the left-wing criticism of the tax structure for its failure to shake
concentrations of wealth and privilege, and in the right-wing criticism that it deprives people of the returns of effort and initiative.
The present system has given us the worst of both worlds with
maximal disincentive effect for minimal redistributive impact. It is
not difficult to propose reforms that would lead to improvements
on both counts, and these we shall discuss in subsequent chapters.

Taxes on gifts and bequests

Inheritance is a major determinant of the distribution of wealth in
Britain. How is its influence mitigated by taxes on gifts and bequests?
The idea of death duties goes back many centuries. Modern legislation dates from the introduction of probate duty in 1694 which
lasted until the famous Budget of Sir William Harcourt in 1894
which brought in estate duty. In the eighteenth and nineteenth centuries two other taxes on transfers at death were enacted—legacy
duty and succession duty—and these survived until 1949. These two
latter duties embodied the principle that the tax paid should reflect
the circumstances of the recipient, or donee, rather than the size of
the estate. Estate duty related the tax paid on transfers of wealth
only to the circumstances of the donor. There have been many
suggestions for replacing estate duty with a tax on the receipts of
beneficiaries. Such a tax is often called an accessions tax and in 1972
the government published a Green Paper (Cmnd. 4930) to stimulate
discussion on the idea of moving towards inheritance taxation. But
when estate duty was finally overhauled in 1975 it was transformed
into capital transfer tax which continued to relate tax liability to the
size of the estate.

Capital transfer tax did, however, bring one very important
change to the system of taxing transfers of wealth in Britain. For
the first time it extended the taxation of estates to cover gifts. Under
the old estate duty the principle was not to tax gifts at all, but in
order to prevent gifts made 'in contemplation of death' avoiding tax
altogether it was necessary to include gifts made just before death in
the taxable estate.[1] If the only loophole were death-bed gifts then a
rule including gifts made within a few weeks of death would be
sufficient. But wealthy individuals and their wealthy advisers are
sufficiently ingenious to plan to give away at least part of the estate
well before the expected date of death, and by so doing they were able
to avoid tax altogether. The government responded by extending the
length of the period before death within which gifts made were
taxable from nothing to three months, then to a year, three years,
five years . . . ! Before it was replaced, estate duty covered gifts
made within seven years of death. Clearly, the taxman favoured the
healthy, wealthy, and well advised.

---

[1] The technical phrase '*inter vivos* gifts' is used to describe gifts made before the
date when they would become taxable as transfers on death.

The addition of gifts to the base of the transfer tax was a logical and necessary step, although since the introduction of capital transfer tax the government has seen fit to reduce the tax rate on gifts to considerably less than the rate applying to transfers on death. Allegedly this was to help ease the problems of the transfer of small private businesses, but it increases the possibility of tax avoidance and reintroduces the creation of rules to prevent death-bed gifts which are now defined to be those made less than three years before death. Another change which followed the inclusion of gifts was the decision to levy tax on the *cumulative* lifetime total of gifts and bequests made. Instead of being an annual tax, capital transfer tax was designed to be a tax on lifetime transfers. But in 1982 the government changed this principle to basing the tax on transfers made within a ten-year period. Hence when a gift or transfer is made, the tax charged is based on a cumulation of transfers over ten years. Although there is a good case for lifetime cumulation, and some case for an annual tax, it is difficult to conceive of any economic justification for basing a tax on transfers cumulated over a period of ten years. Rather, this change, like others introduced in recent years, appears to be aimed at nibbling away at the base of the tax, thus reducing the burden and eroding receipts of revenue. The amount that may be given away tax-free within any ten-year period is £67,000 and in addition there is an annual exemption of £3,000 per individual. In 1982 it was announced that the threshold for capital transfer tax would in future be indexed (over-indexed in fact because the adjusted threshold each year will be rounded up to the nearest £1,000).

The move to replace estate duty by capital transfer tax was inspired by the evident failings of estate duty. Avoidance of estate duty became so easy that it was sometimes described as a 'voluntary tax'. There have been so many changes to the detailed tax legislation, all designed to stop up the loopholes, that the tax avoidance industry has grown as rapidly as any. Yet despite these efforts the tax has done little to bring about a more equal distribution of wealth, and seems relatively unimportant in comparison with the effects of high rates of inflation which we discuss later. The easiest way of avoiding estate duty was simply to hand on wealth to the next generation and hope that you lived for another seven years. That way you would never pay tax at all. In a study of the importance of tax avoidance by *inter vivos* gifts Horsman (1975) found that in the late 1960s the value of gifts made upon which duty was never charged was probably of the order of £330 million a year. The amount of tax avoided was estimated by Horsman to have been £177 million in 1968 compared with actual receipts of death duties in that year of £382 million. Given the importance of avoidance by this means it is strange that the government gave way to pressure and introduced lower rates of tax on *inter vivos* gifts under capital transfer tax.

Gifts were not the only method by which it was possible to avoid paying estate duty. Lower rates of duty were charged on agricultural land and property, assets of private business, growing timber, and works of art. No doubt a good case was made out for the special treatment of each of these classes of assets in turn, but these arguments almost always overlook the basic principle of the capitalization of taxes. If a concession is made to the taxation of growing timber, then wealthy individuals will switch at least part of their wealth from other assets into growing timber. This extra demand will bid up the price of timber until there is no net advantage in passing on wealth in one form rather than another. Tax revenue falls, and those who gain are the people who happened to own the timber when the concession was announced. It is hard to see what is achieved by this, and in the case of farming it can have perverse results. The reason for giving concessions to agriculture is to help farmers continue in the profession. But all that happens is that farms become much more valuable than would otherwise have been the case (thus making farmers even more concerned at the prospect of paying tax) and it becomes even more difficult for the genuine small farmer to borrow enough to purchase his own farm. On top of this, many farmers become millionaires, a fact which they find puzzling because there is no change in their standard of living. The only way in which they can enjoy the benefit of their good fortune is to abandon farming, at which we hope they were skilled, sell out, and go and live in the South of France. We suspect many farmers would be happier on their farms than in the casino in Monte Carlo.

We would have hoped that the introduction of capital transfer tax would have seen the end of these anomalies. Not a bit of it; reduced rates apply to gifts *inter vivos*. Although this concession was given to reduce the 'threat' to small businesses, it applies to transfers of *any* kind of asset. Agriculture too receives special treatment. It is zero-rated for VAT, exempt from rates, receives concessions for capital gains tax, and the value of agricultural property is reduced by 50 per cent for the purposes of capital transfer tax. There are restrictions on those who may benefit from agricultural relief but the definition of 'working farmer' is not too difficult to satisfy. There is also special relief for gifts made to charity and for works of art and historic buildings.

Another method of avoiding tax has been for the wealthy to set up trusts, the trustees of which could distribute the income and capital of the trust in any way they wished to individuals on a list of potential beneficiaries. This sort of trust, called a discretionary trust, could (provided it satisfied certain minimal conditions) escape estate duty altogether and hence was an attractive way of handing on family wealth down the generations without paying tax. It was clearly important to stop up this loophole. Some steps were taken in 1969 and the switch to capital transfer tax (CTT) also brought with it changes in the tax treatment of trusts. It may be that in due course these changes will be seen to have stopped up some of the more serious loopholes. The prospect of this was diminished when in June 1979 the new Conservative government postponed for two years the date when discretionary trusts would be taxed under the full CTT provisions. This was later postponed further until 1983. But the rewards for successful ingenuity in this area are great, and the use of trusts, many of which are set up for the sole purpose of tax avoidance, seems likely to remain a vehicle for the rich to hand on their wealth. Indeed, a leading authority on the subject has written: 'in Great Britain it is probably true to say that 95% of all discretionary and accumulation trusts are created solely for tax-saving reasons' (Wheatcroft, 1965, p. 136).

Although there are high nominal tax rates at the top end of the scale, the numerous possibilities for avoidance mean the system raises little revenue and average tax rates are rather low. As Atkinson has commented, 'Where those with good tax advisers—and perhaps few scruples—can pay little tax while others pay tax at rates up to 80%, there can be little respect for the equity of taxation' (Atkinson, 1972, p. 129). The failure of capital transfer tax to remedy the deficiencies of estate duty can be seen from Table 4.5. From 1963/4 to 1973/4 the revenue from estate duty rose 32 per cent, in contrast to the rise in money GDP of 139 per cent and in total tax revenue of no less than 166 per cent. But since 1973 the revenue from transfer taxes has hardly risen in nominal terms. Between 1973/4 and 1983/4 the combined receipts of estate duty and capital transfer tax rose 47 per cent in a period during which prices rose by 254 per cent!

It is possible for individuals who are obviously far from being paupers to die leaving estates for tax purposes that bear little relation to their real wealth. It is generally believed that the largest sum ever paid in death duties, by a considerable margin, was the £11 million paid on an estate estimated at between £40 million and £60 million on the death of the third Duke of Westminster in 1953. On the subsequent death of the fourth duke, his reported estate was a little over £4 million, on which estate duty came to around £1 million. In fact not even this sum was paid, since after a protracted legal case it was resolved that the duke (who was partially disabled by war wounds received in 1942 and who died of cancer in 1967) was entitled to the benefit of an exemption from estate duty for those killed on active military service. The fifth duke died in 1979, and press reports then estimated that the family fortune controlled by the new Duke of Westminster was between £300 million and £800 million. Again the reported estate was expected to be less than £5 million (*Daily Telegraph*, 20 February 1979).

Table 4.5:   *Revenue from transfer taxes*

	Estate duty	Capital transfer tax
1963/4	312	—
1973/4	412	—
1976/7	124	259
1977/8	87	311
1978/9	46	317
1979/80	32	404
1980/1	27	423
1981/2	17	480
1982/3	15	499
1983/4	9	599

Source: *Inland Revenue Statistics 1985*, Table 4.1.

Another major cause of the failure of death duties to produce revenue is the rate structure. At first sight this may seem surprising because the 'enormously high' rates of up to 8 per cent imposed by Harcourt in his 1894 Budget have steadily risen, and the top marginal rate today is 60 per cent (30 per cent on gifts). But to pay an average tax rate of even 30 per cent requires the transfer of an estate of £300,000, and that is before taking any account of the special concessions to gifts or particular assets described above. If the money is handed on as a gift (provided it is made more than three years before death) the tax rate would never reach 30 per cent. On a gift of a small business worth £5 million the average tax rate (in 1985/6) was 14.2 per cent. In 1985/6 a single person on average earnings pays income tax (including national insurance contributions) at an average rate of about 30 per cent. We should also note that transfers between husband and wife (whether during life or on death) are completely exempt from tax. Gifts to charities are also exempt from tax.

The reason for this disparity between high marginal and low average rates on capital transfers is the very high exemption level below which no tax at all is paid—£67,000—and the slow build-up of marginal rates. With good advice few people need pay much capital transfer tax. The exemption level may remove the 'average' family from the tax net but it also reduces the effective tax rate charged on the larger estates. In real terms the exemption level is much higher now than it was in 1894. Moreover, the effective exemption level can be very much higher than the apparent value of £67,000 every ten years. This is because each year any individual may give away £3,000 tax-free. A married couple can therefore pass on to their children £6,000 each year without incurring tax at all. This is obviously much easier for the wealthy family which can transfer the ownership of stocks and shares, than for the more typical family whose main assets are in the form of an owner-occupied house the ownership of which is difficult to transfer bit by bit. Over a twenty-year period a couple could pass on more than £250,000 without paying a penny in tax! On top of this there is a tax-free allowance of £5,000 for gifts made in 'consideration of marriage'. There cannot be many married couples who anticipate returning from honeymoon to a cheque for £5,000.

The combination of very high exemption levels at the bottom and high marginal rates at the top has not been very effective in redistributing wealth. Redistribution is about average tax rates and raising revenue, and as we have seen capital taxes in their present form are not major revenue-raisers. In 1983/4 the combined revenue from estate duty and capital transfer tax amounted to £608 million, which is about what would be raised by an increase of one-half of a percentage point on the basic rate of income tax.

5

The choice of the tax base

It should be clear from the previous chapter that many of the weaknesses of the UK tax system arise from the absence of a coherent view as to what should constitute an individual's 'taxable income'. We have illustrated this by pointing to several difficulties in the existing structure of the tax system which have become increasingly evident in recent years.

Firstly, there is a case for shifting part of the tax burden from earned income to some wider measure of an individual's wealth, to reflect his total resources or consumption over his lifetime. Secondly, the present taxation of capital income, especially in an inflationary era, is most unsatisfactory. Thirdly, whatever view one takes about the appropriate tax treatment of savings in general, it is clear that the discrimination among different forms of saving has some undesirable effects. These considerations lead us to believe that it is time to take a fresh look at the basis of our tax structure.

Suppose we go back to square one and ask the question 'What principles should guide the choice of the tax system?' In the theory of taxation two different lines of thought may be detected.

One traditional approach is to say that since taxes are levied to finance collective expenditure on services that either cannot be provided by the market, or that the government of the day chooses to supply from public funds, then the amount of tax paid by an individual should be related to the benefit that he derives from public expenditure. This school of thought has become known as the 'benefit theory' of taxation. But it is very difficult to measure these benefits because people can rarely be excluded from enjoying the benefits of many forms of public expenditure. Financing national defence or public television by voluntary subscription is usually found to be impracticable, and the tax authorities and detector vans are called in to help out the state.

The objection to the benefit theory of taxation is not, however, based only on its impossible demands of human nature. We simply do not know the distribution of benefits of public expenditure, and there is little prospect of discovering it. How can we measure the benefits that any particular individual derives from defence, the police, or the Department of Industry? An alternative approach is to say that for a given level of public expenditure, the total cost of financing it should be divided among individuals according to their 'ability to pay'. The idea behind this is that an individual should make a contribution according to the 'sacrifice' which the tax burden imposes upon him, and that individuals should make equal sacrifices. This is not equivalent to saying that each individual should pay the same amount of tax because a rich man can pay much more tax than a poor man while being said to suffer the same 'sacrifice'. The evident difficulty of defining exactly what is meant by 'equal sacrifice' explains why the 'ability to pay' approach, like the benefit theory, has not contributed a great deal to the resolution of practical problems.

One reason for this is the confusion of two quite distinct issues. The first is the question of what is the best index of an individual's 'ability to pay'. Obvious candidates include income, wealth, and consumption. The second question arises once we have chosen a particular index, income for example. How should the tax burden be distributed among people with different incomes? In other words, how progressive should the income tax be? For the moment we shall consider these issues separately. In this chapter we examine the former, returning to the latter question in Chapter 14.

A natural way to measure an individual's ability to pay is his ability to earn. This, however, contravenes a basic criterion for a feasible index, which is that we must be able to *measure* it. What someone actually earns is not necessarily a good guide to what he could earn. A man who has the ability to produce a great deal but chooses to lie on a beach all year round will pay no tax. It would be difficult to prove that he had the ability to earn enormous sums, and impossible to measure at all accurately what he might have earned. Before this approach to the taxation of potential earnings is condemned as unjust and illiberal, we should recall the widely held belief that owners of property should pay full rates even if the property concerned is empty. The owner of an empty office-block is regarded as just as worthy an object of taxation as the owner of a building that is fully used.

Politicians and administrators charged with the responsibility for collecting taxes will be more interested in what measurable indices or tax bases they could use. At this stage we may distinguish three potential tax bases—wealth, income, and expenditure—the values of which measure how much an individual owns, earns, or spends respectively.

Wealth as a tax base

Wealth taxes have a longer history than income taxes. This may seem surprising to those people who regard the idea of a wealth tax as a recent left-wing idea, but monarchs found it easier to measure their subjects' wealth than to perform the more sophisticated calculations that are necessary to compute income. Representatives of the monarch would estimate an individual's visible wealth (acres of land of different types, numbers of servants and cattle), and levy a wealth tax at regular or irregular intervals depending on the Crown's needs.

More recently, wealth taxes have been used in many European countries as a substitute, or partial replacement, for taxes on investment income. A wealth tax was proposed by the Labour government in a Green Paper in 1974 (Cmnd. 5704), and this was examined in detail in a report of a Select Committee of the House of Commons (published in 1975: HC 696-2). The committee was, however, unable to agree upon a report, and the published document contains several minority reports.

One of the motives for the idea of a wealth tax was concern that the distribution of wealth was too unequal. There is no doubt that there is substantial inequality in the distribution of wealth in the UK today. The top 1 per cent of the population owns between 10 and 25 per cent of total personal wealth, depending upon the precise definition of wealth. But it is difficult both to produce such numbers and to evaluate them. (For a careful analysis of the evidence on wealth distribution, and on the difficulties of measurement, see Atkinson and Harrison, 1978.) The standard of comparison against which such concentration should be judged is uncertain. We would expect that older people who have saved for retirement and, in many cases, owned houses for longer would be significantly wealthier than younger people entering the labour market. It is also clear that rich people choose to hold their wealth in very different forms from those of less rich people. Unfortunately, data on the composition of household portfolios for people in different wealth ranges are hard to come by now that the Royal Commission on the distribution of income and wealth has been abolished. In Table 5.1 we show data that the commission produced for Britain in 1976. The table shows how two groups of individuals—those with net wealth in the range £10,000 to £20,000 and those with wealth over £200,000—divide their portfolios between different assets. The first group holds about one-half in the form of owner-occupied houses and another quarter in savings with life assurance companies and building societies. Holdings of shares and other company securities are negligible. For the richest individuals the picture is very different. Company securities comprise over one-third of the wealth of this group, and land 20 per cent.

Table 5.1: *Asset composition of personal wealth in Britain, 1976*

Asset	Range of wealth £10,000–£20,000	Over £200,000	Total for all ranges
Dwellings[a]	49.1	12.5	34.8
Land	1.0	20.0	3.8
Company securities	2.1	36.1	10.5
Life policies	17.6	2.7	15.1
Building society deposits	9.0	1.2	8.9
Cash and bank deposits	4.9	8.5	6.9
Other[b]	16.3	19.0	20.0
Net wealth	100.0	100.0	100.0

[a] Net of mortgages.
[b] Net of personal debts; principal component is consumer durables.
Source: Royal Commission on the Distribution of Income and Wealth, Report No. 7, Table 4.6 (HMSO, 1979, Cmnd. 7595).

It is important to note that Table 5.1 omits any reference to the two most important forms of wealth that most families own. This is because these two components of wealth cannot be measured. The first is simply the present value of the future earnings that an individual may earn, sometimes described as 'human capital'. Apart from the special cases of slaves and football players there are no markets to enable us to put a precise monetary value on the stock of human capital. For this reason it is clear that such wealth is not included in statistical analyses of personal wealth nor is it suitable as a component of taxable wealth.

The second form of wealth that is difficult to measure is wealth held in the form of rights to future pensions. Although an individual cannot sell his or her pension rights (he or she must live at least to retirement age for them to be of any value), they have an actuarial value, and most people would be very upset if their pension rights were taken away. To value a pension right of an individual we have to estimate his chance of survival until the year when the pension will start to be paid, the size of the pension that will be paid after retirement, and the tax treatment of the pension payments that will be in force at the time. Since for most people the pension that they will receive is linked to their final salary, it is very difficult to make accurate estimates of the value of pension rights. In some cases it may be impossible to value such rights at all if there is no contractual arrangement to provide a pension. For example, a director of a small company may have no formal right to a pension but a very high expectation of a good pension, not least because the other directors could decide to award him such payments after retirement. In these cases no valuation could reasonably be made and if formal pension rights were taxed, informal schemes would proliferate. But if pension rights were not regarded as taxable wealth there would be inequities between those with occupational pension rights and those, such as the self-employed, who had to provide their own pension, and, equally important, inequities between those in generous pension schemes and those in poor schemes. Pension rights pose a very serious problem for a wealth tax.

Because of the difficulties that we have outlined, wealth taxes in practice do not attempt to tax either human capital or pension rights. For this reason they are better described as taxes on assets rather than on wealth in its widest sense. A tax that is levied only on assets that can be easily identified and valued is by no means the same thing as a tax on a household's net worth.

Nevertheless, it has been argued that wealth in the form of visible assets gives rise to 'taxable capacity' in its own right. Kaldor (1956), when discussing tax reform in India, cited the example of a beggar and a man who hoarded gold, both of whom received no current monetary income. But it is clear that in some ill-defined sense the man with greater wealth has a larger taxable capacity. If by this is meant that the wealthy man can enjoy a higher standard of living then, although this is obviously true, it is an argument for a tax on expenditure rather than a wealth tax as such. It may be argued that wealth confers power, influence, and security as well as monetary benefits. But it is difficult to relate these non-pecuniary benefits to any monetary evaluation of wealth, and power derives from sources other than wealth. Nevertheless, it suggests the idea that a tax on wealth could be used to tax all the benefits of wealth-holding, both pecuniary and non-pecuniary. With this idea a wealth tax would replace all existing taxes on the holding (though not the transfer) of wealth and the income that derives from it. Taxes on unearned income and on capital gains would be replaced by an annual tax on wealth.

Such a proposal has been put forward by Flemming and Little (1974), and it has evident attractions in principle. But in order to work it would have to be applied to everybody, and this would entail the daunting task of valuing the wealth of each individual every year. Conventions would be adopted, but these would be open to political pressure; and in no time concessions and loopholes for the rich would have been opened up, leaving the rest of the population to pay the tax. Valuation problems have always been considered the major obstacle to the introduction of a wealth tax, even for a tax applied only to the top 1 per cent of the wealth distribution. The problems would become enormous if extended to the rest of the population, and in those European countries that use a wealth tax very generous valuations are made, especially for owner-occupiers.

Since the two largest components of wealth for most people— human capital and pension rights—cannot easily be taxed, it is evident that wealth is not suitable as the base of the main personal tax. This is borne out by the practice of all developed countries.

Income and expenditure as tax bases

In more recent times, as we have seen in Chapter 2, income was used as the index of ability to pay, and this has become the norm in all countries. Nevertheless, there has always been a strong intellectual tradition ranging right across the political spectrum, including such figures as Hobbes, Mill, Fisher, and, more recently, Kaldor, that has argued in favour of the use of expenditure as the measure of an individual's ability to pay. In this tradition two arguments have been deployed for the superiority of a tax based on expenditure over income tax.

The first justification for taxing an individual on his consumption is that it is more just to tax someone on the value of what he takes out of society, in terms of the goods and services that he consumes, than on the value of what he contributes to society, whether in the form of earnings in return for labour services or interest in return for the supply of capital services. This argument is usually supported by reference to the famous question of Hobbes,

What reason is there, that he which laboureth much, and sparing the fruits of his labour, consumeth little, should be more charged, than he that liveth idly getteth little, and spendeth all he gets: Seeing the one hath no more protection from the commonwealth than the other? (Hobbes, *Leviathan*, Chapter XXX)

The answer to Hobbes is twofold. Firstly, there is no obvious reason to regard a tax on what an individual actually consumes as evidently more *just* than a tax on the total economic opportunities of the individual which measure his potential consumption. A one-legged unemployed man who manages to maintain a low level of consumption by begging is unlikely to be seen as just as suitable an object of taxation as a wealthy miser who chooses to spend very little and counts his money each night. A tax on potential consumption has as much claim for the title of a fair tax base as a tax on actual consumption. Secondly, Hobbes's example is very misleading. The injustice arises, so it would appear, because one individual enjoys a good deal of leisure ('living idly' while his neighbour 'laboureth much') and this is not taken account of when his tax bill is computed. This, however, has nothing to do with the distinction between income and consumption. If we consider Hobbes's example and look a year or two into the future, then the man who had worked hard, saved, and now wanted to enjoy the fruits of his work and saving in the form of consumption would, under Hobbes's regime of an expenditure-based tax, find himself facing a heavy tax liability. Both an income tax and an expenditure tax discriminate in favour of the 'idle', and unless we are prepared to tax people on the basis of what they *could* earn there is nothing we can do about it.

A more relevant distinction between an income tax and an expenditure tax is their treatment of saving, and this has been used as the second main argument for a tax on consumption. With an expenditure tax, consumption incurs the same tax liability (for a given schedule of tax rates) regardless of the year in which the individual chooses to consume. There is no discrimination between those who prefer to spend while young and active, and those who prefer to spend in retirement. An income tax, on the other hand, is said to discriminate against saving because it gives rise to the 'double taxation of savings'. The reason for this is the following. Consider a world in which the only tax is an income tax, and two individuals who earn the same amount and hence pay the same tax. The first decides to spend everything this year and pays no more tax. The second decides to save up and spend the money next year. Because he saves he receives some interest on his savings, but under an income tax he is required to pay further tax on his interest income, and this has been described as double taxation. Although there is some force in this argument the position is more complicated than the simple label of 'double taxation' might imply. It should be obvious that what matters is not the number of times tax is paid (whether it be double, treble, or quadruple taxation), but the total tax burden. The important questions are whether taxing interest income discriminates between immediate consumption and deferred consumption, and whether this discrimination is a serious problem. On the first point, we have to decide whether the after-tax interest that the individual receives is less than the rate of return that the nation earns on investment which can be financed out of the individual's savings. In fact this is a complicated issue which depends on, among other things, the taxes and subsidies on investment by companies. Before 1984 the tax system provided, on *average*, no disincentive to saving, although this resulted from a subsidy to institutional savings and a tax on individual saving. Following the 1984 Budget, there is a positive tax on capital income on average, and hence a disincentive to saving.

Whether it is a first priority to remove this discrimination is another matter. There are certainly other distortions in the capital market which affect savings decisions. Access to opportunities for borrowing is not available to all, and in one important market—that for loans for housing—mortgages are rationed among those individuals who would like to borrow more at prevailing interest rates. But if we tried to calculate what would be the best way of taxing interest income, taking account of all the existing market imperfections, we would not only require an extensive and detailed knowledge of how these imperfections affected savings behaviour, but we would be most unlikely to come up with a system resembling the current tax treatment of saving. Hence there is a strong argument for not trying to introduce arbitrary elements of discrimination unless we are sure we are influencing decisions in the right direction. Although we believe that the 'double taxation of savings' implied by an income tax is an argument for an expenditure tax, it is not the only one nor even the most important argument. Indeed, it is necessary to correct a common, but mistaken, impression that the main argument for an expenditure tax is that it would encourage saving.

There have been very large changes in real interest rates over the last decade. In the mid- and late-1970s real interest rates, especially after tax, were negative and often significantly so. In the 1980s real interest rates rose to levels that were almost unprecedented. Yet the savings rate did not exhibit such volatility. It seems implausible, therefore, that the response of savings to changes in interest rates is large. Recent studies in the United States by Boskin (1977) and Howrey and Hymans (1978) yield conflicting evidence about the response of aggregate saving to interest rates, and it seems unlikely that changes in the tax system would have a major effect on savings. The important thing is to distort individual decisions no more than is necessary, and the attraction of an expenditure tax is not so much that it would remove a disincentive to saving in general but that it offers a practicable way of eliminating the differential taxation of particular forms of saving and capital income.

Given that it is unrealistic to think of calculating a special tax rate for each form of saving and each type of income, and given the anomalies that have been introduced into the present system by 'special concessions', there is a powerful case for choosing as the tax base either income or expenditure, but not a mixture of the two. The arguments in principle for choosing between income and expenditure, which we have discussed above, do not seem to us to lean heavily in one direction or the other. Either base can be defended, and the decisive arguments come from a consideration of what the respective tax bases imply in practice. So we shall now examine in more detail the implications of an income tax, and in the next chapter we shall turn our attention to an expenditure tax.

The definition of income and the 'comprehensive income tax'

It may seem too trite to observe that to operate an income tax it is necessary to have a clear definition of what constitutes 'income', but the sad truth is that no single definition of income commands universal assent. Those who either doubt, or are surprised by, this statement are referred to the voluminous literature on the subject (some of which has been brought together in the volume edited by Parker and Harcourt, 1969).

One of the most popular definitions of income remains that of J. R. Hicks (1939) who suggested that 'income is the maximum value which a man can consume during a week, and still expect to be as well off at the end of the week as he was at the beginning' (p. 172). Unfortunately, it is not an operational definition, either for an accountant or a tax inspector. The difficulty lies in the word 'expect'. How can other people possibly determine what I expect? And what are they to do if my expectations are unreasonable? Accountants and revenue officers must work with verifiable facts, and hence they must look, not at what I could have *expected* to consume during a week or a tax year, but rather at what I could *in fact* have consumed while still remaining as well off at the end as at the beginning.

Unfortunately, these two concepts are not the same. If things always materialized as I expected, then there would be no divergence between them; but of course things never do. Consequently, if events go well for me in some particular year—I win the pools, my shares prosper, and my forgotten rich Australian uncle dies—my receipts in that year will be greater than I could have expected them to be, or can expect them to be next year. My 'income', defined in terms of what I could have consumed in that year, will be greater than my income in the Hicksian sense of what I could have expected to consume, and greater than my long-run spending capacity. Conversely, if I have an unexpectedly bad year, in which my shares collapse, I lose my job, and my wallet is stolen, my receipts fall below my permanent income; any one who looks at my accounts will see a gloomy picture—but an unduly gloomy one, because these unexpected adversities are unlikely to happen again. An omniscient auditor or tax inspector would seek to remove from the published figures the influence of such events.

Of course, there is no practicable method of doing this; but in raising the problem we can see why the taxation of capital gains, and capital receipts generally, has posed such difficulties for the income and corporation taxes of this and other countries. The problem is that capital gains may arise for a variety of reasons and we would wish to differentiate between the components of capital gains, some of which are equivalent to other components of income and others of which are not. This is clearly impossible, and in practice we can only adopt some rather crude categorization which is based on things we can actually measure. The normal result is that instead of exempting some capital gains from tax and charging others to income tax, all gains are taxed at a low rate. The distinction between the expected and the unexpected can never be observed, and after a careful consideration of the problems involved Hicks came to the following conclusion about concepts of income, including his own: 'They are bad tools, which break in our hands' (1939, p. 177).

British tax law initially took the view that all capital gains were windfalls and should not be subject to tax, unless they were obtained by traders, in which case they were taxed as income. As we have seen in Chapter 4, it is rather easy to turn investment income into capital gains, and hence the view that capital gains are a different sort of animal from receipts of income has become more and more implausible. The result is the present unhappy compromise in which capital gains are taxed, although at lower rates than income.

Although similar procedures have been adopted in most other countries, there are advocates of the approach of treating all capital gains and most other windfall and capital receipts as income. This view-point has been especially popular in North America, but it also appeared in the Minority Report of the Royal Commission on the Taxation of Profits and Income in 1955. Its goal is to tax an individual on his 'comprehensive income', which is defined as the amount that an individual could consume without running down the value of his wealth. Simons has suggested that 'Personal income may be defined as the algebraic sum of (a) the market value of rights exercised in consumption and (b) the change in the value of the store of property rights between the beginning and end of the period in question' (1938, p. 50). It is this definition of personal income that has come to be known as comprehensive income and we can measure it by the value of what the individual does consume plus the change in the value of his wealth.

A comprehensive income tax (CIT) would remove the present anomalies which arise from the differential treatment of capital gains, but only at the price of introducing substantial anomalies and administrative problems of its own. Capital gains under a CIT would be taxed at full income rates, rather than the current concessionary rates, and, moreover, would be taxed each year as they accrued, unlike the present situation in which capital gains are taxed only when the asset concerned is sold. Such a proposal is clearly impracticable: firstly, it would require that all assets be valued every year; secondly, it would mean that people with illiquid assets (such as houses) would receive tax bills which they did not have the cash resources to meet. We are therefore thrown back on to the taxation of realized capital gains.[1] This is likely to increase the likelihood of 'lumpy' capital receipts which arise sporadically rather than smoothly over time, and increase the need for adequate averaging provisions. On the other hand, the taxpayer benefits because he can defer payment of tax until the date when he chooses to realize the gain.

It also raises the question of what to do about capital losses. One can hardly tax capital gains without allowing losses to be tax-deductible. Yet this might result in some of the less bright or less fortunate City 'financial operators' being the poorest people in Britain in a particular year (such as 1974 when the stock-market collapsed), according to Inland Revenue statistics, even though they were also still among the wealthiest members of society. They simply cut their losses and sold out. Presumably, individuals of this kind, with low or very probably negative comprehensive incomes, would be helped by 'averaging provisions' so that their losses could be carried forward against future income. This, however, would mean that for one, or perhaps several, years certain individuals who would be both wealthy and enjoying a high level of spending would pay no tax. The prospect of finding City financiers who, on returning from a pleasant stay on a yacht on the French Riviera, were met at Heathrow by a chauffeur-driven Rolls-Royce and a note from the Inland Revenue saying that their tax liability for this year had been waived would send Fleet Street wild with excitement and MPs scurrying to put down awkward questions for the chancellor. Comprehensive income is not an idea that it would be easy to put over at Question Time in the House of Commons.

One of the most serious difficulties with a comprehensive income tax is the adjustment of income measurement for the effects of inflation. We discuss what is involved in some detail in Chapter 13; and all the problems considered there are ones that a comprehensive income tax would have to face.

---

[1] The Meade Committee (1978) did, however, suggest a method, albeit complex, for approximating the taxation of accrued gains.

A comprehensive income tax would also seek to deal with the other problems we discussed in Chapter 4 when looking at why the present tax treatment of investment income is so haphazard. It is necessary to ensure that all investment income currently earned by institutions is attributed, by one means or another, to the individual to whom it will ultimately accrue and is then taxed accordingly; only by this means can we reduce the large-scale avoidance of the present investment income tax and reverse the increasing institutionalization of savings. These procedures would have to be applied to trusts, to corporations, to pension funds, and to life insurance companies. This would mean that the income of a pension fund, for example, would be regarded as accruing to the individual who had rights in the fund, although most taxpayers would not appreciate a letter from the Inland Revenue demanding tax on income that they had never seen and that had been received by a distant pension fund. And how could we deal with unfunded schemes (such as that for civil servants) or inadequately funded schemes (such as virtually all UK occupational pension schemes)? The problems involved in 'unmasking' other institutions such as trusts are hardly less acute. In a rather similar way, but with equal difficulty, we could assess rich taxpayers on the 'income' that they derive from the durable goods which they presently buy in preference to more productive assets that yield taxable income; we might re-impose 'schedule A' on houses and extend it to other valuable items like pictures and jewellery.

It is true that what we have been describing is a rather idealized income tax, and that some of these difficulties could be avoided by not following the definition of 'comprehensive income' to the letter. After all, most of the countries that have a rather more successful record of economic management than Britain do manage to run an income tax, and it is clear that we could reduce some of the problems we have noted in Chapters 3 and 4 by moving in the direction of a comprehensive income tax, even if that movement were only a partial one. But the pragmatic approach means that it is only too easy to lose sight of what it is that we are trying to tax, and to ignore the fundamental interrelations between the different parts of the system or to be blind to their consequences. It is, after all, this pragmatism which has brought us to our present state, in which we are faced with high taxes on earned income that fail to tax spending out of inherited wealth, the almost random taxation of income from capital, the institutionalization of personal saving, and the gradual diminution in the tax base and corresponding increase in tax rates. Would an expenditure base for personal taxation offer a solution to these problems?

An expenditure tax

One advantage of choosing consumption expenditure as the tax base is that we require no valuations of an individual's wealth, and hence we avoid all the problems of measuring depreciation of assets (depreciation of consumer durables is less important and is discussed further in Chapter 6), of indexing for inflation, and of our inability to measure some important components of wealth, such as pension rights or human capital. It is no longer necessary to maintain what must inevitably be an arbitrary distinction between capital and income, and this means that we can avoid the complexities involved in the indexation of capital gains and investment income, which, as we shall see, would involve major changes in the organization of capital markets as well as the tax system.

Problems of averaging are likely to be less severe also, because whereas an individual has little control over the timing of receipts of windfall gains he can choose when to spend his resources. Moreover, it seems likely that individuals prefer to maintain a relatively stable pattern of expenditure over a run of years, and not to enjoy a burst of spending in one year followed by relative deprivation in succeeding years. Averaging is achieved not by a set of provisions in the tax system, but by the individual's own voluntary decision on when to consume.

There are two important differences between a personal expenditure tax such as we have outlined and existing taxes on expenditure often called 'indirect' taxes. A common objection to the imposition of indirect taxes is that they take no account of an individual's personal circumstances, and indeed are often, though not always, regressive. What progressivity does exist is achieved by taxing at higher rates of VAT or excise duties those commodities that are consumed relatively more by the rich than by the poor. Since consumption patterns vary between individuals this is a rather arbitrary and haphazard method of redistribution, which is a blessing to the rich man who loves plain cooking and reading, and hard on the poor man who rejects conventional standards of attire and nutrition and adopts consumption patterns more usually associated with the rich by devoting himself to the consumption of whisky. It is important to realize that this objection cannot be levelled at an expenditure tax that is a tax on the total value of an individual's consumption expenditure during the course of a year. In itself it does not discriminate between consumption on different commodities, and can be as progressive as desired in exactly the same way as an income tax is progressive; that is, by the existence of personal allowances and higher rates of tax. The degree of progressivity in the personal tax system is a quite separate issue from that of whether the tax base is to be income or expenditure.

The second difference between an expenditure tax and existing taxes on expenditure concerns the method of collection, and follows directly from the first. Because indirect taxes depend only on the total value of sales of a commodity and not on the identity and circumstances of those purchasing the commodity, they can be collected in the shops at the retail stage, or from the wholesalers (as was the case with the old purchase tax), or from the purchaser at the various stages of production (as occurs with VAT). With an expenditure tax, however, the amount of tax depends upon the personal circumstances of the consumer, and the tax cannot be collected in the shops in the form of an addition to the bill.

How then can the tax authorities measure the value in any given year of an individual's expenditure? The first thing to say is that it does not require the taxman to follow housewives into the supermarket and surreptitiously observe the figures being rung up on the till. We can measure an individual's expenditure by observing what he does with the various cash receipts arising during the course of the year. He might receive amounts in the form of wages and salaries, tips, interest and dividend payments, gifts and bequests from other people, and he might receive cash from the sale of some of his assets (for example, shares or a house) or from borrowing money. Taken together these items form his total cash 'incomings'. We must also be careful to include items received not in the form of cash but 'in kind', whether they be inherited goods (such as houses, paintings, or shares) or perks like free motor cars, lunches, and other fringe benefits. (These problems of identifying transactions and of policing the line between personal and business expenditures arise to the same extent and in just the same way with all broad-based taxes—income tax, expenditure tax, or VAT.) The total 'incomings' are matched by an equal total for 'outgoings' which describe what the individual does with his receipts. Some of these he may give away (to relatives or to charity), some he will use to meet the interest payments or repayments of the principal on loans taken out in the past, and some to save by placing his money in a building society account or by purchasing assets of various types (shares, for example). The remainder will be used to finance his personal consumption. In this way we can see that it is possible to calculate the value of an individual's expenditure by computing his various receipts and payments during the year, and we shall spell out in more detail how this would work in practice in Chapter 6.

It is also clear that some of the other problems associated with an income tax arise from the difficulty of defining an acceptable measure of an individual's *annual* income. In fact we shall now see that if we take a longer view and think of an individual's income over his lifetime, the difference between income and expenditure disappears. To see this let us consider an individual's lifetime accounts and imagine a very careful man who kept a complete record of all his receipts and all his expenditures. On the day after his death we enter his study and find in the left-hand drawer of his desk a complete record of all his receipts over his lifetime filed according to the year in which they were received. We find his salary slips and notes of interest on bank deposits, perhaps some dividends, his pension while in retirement, and all the amounts that he inherited or received by way of gifts from others. In the right-hand drawer we find a similar set of notes, again filed by year, of all his expenditures and payments over the years, including gifts made by him to others. We also find a statement prepared immediately before his death of his net wealth (assets net of liabilities) which is to be bequeathed to his descendants. Into the left-hand drawer we then insert a file with the sale proceeds of the estate and into the right-hand drawer a file containing the same figure which is equal to the value of the estate passed on to his descendants.

Since the items of 'outgoings' in the right-hand drawer must have been financed in one way or another from the 'incomings' in the left-hand drawer, the total of all the figures in the left-hand drawer equals the total of the entries in the right-hand drawer. We enter the world with nothing, and we leave the world with nothing. Our lifetime accounts must balance. The total of the entries in the right-hand drawer is simply the total value of the man's own consumption and gifts and bequests to others over his lifetime. The total in the left-hand drawer consists of his lifetime earnings, gifts received from others, investment income, and the sum of the net sales of assets over his lifetime including the value of his estate. Since we enter the world with nothing the value of net sales is equal to the capital gain the man has made on his assets over his lifetime. Hence the total in the left-hand drawer can be said to measure the man's total lifetime income, and is equal to the total of what he spends on consumption and gifts to others.

From this we can deduce that the effect of collecting a tax on consumption and gifts made on an annual basis is to impose a tax on lifetime income. We might propose an expenditure tax (including gifts in the tax base) as a superior form of income tax!

In effect, what this tax does is to tax an individual on his lifetime use of resources, and for this reason we may describe it as a lifetime expenditure tax (LET). The intellectual basis for the LET is different from that of the pure expenditure tax, although its operation is very similar. It is superior to a comprehensive income tax in that, although it can be described as a tax on lifetime income, it avoids all the problems associated with an annual income tax which we discussed above—the unequal treatment of human and financial capital, the double taxation of savings, and the difficulty of measuring 'income' in times of inflation.

The arguments advanced in this chapter are the reverse of those normally associated with the debate over income versus expenditure. It is usual to argue that in principle expenditure has many conceptual attractions over income for the tax base, but that there are too many practical difficulties involved in measuring an individual's annual expenditure. We have argued that the choice in principle between income and expenditure is finely balanced, that we prefer lifetime income, but that to measure this the appropriate annual tax base is expenditure including gifts made, and that the compelling argument against a conventional income tax is the administrative complexity of measuring an individual's annual income.

To see how the LET would operate in practice, we now turn to a discussion of how an expenditure tax might be implemented.

6

A lifetime expenditure tax

In the preceding chapter we concluded that the most promising direction of reform of the UK personal tax system involved the transformation of the income tax into a direct tax on personal expenditure. Such proposals have been made before—we noted the distinguished intellectual pedigree of the concept—but it has been generally assumed that whatever the theoretical attractions of the expenditure tax the administrative problems of operating it were overwhelming.

Certainly the historical record is not encouraging. The only country to have recent experience of operating a personal expenditure tax—Sri Lanka—has abandoned it. The US Treasury proposed such a tax in 1942, but the reception it received in Congress was so hostile that within a week the suggestion was withdrawn. N. Kaldor, distinguished dissentient member of the Radcliffe Committee of the early 1950s on the taxation of profits and income, invited consideration of the tax. The committee consulted the then chancellor of the exchequer, and was doubtless relieved when he concluded that such a proposal was much too radical to fall within the terms of reference of a royal commission. Kaldor put forward his ideas subsequently (1955), but his work received more attention for its masterly analysis of concepts of income than for its description of taxes on expenditure. Only in India were his arguments found persuasive, but the tax was never a serious one (the number of taxpayers never exceeded 1,000) and was withdrawn in 1966 (Chawla, 1972). But we believe an expenditure tax is a practical proposition, and this is no longer an eccentric minority view. Official reports in Sweden, the USA, and Ireland have shown how such proposals might be implemented in these countries (Lodin, 1967; US Treasury, 1977; Irish Tax Commission, 1982) and the Meade Committee has analysed the possibilities and problems in the UK context.

We should stress that an expenditure tax does not operate by requiring an exhaustive listing of every purchase that has been made during the year of assessment. Many people will be familiar with the rueful reckoning of their expenditure on a foreign holiday. It is certainly possible to try to relive your experiences, recording every-thing you spent—counting the drinks by the swimming-pool, the tip to the taxi-driver, and so on. If your recollections are sufficiently comprehensive, the resulting total will be a good estimate of your total expenditure. But there is a much easier way of reaching a more accurate answer. You simply measure how much foreign currency you took with you, add the amount of currency you bought while abroad, and subtract what was left when you got back. You measure, not the expenditure itself, but the sources of the expenditure, and can thus achieve a simple and reliable measure on the basis of a small number of recorded (and readily verifiable) transactions.

A personal expenditure tax would apply just the same principle. It taxes the sources of expenditure rather than the expenditure. All receipts—whatever their source or nature—are taxable; but any part of them that remains unspent can be deducted in computing liability. We can regard currency you buy as a taxable receipt; the currency you sell back attracts relief. But one problem remains. Some of the things you bring back from holiday have a value that extends beyond the period of the holiday itself. Your expenditure on a bottle of duty-free sherry or on the bull-fight poster that permanently adorns the wall is attributable not so much to the holiday as to the sub-sequent days and years in which you drink the sherry and admire the poster. An accurate measure of holiday consumption would require that you list and value every asset of enduring value which you purchased on holiday and subtract that valuation from the provisional estimate of your spending.

Clearly, this is a daunting administrative task, though a necessary one if an accurate measure of that particular period's consumption is required. But the key to devising a feasible expenditure tax is the realization that it is not important, nor even particularly desirable, that this valuation be comprehensive. Suppose a few pesetas are left in your beach shorts until the following summer; then the allocation of expenditure to particular years is inaccurate but nevertheless ex-penditure over a period of years is correctly measured. And the same would be true if you kept a wallet full of foreign currency for next year's holiday (or purchased a Picasso etching or a bull-fight poster). This year's expenditure would be overestimated, and hence a liability to expenditure tax so computed would be excessive; but all you would have done would have been to make a prepayment on account of your liability next year or in subsequent years, and there is no general reason why a tax authority should take exception to that. Normally people would not want to prepay tax in this way, and indeed you can always ensure that your holiday expenditure is accurately measured by returning your unspent notes to the bank so that the amount you did not spend is recorded. But there may be good reasons why taxpayers may choose to make prepayments. It might simply be convenient to do so—and in the case of durable goods (the poster or the Picasso) such prepayment when the purchase occurs is much the easiest way to collect the tax due. Or they might wish to prepay because they expect to pay tax at higher rates in future as their expenditure rises, and they would rather incur liability at their lower current rates. In all these cases, prepayment of tax would be acceptable—and indeed desirable, since it provides an opportunity for those with uneven patterns of expenditure to average their taxable expenditure. The objective of progressive taxation is to impose a higher average rate of tax on those with a higher average level of income (or expenditure). An incidental side-effect is that those whose average income (or expenditure) is no higher but is more variable also pay a higher average rate of tax. The possibility of prepayment diminishes this inequity.

An annual expenditure tax, which seeks to measure an individual's spending in each separate year of assessment, poses very serious administrative problems, because it requires that his assets be assessed annually. A lifetime expenditure tax, under which payments over the lifetime depend on spending during the lifetime but where payments in any particular year are not necessarily related to spending in that year, is a much more feasible proposition. It is also potentially a fairer tax than either an annual income tax or an annual expenditure tax, even in their idealized versions. We now consider more specifically how such a tax would operate.

The introduction of a lifetime expenditure tax would involve the creation of a class of 'registered assets'. These would include business assets and negotiable securities; some deposit accounts with banks, building societies, and other financial institutions would be registered, though we anticipate that current accounts with banks and balances held for day-to-day requirements and short-term savings would not normally be registered assets. The basic principle is that all receipts obtained during a year would be subject to tax, but after summing these receipts the taxpayer would deduct his net purchases of registered assets during the year. The resultant figure would be his taxable expenditure. The structure of the tax is illustrated in Figure 6.1. Arrows indicate flows of receipts and payments. Transactions that cross unbroken lines are the subject of tax payments or deductions, and it is these transactions and these only that the tax collector monitors. Those that cross broken lines do not interest him. It is important to note that these criteria relate simply to cash flows, and that there is never any inquiry into or distinction between flows of capital and flows of income. The tax base is simply the sum of all net receipts which come across the unbroken lines: earnings and gifts, net surpluses from trading, and net receipts from dealing in registered assets. Since lifetime accounts balance, this is equal, over the lifetime, to the sum of all personal expenditures and gifts to others.[1]

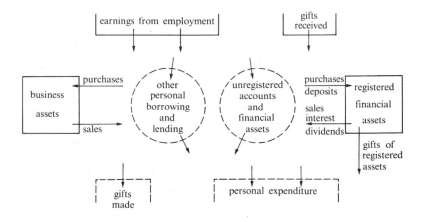

Fig. 6.1. The sources of personal expenditure

The easy questions on the present income tax form would go over to an expenditure tax form more or less unchanged. The first question would still be 'How much did your employer pay you during

---

[1] If both registered and unregistered assets exist, and either (a) returns on unregistered assets are certain or (b) the tax is proportional, the lifetime expenditure tax is exactly equivalent to a lifetime income tax, as discussed in Chapter 5. If neither of these assumptions holds, there may be divergences.

the year?', and people with incomes only from employment and negligible savings or dissavings would notice no real difference. It is the treatment of savings and investment income that is drastically altered, and the changes mostly represent simplifications. At present, the taxpayer must record the proceeds of sales of securities during the year of assessment, and obtain from his records the corresponding acquisition costs at various different dates in the past; additionally, he must declare his purchases during the year so that these can be recorded and related to his subsequent disposals. The gains thus computed are then taxed on a separate basis with a number of available optional treatments and complications. Under an expenditure tax he would simply write down the gross figures for sales and purchases during the year and the net proceeds would be added to his other receipts. The questions would relate to his year's transactions alone.

Similarly, the tax treatment of his trading activities would be much simplified. Tax would be based on the cash accounts of the business, and the proprietor would simply pay tax on the net amount that he withdrew from the business during the year. Life insurance policies would generally be registered assets, so that the whole of any premiums paid would be deductible against tax, but all receipts from policies would be taxable. This would seem to impose a heavy liability when a policy matured, and if the proceeds were spent there would (and should) be such a liability. But if they were not all dissipated immediately tax could be deferred until they were used for expenditure by depositing them in registered accounts, and life insurance companies would no doubt be quick to facilitate such arrangements. Figure 6.2 gives some impression of what an expenditure tax return might be like.

There would be two new sets of questions. One would ask for details of gifts received during the year, including gifts of valuable assets, subject of course to some exemption limit. Receipts would no longer escape tax simply because they had not been earned. Details of accrued interest would not be requested (so those with forgotten bank accounts would no longer be embarrassed when they or the Revenue remembered). Instead, institutions authorized to operate registered accounts would at the end of each tax year notify both taxpayer and Revenue of the amount of net additions or withdrawals, and the form would ask for this information.

The simplifications involved in moving from an income basis to an expenditure base arise principally from the shift from an accruals base to a cash-flow base. It does not matter whether a receipt is an item of capital or income. It is unnecessary to determine the date of the *transaction* to which any particular item relates; the issue is simply when and whether a particular cash payment occurred. Every question on the expenditure tax (ET) form asks only about actual cash payments that took place during the year of assessment. The result is that for taxpayers with simple affairs, the procedures involved in completing an ET form would differ very little from those that are required at present; and for those with more complex circumstances—people who participate in businesses and have substantial investment incomes—the return in Figure 6.2 would be easier to complete.

Nevertheless, the form raises difficulties through its unfamiliarity, and this is not a negligible consideration. Unsatisfactory though the present income tax system is, a few individuals and most accountants have experience and understanding of its operation. No such expertise is presently available for an expenditure tax system. Taken too seriously, of course, this argument would imply that no change in the tax system could ever be made, however miraculous the expected improvement. But it does highlight the central administrative difficulty raised by the expenditure tax. This is not the traditional 'How would it work?'—the answer to that is 'better than at present, at any rate'—but 'How do we get there from where we are now?'

A radical transition to an expenditure tax

This transitional problem is a serious one. We have described how an expenditure tax could be operated by simply monitoring those transactions that cross the solid lines of Figure 6.1, and once the new tax system was fully functioning this would indeed be true. Expenditure could only be financed out of sources that were either the subject of a tax charge now, or that had been the subject of such a charge at some date in the past: present or past employment income, trading surplus or gifts, or withdrawals from registered assets. But this would not be true on the day when the expenditure tax was introduced. On that day there would exist a substantial stock of assets which could, unless some procedure were devised for recording its existence and monitoring its subsequent disposition, be

Receipts

1. *Employments* Enter here the total of all payments from your employer (attach from E2) ☐

   Taxable benefits in kind: see note X ☐

2. *Businesses* Enter here the gross sales proceeds of all businesses owned or operated by you (list details on form B1) ☐

3. *Partnerships* If you are a partner in any business, enter here the total of all distributions to you ☐

4. *Gifts* Enter the total of all gifts and inheritances received. You may neglect the first £100 from any person (list details on form G1) ☐

5. *Pensions, social security, and national insurance benefits.* See note 5. ☐

6. *Securities* Enter the total sales proceeds of securities sold during the year ☐
   Enter here the total of all dividends and interest payments received (list details on form S1) ☐

7. *Registered accounts* Total of net withdrawals from each account (list on form R1 and attach forms R2) ☐

8. *Life insurance policies* Total of maturities (attach forms L2) ☐

9. *All other receipts* See Notes ☐

10. *TOTAL RECEIPTS* (Total of lines 1–9) ☐

Payments

11. *Employments* All admissible expenses connected with your work (see note Y) (list on form E1 unless you claim the standard deduction) ☐

12. *Businesses* Total admissible expenses of businesses owned or operated by you (give details on form B1) ☐

13. *Securities* Total acquisition cost of securities purchased (list on form S1) ☐

14. *Registered accounts* Total net deposits in registered accounts (list on form R1 and attach forms R3) ☐

15. *Life insurance policies* Total premiums paid in the year (if the policy is a new one, attach form L3) ☐

16. *Other payments* See notes. Give details on form P1 ☐

17. *TOTAL PAYMENTS* (total of lines 11–16) ☐

18. *NET TAXABLE EXPENDITURE* (Subtract line 17 from line 10) ☐

Extracts from notes to taxpayers

4. Gifts of registered assets that you have received must be listed on form G1 but need not be included in the total.

5. If you received a pension or social security or national insurance benefits in 1988, you should have received form SS1 at the end of the year. If so, enter the total from it in line 5. If you have not received SS1, contact your local tax or social security office.

6. Gifts of registered assets that you have made count as disposals for this purpose.

9. You must list here all other receipts in 1988 unless (i) they are returns of or on money you have yourself already paid and (ii) you have not claimed tax relief on that payment in this or any previous year (e.g. tips and bonuses must be entered; receipts of principal or interest on loans need not be included *unless* you claimed tax relief when you made them).

11. You may claim a standard deduction of £50. If you wish to claim more you must provide full details on form E1.

Notes to reader

Forms B1, G1, S1, P1 etc. are supplementary statements which need be completed only by those who have items in these categories: the total is then brought forward to the main form.

Forms E2, R2, etc., are supplied by the institutions involved, and the taxpayer need only transfer the total figures to his tax return.

Fig. 6.2. An expenditure tax form

used for subsequent consumption, and which could be spent without involving its holder in any liability to expenditure tax at any time. Indeed the whole of existing personal wealth would potentially be available for this purpose.

Although the owners of this wealth would not have paid expenditure tax on it, they might in accumulating it have paid income tax; and it would be fair and consistent with the spirit of the tax that this should be regarded as prepayment of expenditure tax. If savings had been derived from taxed income, it is unjust that expenditure from them should be taxed also. As we saw in Chapter 4, however, the proportion of personal wealth in the UK that has been accumulated from taxed income is probably rather small. Nevertheless, some of it has been; and the smaller the total amount of the wealth, the larger the proportion of it which is likely to have been subject to income tax at some time. But there are no rules by which we can hope to distinguish between wealth that was saved out of earnings and wealth that originated from capital gains or from ancestors who picked the right side in the Wars of the Roses. It is possible that one could attempt, as the Meade Committee (1978) did, to devise some very crude rules for separating 'life-cycle' and other components of wealth: capital up to some rather arbitrary figure, perhaps related to age, could be deemed to have been derived from earnings, and amounts in excess of that a proper object of taxation, so that a credit of that amount would be given against future expenditure. But the rough justice which would be done would be extremely rough.

Combined with this problem of equity is a straightforward problem of enforcement. Wealth that is concealed on the appointed day for the transition can be spent thereafter without involving its owner in a liability to expenditure tax, and indeed can even be a source of tax relief if it is subsequently converted into registered assets: wealth that attracts the attention of the tax inspector would be substantially less valuable. Thus there would be a strong temptation as the transition approached to convert assets into inconspicuous forms: jewellery, gold coins, bank-notes stuffed under the mattress. Kaldor (1955) was prepared to deal with the last problem by calling in the currency on the appointed day, noting that if the threat were believed it would be unnecessary to carry it out. But devices of this kind are very far-fetched.

Moreover, the problems of equity and enforcement are by no means unrelated. If measures are thought to be fair, then they will be less widely evaded and there will be general support for effective action against those who try to get around them. There seems to us no possibility of devising transitional arrangements which would not be grossly inequitable in many particular cases, and which would not be seen to be inequitable in many particular cases. This is not only a serious objection in itself, but one which more or less precludes effective action to enforce whatever transitional rules might be devised. It would be a remarkably selfless opposition political party which, faced with the manifest injustices of the transition, did not promise to abandon the tax or to undermine whatever specific transitional arrangements were proposed. If this is the only route by which an expenditure tax can be reached then, however alluring the prospect at the end may be, we shall never go down it. We therefore devote the remainder of this chapter to an analysis of evolutionary proposals by which, in time, the present tax system might be transformed into an expenditure tax.

Gifts and bequests under a lifetime expenditure tax

One of the common objections to an expenditure tax by those concerned about the distribution of wealth is that it allows individuals to accumulate tax-free. If such accumulated wealth is used to finance consumption at a later date, then tax will be charged on the expenditure when it is made. Suppose, however, that the assets are either given away or bequeathed to others on death. In the absence of a tax charge on capital transfers of this kind it is likely that wealth would be highly concentrated and handed on from one generation to the next. But is this not exactly what happens under the present tax system? Are the people who are rich today the sons and daughters of those who were rich in the previous generation? This question has been extensively investigated by Harbury and his collaborators who examined the estates of sets of fathers and sons (Harbury and McMahon, 1973; Harbury and Hitchens, 1976). They found that there was a highly significant correlation between dying rich and having had a rich father. Inherited wealth remains an important determinant of the distribution of wealth at the top of the distribution, although its influence may be declining slightly. Harbury and Hitchens (1979) found that 60 per cent of those who died wealthy had themselves inherited a large amount; so large in fact that had their fathers been a random sample of the male population the figure would have been less than 1 per cent.

In the light of this evidence we are inclined to put more weight on inequalities of wealth caused by inheritance than on inequalities resulting from differences in lifetime accumulations. This leads us away from an annual wealth tax and towards the taxation of gifts and bequests. We shall now consider ways of reforming the taxation of transfers.

The first, and most obvious, change is that gifts *inter vivos* could be taxed at the same rates as apply to estates or gifts made within three years before death. A more important change, however, is to examine closely the rate structure. Too much attention is paid to the high marginal rates at the top end which gives rise to the myth of the terrible burden of death duties. The very high exemption level means that the bulk of wealth that is transferred either on death or by gift pays a very low average rate of tax. We feel that it is important to consider carefully the idea of including all transfers in the tax base. One way of doing this is by a comprehensive income tax which counts as an individual's income all receipts of gifts and bequests during the year. Since an individual may have little control over the timing of receipts of gifts and inheritances, his income defined in this way may fluctuate wildly from year to year. Under a progressive tax system this may mean that he would pay more tax than if he had received the same amount in equal instalments. This possibility has led to an acceptance of the need for averaging provisions under a comprehensive income tax. In Chapter 5 we discussed a better way of measuring an individual's lifetime comprehensive income which we saw was equal to the total use of resources over his lifetime. This can be measured by the sum of his consumption plus gifts and bequests made. So if we wish to impose an annual tax on a measure of the individual's lifetime use of resources, a better way of achieving this objective is to impose an annual tax on consumption plus gifts made during the year—the lifetime expenditure tax. Like the comprehensive income tax it includes transfers in the main personal tax base but the amount included refers to gifts made, not those received, and hence the donor can smooth the timing of gifts if he so wishes which reduces the need for averaging provisions.

There are three main virtues of the lifetime expenditure tax. First, it is genuinely a tax on an individual's lifetime income or uses of resources, and in that sense is superior to a comprehensive income tax. Second, it would widen the tax base quite considerably because all transfers (except for some very small exemption on gifts which had to be included) would come within the tax net. Third, since all transfers would be taxed, such a scheme holds out the hope of a reasonably equitable way of taxing owner-occupiers. As we have seen, other attempts to remove the tax subsidy are problematic because the concessions have already been capitalized, and existing home-owners do not have the resources to cope with the removal of the tax concessions to mortgage interest payments. But to tax the value of owner-occupied property transferred by gift, or more usually on death, is a relatively painless way of recouping some of the revenue. This proposal would generate enough revenue to enable a reduction to be made in the tax rate on earned income (or expenditure out of earned income), but it would impose very much heavier taxes on gifts and inherited wealth than currently exist. The extra revenue would arise because the 'typical' estate consisting, say, of a house and little else, would pay tax at full personal tax rates and because a much heavier tax burden would be imposed on medium-sized and large estates resulting from the abolition of the high exemption level. Even with a top marginal tax rate under the lifetime expenditure tax (LET) of 50 per cent, virtually all large estates would pay more tax than at present. Gifts would be included in the annual LET computation, and the value of the estate resulting from death could be considered as the expenditure of a separate tax year.

Towards an expenditure tax

In Chapter 2, we suggested a number of administrative reforms which were desirable if income tax were to be operated more efficiently and effectively. In particular, we advocated the abolition of cumulative PAYE and the schedular system, and the institution of a single annual return of the whole of a taxpayer's income. We would favour these reforms whether or not any other changes are made in the structure of income tax. They would certainly be desirable and probably necessary if progress were to be made towards an expenditure tax, since only by means of an annual return would it be possible to be confident that individuals obtained the reliefs to which they were entitled and paid the tax to which they were liable. We assume that such changes would be accompanied by extensive computerization of UK income tax administration, which has already occurred in most comparable countries and is slowly being introduced in Britain (although the schedular system makes the process more difficult).

At the same time, we would like to see progress in the following directions: firstly, in acknowledging that expenditure is the most appropriate base for the main direct personal tax; secondly, in assimilating the existing unsystematic reliefs for saving to the expenditure tax arrangements; and thirdly, in extending these arrangements to other forms of saving. We have described the three main forms of 'privileged' saving in the present UK tax system: pensions, housing, and life insurance, although the privileges of the latter have been reduced. As we move to an expenditure tax, new life insurance policies would obtain full tax relief on premiums paid, and proceeds of the policy, whether by surrender or maturity, would be taxable in full. As we noted on page 94, this would probably lead to some changes in the institutional arrangements made by companies to deal with policy maturities, so that the whole sum due need not be drawn from the policy proceeds immediately it matured. Unfortunately, it would be necessary to continue the present very complicated rules for existing policies, at least for some years, since otherwise current policy-holders would suffer the disadvantage of the new procedures (the tax on proceeds) without having received the benefits (relief on premiums and accumulation).

We have also described housing as a 'privileged asset'. The Meade Committee has discussed in detail the most logical treatment under various tax arrangements. But it is not clear that tinkering with the tax treatment of housing would improve the efficiency of the much-distorted housing market, and because tax concessions in this area have been largely capitalized, as we noted in Chapter 1, any change in the *status quo* would be likely to involve major inequities and hardships to particular individuals. If we were to describe what might be done about the UK housing market we should need to write a book, and this is not it. The UK is by accident or design committed to an outcome in which those who can buy their own homes do so, and those who cannot are housed by local authorities; and no foreseeable tax changes will alter that situation.

Pension funds are already taxed on LET principles—contributions are exempt but the proceeds are taxed—and therefore no change in these arrangements would be required. But there are at present substantial restrictions on the benefits which can be provided from schemes that qualify for Inland Revenue approval; these restrictions could be abandoned and the associated administrative machinery abolished, since if people can save in this way for themselves there is no need to limit the amount they save in this way via a pension fund. Equally, once people have the opportunity to save in this way for themselves there is little reason to compel them to make such provision through a pension fund. Under an expenditure tax, it is very much easier for people to make 'life-cycle savings' to ensure that part of their income is available to them after their retirement. So we expect that there would be less demand for extensive occupational pension schemes, and people who were offered good schemes of this kind would no longer be at a great advantage relative to those who were not. We expect that state and private schemes would continue to provide basic pensions to ensure against poverty in old age, but would envisage that more elaborate provisions might become voluntary. If this happened, the present extreme complexity of pension fund administration could be reduced, and the proportion of personal wealth that was held in pension funds would diminish while that held directly by individuals would rise.

In addition to these changes, it would be essential to bring other types of savings into the expenditure tax framework. The procedure for dealing with land and negotiable securities would be as follows. After some appointed day—A day—the new rules would be applied. Purchase costs would be deductible and proceeds would be taxable. (Some limits on the purchase of registered assets which would qualify for a deduction would be necessary during a transitional period.) Any seller of securities subsequent to the appointed day would therefore be liable to tax on the whole of his receipts from the sale, unless they were reinvested in other securities or registered assets. If he had purchased his securities after A day, he would obtain no relief against this liability, since he could already have claimed their cost as a tax deduction; but if he could show that they represented a pre-A-day acquisition, he might be allowed to deduct the purchase price from the proceeds. This means that for securities that he had purchased under the previous income tax regime, he would be taxed on the capital gain as at present but at income tax rates. This means that in spite of the relatively conservative nature of the transition to an expenditure tax involved in these proposals, many people spending out of accumulated wealth would pay more tax than they do under the present tax structure right from the start.

Changes would also be needed in the taxation of unincorporated businesses. The base for taxation would be shifted from the profit of the business to the net amount withdrawn from the business during the year by the proprietor, since all sales proceeds would be taxable (whether capital or current in nature) and all expenses would be deductible (whether capital or current in nature). The small business man would pay only on that part of his profit that he chose to withdraw for his own consumption, and would be fully relieved of liability on what he reinvested in the future growth of his firm. He would therefore obtain the twin benefits of a system vastly more conducive to the expansion of small business (aided by an increase in the importance of personal saving relative to that of institutions) and a substantial reduction in the administrative burdens involved in preparing tax accounts. There are opportunities to make similar simplifications in the taxation of incorporated businesses.

The other major category of personal saving is deposits in accounts with banks, building societies, and other financial institutions. In general, it seems to us undesirable that current accounts and balances used for transactions purposes should be registered assets: monitoring the balances on accounts that are the subject of frequent small transactions would be a nuisance for the taxpayer, the financial institution, and the Revenue alike. But both the logic of the tax and the desirability of allowing as much freedom of choice as possible in savings behaviour suggest that taxpayers should have the opportunity to make deposits in registered accounts. All payments into such accounts would attract relief; all withdrawals would be taxed. But these accounts would mainly be intended for long-term and contractual savings, not for day-to-day purposes. These objectives can be achieved by requiring that basic rate tax be withheld from withdrawals from registered accounts, with provision for rapid refunds from the Revenue in cases of hardship. This would have the effects of making it inconvenient to operate frequently on registered accounts, and of ensuring that people who did so did not end up with tax liabilities that they could not pay because they had already spent the full amount which they had withdrawn. In due course it would be desirable to assimilate unregistered accounts fully to the expenditure tax system by abolishing tax on the interest derived from them; registered accounts would then fall within the right-hand box of Figure 6.1, unregistered accounts into the right-hand circle.

Once all these changes had been made, the British income tax would have been transformed into a direct tax on personal expenditure. It is interesting to note that, with two exceptions (the more extensive monitoring of gifts and the treatment of registered deposit accounts), every change involved is a simplification. The taxation of life insurance policies and companies is much more straightforward. Most of the burdensome aspects of pension fund administration disappear. The tax treatment of capital gains and of small businesses, which are the most difficult parts of the present income tax system to understand and to administer, is greatly simplified.

Why do so many people believe, as we used to believe, that an expenditure tax might be fine in theory but could not work in practice, when in reality it is likely to be rather easier to operate than the existing income tax? We think there are two reasons. One is that the expenditure tax has not been explicitly compared with the present tax structure, but rather with some idealized income tax system which was not too precisely defined but which was assumed to be working smoothly and efficiently. We had simply forgotten how complicated and unsatisfactory the system was at the moment.

The other reason is that it is common to view any proposed change to the tax system in isolation. If we take for granted that every other aspect of the tax structure is to be operated more or less as it is now, then it is almost inevitable that any change will seem difficult and expensive to make. But if we take a broader view of the system as a whole and look at sets of interrelated changes, a much wider range of possibilities is feasible. For example, we shall observe that there are many changes (such as the introduction of local income tax) that are costly with cumulative PAYE and cheap without it. This is one reason why it is essential, even for an understanding of the administration of taxation policy, to be aware of the underlying principles of taxation involved, since only then is it possible to see these interrelationships and the effects of the system as a whole. It is also for this reason that a tax system which is to be fair, simple, and efficient in administration must stick closely to a well-defined set of underlying principles. When we depart from these—for good or bad reasons—we begin to generate anomalies and loopholes; these demand *ad hoc* solutions which give rise to further anomalies and loopholes; and so on down a path of ever-increasing complexity. A principal merit of an expenditure tax is that it really can be operated in a way that is close to such basic principles, while as we saw in Chapter 5 a comprehensive income tax presents many more problems; spending is easier to measure than income, and cash flows are easier to recognize than accruals. A satisfactory annual income tax would be difficult to operate even in a perfect world, which is why it does not work very well in the UK.

7

Social security and taxation

We noted in Chapter 2 that before the Second World War a married couple on average earnings paid no income tax. Nor did they receive any state benefits, although they might be eligible for a modest retirement pension. Tax and social security were entirely separate activities, administered by different departments with very different styles of operation, for different groups of clients.

All this has changed. Almost everyone in employment is now a taxpayer, and post-war reforms based on the Beveridge plan extended the benefit system to the whole population. Initially, the relationship between tax and social security was not a major concern. Most benefits were contingent—they were paid on the occurrence of a specific event, like unemployment, old age, or sickness. But as pressure grew to achieve value for money within the social security system, benefits were increasingly tailored to household needs and resources. Thus the information needed to assess benefits came to look like the information needed to assess tax. And as the range and scope of benefit paid to low-income working households grew, so did the range within which the tax and benefit systems overlapped. In this way the interaction of tax and social security—an issue that fifty years earlier no one would have imagined could arise—became one of the principal questions in tax policy in the 1980s. In this chapter, we describe the main elements of the social security system as it is today, and argue that closer integration of tax and social security is both an inevitable and a desirable development.

The present system

Most adults who are not in work are in this position because they are elderly, or sick, or unemployed. There are contingent benefits designed to deal with each of these situations. A single man or woman obtains a retirement pension of £38·30 per week. Most married women have little pension entitlement of their own and their pensioner husbands receive an additional £23 per week; on the death of her husband, a widow is entitled to a pension of £38·30 of her own. Since 1978, however, married women can no longer opt out of the state pension system and may credit up twenty years of family responsibilities towards their career record; this means that in due course most married women will receive single pensions in their own right when they reach retirement age.

If you are unemployed, but have worked for at least half the previous fiscal year, you will be entitled to unemployment benefit at the weekly rate of £30·45, increased to £49·25 if you have a dependent spouse. You can recive unemployment benefit for up to a year. You are not entitled to unemployment benefit at the end of this period of a year, or if you did not have a job before you became unemployed. The long-term unemployed and school-leavers who have never held a permanent job are therefore excluded.

Most employers provide some sick pay during a short spell of illness. For the first eight weeks, the cost of this is partly defrayed through the Statutory Sick Pay scheme. Thereafter a worker may be entitled to sickness benefit, at rates slightly lower than those paid to the unemployed. Sickness benefit can last for a year and, depending on the cause of your illness, you may be able to obtain other benefits thereafter.

All these benefits are purely contingent benefits. Even if you are a millionaire and receive dividend cheques in the post every day, or are married to someone whose income makes him or her liable to a higher rate of tax, you will receive these benefits provided you are elderly, or sick, or unemployed, and meet the other conditions. However, most people who are elderly or unemployed, and many who are sick, have very few resources other than state benefits. For such people, these benefits are generally insufficient. Certainly they are below the safety net provided for everyone by supplementary benefit.

Supplementary benefit is available to any one who is in work. The basic rates are slightly less than the standard rates of unemployment benefit, and there is a long-term rate, principally for pensioners and single-parent families, which in turn is slightly less than the rate of retirement pension. However, the supplementary benefit scale provides for housing costs in addition, and so the effective standard it implies is substantially above the rates of national insurance benefit. Any one who is not entitled to national insurance benefit, or who is entitled and lacks the support of assets or a partner's income, will therefore have a right to supplementary benefit. Table

7.1 shows how many of those who were not working in 1985 came into these various categories.

Table 7.1:   *Benefit levels, November 1985*

Benefit	Weekly rate (£)	Number receiving (m)	Cost, 1985/6 (£b)
Child benefit	7.00	12.2	4.4
Family income supplement	97.50 (qualifying limit)	0.2	0.14
Retirement pension:		9.4	16.7
single	38.30		
couple	60.80		
Supplementary benefit			
long-term:		2.6	2.7
single	37.50		
couple	60.00		
short-term:		2.2	4.6
single	29.50		
couple	47.85		
Unemployment benefit:		1.0	1.6
single	30.45		
couple	49.25		

Those who are in work may not receive supplementary benefit. The principal benefits to which they are entitled are for housing costs and for their children. Housing benefit provides a proportion of both rent and rates which is based on the difference between household income and a needs allowance related to household size. (This is 'non-certificated housing benefit', which goes to those in work and others who are not receiving supplementary benefit; those who do qualify for supplementary benefit obtain 'certificated housing benefit' which can cover their full housing costs.) All families, whatever their income or work status, are entitled to child benefit of £7 per child per week. Low-income working households may be entitled to family income supplement. This provides for a payment of half the difference between a prescribed amount—also related to household size—and actual income. As Table 7.1 shows, relatively few working households receive these means-tested benefits.

Pensions

The 1950s saw a rapid increase in the proportion of pensioners in the population. This continued in the two following decades, although stability can now be expected till the end of the century as the low inter-war birth rate which caused so much concern in the 1930s results in a correspondingly small number of people reaching retirement age. With unemployment at much lower levels than had been anticipated—or had been believed possible—the focus of attention in the development of social security policy became the position of the elderly.

There was concern that an increasingly large proportion of poor households were elderly people with inadequate pensions, and that the rapid extension of occupational pension schemes in the public sector and among middle-class employees would leave other workers behind and exacerbate inequality in old age. In 1959 the Labour party proposed an ambitious scheme of national superannuation and although Labour lost that election the architect of the proposals, Richard Crossman, advanced a similar scheme when he became secretary of state for social services in 1968. Although approved by Parliament, the Crossman proposals were abandoned after the Conservatives won power in 1970. A new scheme was devised, giving a much greater role to the private sector. This too passed into legislation, and was also abandoned when its sponsors were defeated in the 1974 election.

With this history, the primary concern thereafter was not to find the best pension scheme but to find a scheme on which everyone could agree; and this was reflected in the design of the State Earnings-Related Pension Scheme (SERPS) which came into operation in 1978. It provided for a pension based on average revalued lifetime earnings. Good occupational pension schemes could 'contract out' of SERPS, which meant that your state pension was reduced but the private scheme must guarantee at least to make up the difference. Contracted-out workers pay lower rates of national insurance contribution and so do their employers.

The scheme was extremely complicated and was not adequately costed at the time of adoption. Projections of the expenditure involved (Hemming and Kay, 1982; Government Actuary, 1982) caused increasing concern as to whether the proposed pensions could be afforded. As part of the 1985 Social Security Reviews, the government announced the abolition of SERPS. Existing accrued rights would be honoured (which implied that some SERPS pensions would be paid until the twenty-second century), but no new ones would be earned after 1990. Instead, all employees would be obliged to make some pension provision of their own with a minimum contribution of 4 per cent of earnings. The proposal aroused fierce opposition, however, and the government withdrew its proposal, favouring substantial reductions in benefits paid instead.

The interaction of tax and benefits

The interaction between the tax and social security systems is a difficult issue. For many, it may seem surprising that there is any interaction at all. Is it not absurd that people with incomes below the supplementary benefit level should be liable for income tax? Surely it is nonsensical that many households are simultaneously paying income tax and receiving means-tested benefits? The inter-relationship appears to be the product of some administrative muddle in which the left hand of the government—the Department of Health and Social Security—does not know what the right hand—the Inland Revenue—is doing.

Although there is no shortage of administrative muddle in this or other areas of the tax system, this picture is somewhat over-simplified. If the tax threshold were raised to a level at which no one who was poor was liable for tax, this would benefit not only the poor but everyone who paid income tax, whatever their income level. As a result, increasing the threshold is a very expensive method of helping the poor. We might try to claw back the gains from those with incomes above the tax threshold, but this involves sharply increasing the marginal rate of tax paid at this point in the income distribution. This would make it difficult for poor households to escape poverty by increasing their earnings—it would exacerbate the poverty trap, which we discuss below. Related difficulties would arise in trying to eliminate the overlap between tax and means-tested benefits. It is important to recognize that most of those taxpayers whose incomes are at or a little above the tax threshold are not poor at all. The tax thresholds—around £42 per week for a single man and £66 for a married couple—are very low, and very few bread-winners have incomes as low as that. Most of the people who do are secondary earners—married women woring part-time, juveniles,

people moving into retirement (Kay, 1984). There is nothing necessarily irrational about collecting tax from all these people and refunding part or all of it through family income supplement to the
small minority of them who do indeed have household responsibilities. It may therefore be a perfectly economical administrative
procedure to have some people who both pay tax and receive
benefits.

Nevertheless, some aspects of this interaction of tax and social
security are clearly unsatisfactory. The poverty trap is one of these.
As income increases, entitlement to means-tested benefits falls, and
this imposes an implicit marginal tax rate on extra earnings additional to the explicit rate imposed by the tax system itself. This
rate can be 50 per cent for family income supplement (FIS), 29 per
cent for rent rebates, 9 per cent for rate rebates. These rates cannot
simply be added to each other because there are interrelations between them. The combined effect is shown in Table 7.2. A household
with a gross income of £140 per week could actually be worse off
than one with only £60 per week—an implicit marginal tax rate over
this range of over 100 per cent. As a result of measures to limit the
cost of housing benefit and progressive national insurance contributions, this poverty trap has become steadily more severe.

Table 7.2:   *The poverty trap, November 1985*

	(£ per week)		
	Gross earnings	60.00	100.00	140.00
Plus	Child benefit	14.00	14.00	14.00
	Housing benefit	21.88	15.03	—
	FIS	25.00	5.00	—
	Free school meals	6.00	6.00	—
Less	Income tax	—	10.07	22.07
	National insurance	4.20	9.00	12.60
		122.68	120.96	119.33

Note: Calculations are for a married man with two children aged 10
and 13, rent of £20 per week, and rates of £7 per week.

These implicit marginal tax rates are very difficult to work out, not
least for the individual concerned. Means-tested benefits are not

awarded at the same time as tax is collected, and the periods over which they are calculated differ from the fiscal year. Some benefits, such as FIS and free school meals, run for up to twelve months once eligibility has been determined. Consequently an increase in wages does not necessarily affect benefits received for several months, and a temporary increase might not affect them at all, or alternatively might affect them for a very lengthy period. This complexity makes it possible that many people are unaware that their marginal tax rate is so high, and hence the disincentive effects are reduced. Whether a system that works only because people do not understand it is desirable is another matter.

Although the poverty trap covers a wide range of incomes, the number of people affected by it is not large. Table 7.3 shows the estimated distribution of marginal rates of tax faced by heads of households in 1985. These marginal rates include not only the direct taxes—income tax and national insurance contributions—but also the implicit taxes which result from the withdrawal of means-tested benefits. It is apparent that most households face a rate between 30 and 45 per cent. Higher rates apply to those affected either by the higher rates of income tax or by benefit withdrawal; only a very small minority are in the position of the hypothetical household of Table 7.2 which is subject to a rate over 100 per cent.

Table 7.3: *Distribution of marginal tax rates for heads of tax units, December 1985*

Marginal tax rate faced by head of household	Per cent of population
< 10%	6.1
10%–30%	14.1
30%–45%	73.1
45%–60%	3.4
60%–80%	1.7
80%–100%	0.8
> 100%	0.7
Average 36.2%	100.0

Note: Rates include implicit rates from withdrawal of means-tested benefits.
Source: Estimates from IFS tax and benefit model.

This poverty trap is also rather intractable. We have shown how it is possible that a man with gross earnings of £140 per week is no better off than someone with £60 per week. We can reduce the poverty trap either by making the £60 per week man worse off or by making the £140 per week man better off. The first of these is presumably unacceptable—it relieves the poverty trap by exacerbating poverty. The second of these can only be done at reasonable cost if we avoid making people with incomes a little over £140 per week any better off—which means extending high marginal rates of tax into a broader range of the income distribution, and one in which much larger numbers of households are to be found.

The poverty trap and the unemployment trap are often confused. The poverty trap affects households in work; the unemployment trap affects households out of work. The poverty trap reflects the lack of incentive for low-income households to increase their earnings. The unemployment trap reflects their lack of incentive to find a job at all. This affects people who have high *replacement rates*. The replacement rate is the proportion of your net income that will be 'replaced' by the benefit system if you lose your job (or, for someone who is already out of work, the ratio of current income to expected net wage). A simple illustration of how a replacement rate is calculated is given in Table 7.4. Since there are usually costs associated with holding a job, such as travel to work and meals while there, someone with a replacement rate of 90 per cent or more is probably better off on the dole. Of course, many people dislike work and might welcome the opportunity to give it up even if they were somewhat (but not too much) poorer, and the benefit system attempts to restrict the entitlement of people who quit jobs voluntarily or refuse or do not seek reasonable offers of employment. There are other people who might want to work even if it made them worse off.

The household shown in Table 7.4 is significantly worse off out of work than it would have been in work, and Table 7.2 suggests that it would be at least £15 per week better off with almost any job, however poorly paid. This suggests that some scepticism about claims that the relationship between tax and social security is the cause of high levels of unemployment (see, for example, Minford, 1983) is in order. However, the size of the possible disincentive effects cannot be deduced from hypothetical examples; it is necessary to look at the actual distribution of replacement rates over the population as a whole.

Table 7.4: *Calculating a replacement rate, December 1985*
(£ per week)

In work		Out of work	
Gross income	100.00	Unemployment benefit	49.25
Child benefit	14.00	Child bencfit	14.00
Housing benefit	15.03	Housing benefit	27.00
Family income supplement	5.00	Supplementary benefit	9.80
Free school meals	6.00	Free school meals	6.00
Income tax	−10.07		
National insurance	−9.00		
	120.96		106.05

$$\text{Replacement rate} = \frac{106.05}{120.96} = 88\%$$

Note: Household as in Table 7.2.

Careful calculation of replacement rates is an extremely complicated exercise. The figures in Table 7.4 reflect a snapshot of an early week of unemployment, which may be misleading. Because both earnings and benefits are taxable, but in different ways, a spell of unemployment can have effects on tax liabilities after it has ended (or before it started). Benefit entitlements are themselves a function of the length of the spell of unemployment. To measure a replacement rate accurately, it is necessary to specify the length of time for which a household is unemployed and past work experience, and to measure its effect on net income over a period which may extend for several years.

These calculations form the basis of the figures reported in Table 7.5. The 13-week average replacement rate reflects the experience of someone who is unemployed for a relatively short period. In 1968, 35 per cent of the population had replacement rates in excess of 90 per cent, and the average for the population as a whole was 87 per cent. Ten years later, 21 per cent were still above 90 per cent and the population average was 79 per cent; but by 1983 this average was only 60 per cent, and very few people had high replacement rates.

There are three main reasons for this. The level of benefits has fallen somewhat relative to wages. Earnings-related supplements to national insurance benefits have been abolished. Most importantly, unemployment benefit became taxable in 1982. This does not mean that large amounts of tax are collected from the unemployed—someone who is out of work for a lengthy period will not normally receive enough benefit to incur a tax liability. But for someone who had both earnings and unemployment benefit receipts in the course of a fiscal year, the fact that additional earnings might be taxed at around 40 per cent while benefits were not taxed at all made short-term replacement rates high for many taxpayers, and this anomaly has now been removed.

Table 7.5:   *The development of replacement rates over time*

	13-week average			53-week marginal		
	Average	% with >0.9	% with <0.5	Average	% with >0.9	% with <0.5
1968	0.870	35.2	0.5	0.537	2.8	30.7
1975	0.751	17.2	5.9	0.498	2.5	50.5
1978	0.790	21.0	2.3	0.519	2.2	44.0
1980	0.727	12.0	8.0	0.503	1.9	47.8
1982	0.597	3.2	28.0	0.510	2.2	52.3
1983	0.600	2.9	21.0	0.504	1.9	53.2

Source: Dilnot, Kay, and Morris, 1984.

The efficiency of the social security system

The efficiency of the social security system can be measured in a variety of ways, and in Table 7.6 we attempt to summarize several indicators. The narrowest concept is concerned with direct administrative costs. These are costs of social security which do not result in any direct gain to the recipients. The cheapest benefits to administer are retirement pensions. The entitlement of a beneficiary need only be determined once, and then continues for the rest of his or her life—the procedure thereafter is more or less automatic. The costs per pound of means-tested supplementary benefit and family income supplement are up to twenty times higher. Assessing entitlement is a more complex process, the circumstances of beneficiaries are more likely to change, and while retirement pensions are usually the recipient's main source of income, many people obtain—as the names suggest—only small amounts of supplementary benefit or supplementary pension to top up other benefits or sources of income. These variations in administrative cost are likely to be reflected also in variations in compliance costs to recipients. The costs of operating sickness and unemployment benefit are closer to those of the means-tested benefits than to other national insurance benefits.

Table 7.6: *The efficiency of the social security system*

	Administrative cost (1981/2) per £ benefit (£)	Take-up (%)	Percentage to non-poor (1981)
Supplementary benefit	.105	74	—
FIS	.045	50	—
Pensions	.013	→100	41
Unemployment/sickness etc.	.092	?	58
Child benefit	?	→100	75
Housing benefit	?	70	50

Source: Dilnot, Kay, and Morris, 1984.

Do those who are entitled to benefits actually receive them? This is another measure of the efficiency of the system, and one that is generally described as the problem of 'take-up'. For pensions and child benefit, take-up approaches 100 per cent; but for means-tested benefits it is generally much lower: official estimates put the figure for family income supplement as low as 50 per cent, and for some other benefits, such as welfare foods, the figure is much lower than that. As noted above, however, many households have quite small entitlements to means-tested benefit. It is less surprising, and less disturbing, if these entitlements are not pursued than if people fail to claim benefits on which they are almost wholly dependent.

Take-up examines whether people who need benefits receive them; do those who receive benefits need them? The final column of Table 7.6 considers what proportion of each benefit is paid to households that are not poor. The procedure adopted in calculating these figures is to estimate for each household a poverty line based on its supplementary benefit entitlement, and then to measure the extent to which benefits are paid to those who are already above the poverty line or are in excess of the amount needed to take them to it. The design of supplementary benefit and FIS ensures that practically all of these benefits accrue to the poor. However, most other benefits are paid to households that are not poor, and for child benefit this proportion rises to three-quarters. Of course, benefits have objectives other than the relief of poverty, but these estimates provide a measure of the efficiency of different ways of achieving this primary objective.

Contingent benefits are relatively cheap to administer, have high take-up rates, but are not very effective per pound spent at relieving poverty. Means-tested benefits are more costly to operate, and are not always received by those who need them, but are relatively efficient at targeting assistance on those who are poor.

Fundamental reforms

The discussion above has demonstrated the advantages and disadvantages of contingent income-related benefits. Most proposals for fundamental reform of social security choose to pursue one or other of two alternatives. There are those that reduce the number of contingent benefits, and rely on a single means-tested system to deliver support to those with inadequate resources. Tax credit proposals, social dividend or minimum income guarantee, and negative income tax schemes are in this group. The opposite direction of reform is to plan a more generous and extensive network of contingent benefits and to reduce the number and extent of means-tested benefits. This is frequently described as a 'back to Beveridge' plan, although what is proposed is generally rather far removed from the austere pursuit of the social insurance concept which characterized the Beveridge Report.

Before considering either of these groups of proposals in more specific detail, we should note a fundamental problem common to both. The merit of contingent benefits is that it is easy to see that the unemployed or the old have, as a class, greater need for income support than the working population. The merit of income-related benefit is that within any of these categories there are some people who need state support to achieve adequate income levels and others who do not. It follows that a move to a system that predominantly relies on one kind of benefit at the expense of the other involves discarding information about either means or status that enables the social security system to be targeted more effectively on those with the greatest needs.

For this reason both types of proposal tend to be less cost-effective than the present system. Moreover, schemes in the negative income tax or social dividend group tend to hurt the poorest people in needy categories—such as the old or unemployed with no other source of income—and to help poor people in less needy categories—such as households in work but with low incomes. Conversely, 'back to Beveridge'-type schemes tend to favour rich people in needy categories—affluent pensioners or large families—and to hurt poor people in less needy categories—low-income working households. For these reasons, those who support predominantly income-related schemes often retain some contingent benefits, and those who favour contingent benefits recognize that adequate levels are difficult to achieve if they are paid to all. Proposals that begin as fundamental reforms therefore tend to become modified in ways which lead to results not necessarily much less complex than, or different in effect from, the present system.

The appeal of one single comprehensive scheme of income maintenance is obvious. One such proposal (originally put forward by Lady Rhys Williams during the last war) is to scrap all existing social security benefits and replace them by a single payment for each member of the household. This payment would be a kind of 'social dividend'. It would be paid automatically to all households regardless of circumstances, and would be tax-free, thus representing a guaranteed minimum income for each household. All personal tax allowances would disappear and income tax would be imposed on all income other than the social dividend. We shall assume for purposes of exposition that all income is taxed at the single basic rate. The operation of a social dividend scheme is illustrated in Figure 7.1. This shows how a family's income after tax depends on its income before tax and the social dividend. If there were no tax or benefit system at all, each family would find itself on the 'no-tax' line on which income before tax equals income after tax. With the social dividend scheme a family receives the guaranteed minimum income shown by the distance OA in the figure. As its earnings rise, part of the increase is taxed away and so net income rises less fast than gross income—the slope of the line AD is less than the sloe of the no-tax line. At some level of income, shown in the figure as OC, the amount of tax paid equals the social dividend received. This is the break-even level of income. Below this level of income families are net recipients and above it they are net contributors to the public purse.

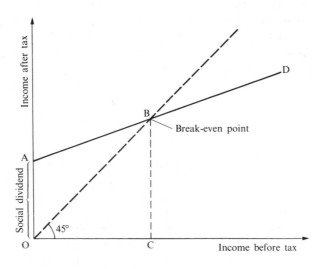

Fig. 7.1. A social dividend scheme

A universal tax credit scheme would have just the same effect. The idea of a tax credit is that instead of receiving a personal income tax allowance of say £40, an individual would be given a weekly tax credit of £12 (which is simply the value of a £40 allowance to someone who pays a basic rate of 30 per cent). All income would be taxable but he could offset the credit against his liability; so that if his income for the week was £80 he would pay £24 − £12 = £12. For someone who earned as much as this the system would work just as it does at present; the difference is that those with low incomes could reclaim the credit, so that a man with an income of £20 and a tax liability of £6 would receive a refund of £6. If the scheme were extended to the whole population, then it is exactly equivalent to a social dividend for everyone of £12.

An alternative approach, but one which is again the same in its effects, is a negative income tax. The basic idea behind this is to extend the tax system to cover people whose incomes are below the tax threshold. With a negative income tax the liability would become negative; while others continue to have tax deducted from their earnings they would receive weekly additions to their income from the government. The amount of these payments would be the basic rate of tax multiplied by the shortfall of the taxpayer's income from the tax threshold. The equivalence of negative income tax and social dividend can be seen from Figure 7.1. The tax threshold is the point at which no net tax is paid, and is therefore the break-even point of the social dividend scheme. This is at gross income OC. Above this point tax is paid and net income increases along the line of BD. Below the threshold a family receives payments of negative tax which help to offset the fall in its earnings and it moves down the line AB. A family with no income has a negative tax payment of OA, equal to the tax rate multiplied by the tax threshold. This is precisely equivalent to a social dividend OA. These systems appear simple, easy to understand, and capable of providing a minimum income for all. Their drawback is obvious. The existing personal income tax allowances imply a universal tax credit, or a social dividend, or maximum payment of negative income tax of £13 per week for a single person and £20 for a married couple. This is quite inadequate for subsistence of any kind; the corresponding supplementary benefit rates (including average housing costs) are £45 and £70. In order to bring these rates into line, it is necessary to be enormously more generous to those in work, or very much more parsimonious to those out of work; the system either becomes much more costly, or is much less effective in relieving poverty. We must either contemplate basic rates of tax of 50 to 60 per cent, or be less ambitious in our view of what the social security system can achieve.

Regarded as a social dividend scheme, the present system in effect pays a much lower social dividend to those in work than to those out of work. Since most people are in work, this saves a great deal of money; but it is unfavourable to those in work with very low earnings. Anyone with earnings of less than £40 per week is likely to be better off on supplementary benefit; but because virtually no one in full-time work does in fact earn as little as this the anomaly is not particularly serious.

For these reasons the Meade Committee contemplated a 'two-tier' social dividend scheme, under which a lower rate of dividend would be paid to those in employment. This illustrates the general point made at the beginning of this section. By making the rate of social dividend contingent rather than universal, we can make the system offer better value for money. We begin to consider different rates of social dividend for the old, for single parents, for the chronically sick, and so on. We have moved steadily back from the pristine simplicity of the social dividend to a system of partly contingent benefits much closer to the present system.

The alternative radical reform proposal is 'back to Beveridge'; this implies raising purely contingent benefits to levels which ensure that those who receive them always have incomes above the supplementary benefit (SB) level. National insurance benefits would be set clearly above SB scale rates, and child benefit would be increased (broadly doubled) in line with the provision for children in the SB scale. There are two main difficulties with this approach. The first is cost. Raising pensions or child benefit is very expensive; and it is expensive because the money is distributed to all pensioners or all families with children, most of whom are not poor. Just as discarding contingent information raised the cost of relieving poverty by means of income support mechanisms, so discarding information on incomes raises the cost of relieving poverty through contingent benefits. It is cheaper to support poor families by providing higher payments to the children—as happens with FIS and SB—than to support all children. One suggestion for financing higher child benefits is to abolish the married man's allowance, and we discuss this in Chapter 14.

The second difficulty is the treatment of housing costs. The principal reason SB scale rates are above national insurance benefit levels is that the former includes payment for housing while the latter does not. If there were a competitive housing market, national insurance benefits could be raised by some average price of housing services of a certain minimum standard, and the Beveridge principle adopted. But the housing market is in such a mess that any average allowance for housing costs would, on the one hand, leave many families with inadequate resources to meet their actual housing costs, and, on the other hand, be much too generous to many families living in heavily subsidized accommodation. The only real solution is the reform of the housing market, but in the absence of this those responsible for running the social security system have to carry on as best they can and one can only sympathize with them.

Integrating tax and social security

We have described how the tax and benefit systems have become more like each other—in the information that they require, in the ways in which they use it, and in the clientele with which they deal. We have noted the arbitrary and unintended interactions in the way taxes and benefits relate to each other. We have concluded that it is necessary that a well-designed benefit system, like a well-designed tax system, should make use of information both about contingencies and about household incomes and resources. All these arguments point to the integration of tax and social security.

The first proposals of this kind were contained in the tax credit scheme, proposed in a Green Paper in 1972. This would have transformed the personal allowance into tax credits in precisely the manner described on p. 120 above. This immediately encountered the difficulties there described: the tax credit that this permitted was very low, and so the scheme could only apply to those in work. Even then, the credits were insufficient for those on low earnings, who would have lost more from the abolition of the then newly introduced and rather limited FIS than they would have gained from the credit. This problem was to be met in part by increasing the rates of credit, at a considerable net revenue cost; and as critics of the scheme pointed out (Atkinson, 1973c), because the credit went to everyone most of this additional expenditure went to households that were not at all poor. Even so, very low earners were excluded from the proposals.

An alternative way of dealing with this difficulty is to give higher rates of credit which are then withdrawn more rapidly against the first tranche of earnings. This proposal, as put forward in Dilnot, Kay, and Morris (1984), would enable both a wider range of benefits and a wider range of households to be brought into the system. By differentiating credits in line with factors that now determine benefits—principally family composition and housing costs—a tax credit or 'benefit credit' scheme on these lines could replace the majority of existing benefits and achieve a wide-ranging integration of tax and social security benefits.

First steps along this road were proposed by the government in a White Paper in 1985 (HMSO, 1985). This suggests the replacement of family income supplement by a family credit, the size of which is to be determined by the number of children in the household. Family credit is to be paid through wage packets and offset against tax deductions, and to be withdrawn as income (net of tax and national insurance) increases. However, although the payment mechanism is to be integrated with PAYE, the assessment process is not. DHSS is required to obtain information about household income on its own behalf and then notify the employer of the adjustment to be made to the employee's earnings. This extraordinary arrangement, which involves both administrative duplication and an inefficient assessment procedure, appears to result from the Inland Revenue's unwillingness to accept substantive tax and benefit integration (see evidence by the secretary of state to Social Services Committee, 1985).

The White Paper also proposes reforms to housing benefit which, although stopping short of integrating payment with tax deductions, take proper account of the interaction of tax and benefits. The distinction between certificated and non-certificated benefit is to disappear, and housing costs are to be met on a common basis for those in and out of work. Housing benefit is withdrawn as net income (after income tax, national insurance contributions, and family credit) increases, so that those with no other income will continue to have their housing costs met in full (subject to some other restrictions). Although there is still a long way to go, the 1985 Social Security Reviews, if implemented, represent important initial moves in rationalizing the incoherent relationships between the tax system and social security.

8

Indirect taxes

Direct and indirect taxes

The *Oxford English Dictionary* defines an indirect tax as one which is 'not levied directly upon the person on whom it ultimately falls, but charged in some other way, especially upon the production or importation of articles of use or consumption, the price of which is thereby augmented to the consumer, who thus pays the tax in the form of increased price'. We argued in Chapter 1 that the economic analysis contained in this definition is shaky, and in general such a distinction cannot be made. We mean by indirect taxes only what is usually meant by them and attach no special significance, and particularly no economic significance, to the classification.

Nevertheless, many people do. Indeed, it almost became part of the conventional political wisdom of the UK that the tax structure relied too much on direct taxation—especially income tax—and too little on indirect taxes. In a period of inflation, a progressive income tax takes an ever-increasing proportion of real incomes while the real yield of indirect taxes (which are in many cases levied as fixed monetary amounts) declines. This shift was not intended, and it reinforces the case for indexation, which is the only way in which inflation can be prevented from accidentally bringing about changes that no one wants to bring about by design. So it is not surprising that the balance of direct and indirect taxation should have been a subject of attention.

But some of the reasons that people had for believing that the balance of direct and indirect taxation was wrong were bad ones. One is that it is thought that the disincentive effects of high rates of direct taxation can be reduced or avoided by a shift to indirect taxes. This argument is quite simply false. Let us ignore for the moment the role of savings, since it is the incentive to work rather than the incentive to save which is at the centre of this concern: we have dealt with savings incentives at greater length in Chapter 5. Then any one considering whether to work longer hours or assume more responsibility will weigh the obvious costs against the benefits in terms of increased consumption which he or she would derive. The additional effort would, we shall assume, generate additional earnings of £10 per week. Now compare a 50 per cent tax on all income with a 100 per cent tax on all expenditure, since that is the rate which is needed to maintain the same revenue. Then our worker would discover that the extra £10 per week was reduced to a net £5 per week by the income tax; with taxes on expenditure, it would remain £10 but would only buy the same bundle of goods, the additional £5 being absorbed by the indirect taxes. The reality of the final outcome is exactly the same in both cases. It is possible that for a time people might be misled into working harder to earn larger monetary amounts before they noticed the reduced purchasing power of what they were receiving; but it is improbable that this irrationality would persist for long. If it did, then inflation—which puts larger quantities of less valuable money into wage-packets in just the same way— would have precisely the same beneficial effect on incentives to work, and few people would find this easy to believe.

The hope that the disincentive effects of high marginal rates of taxation can be reduced by recasting direct taxes as indirect ones is therefore quite chimerical. We should note also that the view that shifting from income tax to a payroll tax (like employers' national insurance contributions) would confer benefits, or even make a significant difference in anything but the short run, is erroneous in just the same way and for just the same reasons. A payroll tax on all forms of employment will lead partly to employers being unable to pay the same money wage as before—and hence to lower earnings than would otherwise have occurred—and partly to an increase in labour costs which will be reflected in higher prices for all goods and services. It is not easy to say which of these effects will be predominant, but this determines only whether we have (in the first case) slightly lower wages and lower prices or (in the second case) somewhat higher wages and higher prices, and the disincentive effects will be the same regardless of whether its incidence resembles more that of an income tax or a general commodity tax. One cannot remove the disincentive effects of taxes by disguising them under a different name, and those who look at our EEC neighbours and are attracted by the combination of lower rates of income tax and higher payroll taxes are guilty of an error which is certainly not made by continental managers and trade-unionists. What matters is the relationship between take-home pay and prices in the shops, and this seems to be understood much better by the ordinary person than by many tax experts.

There are, however, two possible grains of truth in these arguments. One is that people may be more resentful of the fact that over half the product of their extra effort goes in tax if this fact is intimated to them on their pay-slip than if the same money is extracted by their shopkeeper in a slightly more roundabout way, and that this resentment itself leads them to do less work—that people are willing to deprive themselves if they can also see that they are simultaneously depriving the taxman. (Musgrave, 1959, describes this as the 'spite effect'.) Some people may have this psychological make-up, but the Social Survey (Radcliffe, 1954) found that more people cited high prices than high taxes as an adverse influence on their incentive to work, and it is a weak argument for a particular tax structure that it would help to conceal the realities of the tax system from people who have pathological views about it.

The second point is that indirect taxes are generally less progressive than direct taxes—mainly, though not entirely, because there is a threshold of income which is exempt from income tax while all expenditure, however small, is vulnerable to commodity taxation: we pay taxes on every penny of expenditure but not on the first £2,205 of income. This means that the marginal rate of income tax is generally substantially above the average rate, while for commodity taxes there is little difference between the two. Thus indirect taxes can yield the same revenue from lower marginal rates, and hence disincentive effects (which depend on these marginal rates) would be reduced if this were done. This argument is perfectly valid, but it rests on the reduction in progressivity, not on the shift in the structure of taxation, and this reduction could be equally well—and more honestly—achieved by altering the rates of direct tax than by changes to different kinds of tax.

The second bad argument for preferring indirect to direct taxes suggests that the former are voluntary in a sense in which the latter are not; this notion is reflected in an older terminology which distinguishes 'escapable' and 'inescapable' taxes. It is true that any particular indirect tax can be avoided by any particular individual who chooses not to consume the taxed good. But it is also true, given that a certain amount of revenue is required, that taxes in general cannot be avoided by individuals in general. So an 'escapable' tax leaves the person who escapes it worse off—since he would have preferred, in happier circumstances, to have consumed the good which is taxed—and it makes everyone else worse off too, since it requires a higher rate of tax on those who continue to consume the good. Thus the tax structure to which this argument would lead is the worst possible in terms of economic efficiency—it maximizes the welfare loss which is additional to the basic and inescapable burden of the tax.

Principles of indirect taxation

What then would an efficient system of commodity taxes be like? A first principle is that there should be no taxes on intermediate goods—on items like sheet steel or turbo-generators which are sold to other producers rather than to final customers. Taxes on things must of course ultimately be paid by people, so that levies on producers must finally be borne by taxpayers generally in one capacity or another, as consumers, workers, or owners of firms. Hence the imposition of taxes on producer goods does not reduce the tax burden in any way; in fact it will actually increase it by inducing producers to make different and (from a social view-point) less efficient choices of inputs. Essentially, the principal objectives for indirect taxes—raising revenue, achieving some distributional aims, or encouraging or discouraging particular consumption patterns— can all be more efficiently achieved by the imposition of taxes on final goods alone (Diamond and Mirrlees, 1971).

The burden of commodity taxation should therefore be confined to final goods; how should it be distributed among them? Economic efficiency requires that indirect taxes should be cast so as to minimize the distortion of consumer choice involved—that as far as possible, revenue should be raised without diverting taxpayers into less preferred patterns of consumption in their (collectively unsuccessful) attempts to avoid tax. At first sight, it might appear that this implies that all commodities should be taxed at the same rate and this has often been assumed, but there are at least two reasons why such an argument is false. First, while a uniform tax on all commodities will minimize distortion of the consumer's choice between different commodities, it will nevertheless have disincentive effects on his choice between leisure and work. So if a heavier tax is levied on commodities for which demand is inelastic—goods which the consumer will buy in any case—a lower rate of tax can be imposed on other goods and the disincentive to work reduced with little consequential distortion of choice of commodities. And if heavier taxes go on goods which are in some respects substitutes for work—like camping, sports, and yachts—and lighter ones on complementary activities—like overalls, travel to work, and this book—then this too will tend to ameliorate the disincentive effects of commodity taxation. These considerations underlie the 'Ramsey rules' (Ramsey, 1928; Baumol and Bradford, 1970) which say, very roughly, that commodity taxes should have the effect of reducing demand for all commodities in the same proportion.[1]

But these rules overlook the second weakness of the case for uniform commodity taxation—that it ignores the distributional impact of such taxes. This is a basic objection not only to uniform taxation, but to the Ramsey rules themselves. These are the answer to the question 'If we are not concerned about the source of tax revenue, but simply aim to raise a given amount of revenue with minimal disincentive effect, what commodity taxes should we impose?' But if we are really not concerned about the source of our tax revenue, we should not impose commodity taxes at all; we can simply divide public revenue requirements equally among the whole population and raise them by means of a universal poll tax which avoids distortion altogether. Of course, the distributional consequences of this would be unacceptable, and that is why we adopt income and commodity taxes instead. But this means we cannot choose rates for these taxes independently of our view of distribution, so that commodity taxes must be chosen according to principles which take account of the distributional characteristics of goods as well as their demand elasticities.

Since the commodity composition of expenditure changes as income rises, indirect taxes can be used to influence distribution by imposing higher taxes on goods that attract a higher proportion of the expenditure of the rich. It need hardly be said that this too cannot be accomplished without disincentive effects—if managing directors spend a larger fraction of their income on caviar than their deputies then a heavy tax on it will discourage the latter group from aspiring to the positions of the former. And further analysis suggests that there may not be much advantage in using commodity taxes in this way. Adjustments to income tax can achieve similar effects more

---

[1] The rules take this precise form only for small tax revenue and compensated changes in demand.

sensitively, and without diverting rich and poor alike into celebrating festive occasions with cider and fish paste rather than champagne and caviar. We might still, however, see some case for taxing 'prestige goods', such as Rolls-Royces, whose attraction is derived not so much from their intrinsic utility but from the prestige that their limited availability confers on the owners.

Differential commodity taxation does not look a promising method of redistributing income, but there is a further possibility we should consider. We saw in Chapter 5 that an ideal tax system might be one that avoided disincentive effects entirely by taxing not earnings but the ability to earn. If we look at the kinds of goods that are consumed in relatively large quantities by the affluent, we might try to distinguish two categories. There are goods like large houses, expensive motor cars, and yachts that most people would like to buy if they could afford to. But there may also be other goods which are consumed only or mainly by people with high earning ability. Books and opera tickets might come into this category. We have seen that it is impossible to levy taxes on the first kind of good without disincentive effects; but it is possible to avoid them by taxing the second. Taxes of this kind represent a method—the only method—of relating tax liability to earning capacity as distinct from earnings. For example, if certain social groups send their children to public schools and if appointment to lucrative jobs in the City is made from this group, then we would wish to impose a heavy tax on public school fees. We might also redistribute by subsidizing goods which people with high earnings potential tend not to buy at any price— such as bingo sessions and certain Sunday newspapers. The difficulty with such a policy is immediately evident. We are confident that readers of this book have above-average earning capacity. But are they reading it because this is the kind of book that people of superior intellect and ability like to read, or is it that they have acquired their superior intellect and ability as a result of their taste for reading books like this one? Probably both are true; but in the former case we should wish to tax the book heavily and in the latter case to subsidize it heavily.

Whatever category readers actually do comprise, they may by now share our scepticism as to whether there are in fact large gains to be obtained by departures from a general principle of uniformity in commodity taxation. The administrative arguments against doing so are substantial. In order to exploit differences in the distributional characteristics of goods, it will be necessary to adopt a rather fine commodity classification—to distinguish not only cheese from other dairy products but Cheddar from Camembert and White Stilton from Blue. (The 1974 cheeses subsidy scheme attempted just that.) Such distinctions are likely to lead to administrative nonsense and to large and pointless distortions of consumer choice. It is not easy to believe that the information required to devise an optimal scheme is likely to be available, or likely to be used to good effect if it is.

There remain some arguments for taxes or subsidies on particular commodities. One is simple paternalism—I, as chancellor of the exchequer, think that people (presumably other people) drink too little milk or too much beer, and seek to remedy the situation by fiscal incentives. Another justification for these corrective taxes can arise if they allow prices to be adjusted so as to ameliorate the effect of inefficiencies elsewhere—if electricity for space-heating is too cheap, then one way to stop excessive use of such electricity is to impose a tax on space-heaters. As the example suggests, it is usually preferable (though not always possible) to tackle such problems directly rather than to adopt 'second-best' policies of this kind. A slightly different argument concerns goods whose production or consumption imposes costs or benefits on those who are not themselves directly involved in buying and selling them—goods which are made in smoky factories, transported in juggernaut lorries, or grown in attractive orchards. The 'external effects' of these goods are not fully accounted for by the person or organization who provides them. Hence they will tend to be over- or under-supplied—there will be too many juggernauts and too few orchards. Economists have long argued (with rather little practical effect) that these problems might more appropriately be dealt with by means of taxes and subsidies on the products concerned than by administrative regulation. Taxes of these kinds are an exception to the general rule that taxes on intermediate goods should be avoided.

A further reason for indirect taxes may be to act as a tariff: to improve the balance of payments by discouraging imports and to give advantages to British producers of competitive goods. This consideration may have been one motive for the so-called 'luxury' rate of VAT (p. 134 below), which fell heavily on imported goods. In 1983, the European Court found Britain guilty of this in taxing (mainly imported) wine more heavily than beer (which was mainly

domestically produced), following a complaint by the Italian government that Britain was engaged in protection which violated the
Treaty of Rome. Wine drinkers benefited from a tax reduction of
around 20p per bottle.

Indirect taxes in Britain

If we examine the structure of commodity taxes in the UK, we find
one general sales tax—VAT—and heavy duties on three products—
tobacco, alcoholic drinks, and petrol. Table 1 in the Introduction
shows their relative contributions to revenue. We consider these
major indirect taxes in turn.

The basic principle of VAT is that it is a sales tax chargeable to
the sellers of all output, with the proviso that in computing their
liability firms may deduct any VAT that has been levied on inputs
into their products. We can see how this works by considering a
simple example with a standard rate of VAT of 15 per cent. Suppose
a man discovers a block of iron which with the aid of a magic wand
(provided free of charge) he turns into steel worth £100. Adding
VAT at 15 per cent he sells this to a motor car firm for £115. The
firm buys additional components which cost £500 to make and on
which it is charged £75 VAT, and employs labour at a cost of £400.
It sells the car for £1,300, charging 15 per cent VAT, to make up a
total price to the purchaser of £1,495, and secures a profit of £300.
The firm now assembles its accounts for this set of transactions,
which are given in Table 8.1.

Table 8.1:   *Accounts for a simple example using VAT at 15%*

	Revenues (£)	VAT		Costs (£)	VAT
Car	1,300	195	Steel	100	15
			Components	500	75
			Labour	400	
			Profit	300	
				1,300	90

It must now account to the Customs and Excise for the difference between the VAT levied on its outputs (£195) and the VAT charged on its inputs (£90) so that it makes a payment of £105. This amounts to 15 per cent of the £700 of *value added* in the car factory—the difference between the values of inputs and outputs, made up of £400 of labour costs plus £300 profit—and indeed it would be possible to compute the tax in this way. (This would be an *accounts* basis for the tax, in contrast to the *invoice* basis which is what we are describing and which is used in the UK and in the EEC.) At the same time as the VAT man receives the car firm's cheque for £105, he also gets £75 from the component manufacturer and £15 from the steel producer, so that in aggregate £195 (15 per cent of the value of the final output) is levied on the sequence of transactions involved in the production of the car. It is easy to check that this amount would remain the same however few or many transactions are involved in the chain of production.

Thus the main advantage of VAT is that it is a method of levying a tax on all commodities that enter consumption while effectively exempting all intermediate goods—those who buy goods for further processing receive a refund of the tax that they have been charged, and only those who are the final consumers of the goods actually pay it. Thus it seems an ideal tax judged by the first of the principles of indirect taxation described above—the taxation of producer goods is systematically avoided. The price paid for this is a high one, however. As will be clear from the exposition above, the tax is complex and, as is inevitable if a charge is levied on every transaction in the economy and refunded on most of them, it is expensive to administer. Initially, VAT cost about twice as much to collect per pound of revenue as did the purchase tax which it replaced (cf. Customs and Excise, 1976, and estimates of Richardson Report, 1964). The near doubling of the rate in 1979 made this picture look less bleak. Since it costs little more to collect VAT at this higher rate, the outcome was a reduction of nearly one-half in cost per pound collected. If rates of purchase tax had been doubled, then much the same would have happened. But the administrative burden is much greater than this. VAT is a self-assessed tax—forms must be completed and tax paid or refunds claimed by the taxpayer himself, subject to routine checks by control officials. Total compliance costs were put by Sandford *et al.* (1982) at 10 per cent of revenue collected. This figure predates the increase in the rate in 1979 and is also likely to have fallen considerably, but it remains a disturbingly high proportion. The number of taxpayers increased from 74,000 in the last year of purchase tax to 1·4 million under VAT; and the number of collectors rose from 2,000 to 12,500.

The Richardson Committee concluded in 1964 that VAT had no merits sufficient to compensate for these acknowledged administrative problems, and proposals to introduce it were rejected at that time. Two developments led to its implementation in the UK. The first was the adoption of the French VAT by West Germany and subsequently by other members of the EEC. In both France and Germany, VAT replaced unsatisfactory turnover taxes, levied cumulatively at each stage of production, which were both expensive to run and inefficient in economic effects (the rate of tax depended only on the number of stages in the production process). In Britain, however, purchase tax, a single-stage, broadly based commodity tax levied on wholesalers, had developed into a relatively cheap and simple fiscal instrument. The second development was the failure of an attempt to tax services (purchase tax was levied only on physical commodities). SET (selective employment tax) was a weekly tax per employee, chargeable to firms in service industries, and administered by levying it on all employees and refunding it to manufacturers. The case for SET was poorly presented (mainly in terms of a desire to transfer labour from service to manufacturing industry), the definition of the border-line between the two sectors gave rise to constant anomalies, and the tax proved wildly unpopular. VAT offered a mechanism by which the taxation of services could be integrated into a general system of commodity taxes, and when it was introduced in 1973 SET disappeared, unlamented.

There are two rates of tax—zero and the standard rate of 15 per cent. A 25 per cent 'luxury' rate was introduced in 1975, reduced in 1976, and abolished in 1979. Additionally, some products—such as financial services, education, and funerals—are exempt. Exemption is not the same as zero rating, since while the exempt trader need pay no tax on his outputs his zero-rated colleague can reclaim the tax paid on his inputs as well; so it is always better to be zero-rated than exempt, and (if the value of output sold to final consumers is less than the value of taxed inputs) it may even be more beneficial to be standard-rated than exempt. Consumption of food does not rise in proportion to income and because it is both zero-rated and a substantial part of the budgets of poorer families the distributional impact of VAT is slightly progressive.

Table 8.2: *Rates of VAT*

Zero	15%	Exempt
Food	All other	Land
Water	commodities	Insurance
Books		Postal services
Fuel and power		Betting
Construction[a]		Finance
Exports		Education
Transport		Health services
Children's clothing		Burial and cremation
Protective clothing		
Large caravans		

[a] New construction is zero-rated, but improvements, alterations, and repairs are subject to tax at the standard rate.

As Table 8.3 shows, the difference between the rates of tax imposed by VAT on the major part of consumers' expenditure and the rates on items subject to excise duty is very great: tax accounts for the major part of the price of cigarettes and whisky, and the effective rates on beer and petrol, though lower, still mean that the prices of these commodities relative to others are wildly different from what they would be if the structure of indirect taxation were non-discriminatory. The taxes on alcohol and tobacco are not, of course, imposed for reasons that are recognizably economic in character. There is some talk of the inelastic demand for these commodities (demand for tobacco is inelastic—a 10 per cent price rise might reduce consumption by $1\frac{1}{2}$ per cent—and the same may be true for beer, but consumption of wines and spirits is rather sensitive to price: see Deaton, 1975). The unpleasant consequences that their consumption has for others may also be cited (although smokers make reduced demands on public services by dying prematurely and alcohol as social lubricant has beneficial as well as adverse external effects). But the real reason these taxes exist is that it is rather easy to induce feelings of guilt about these forms of consumption; and as a result it is more acceptable to raise revenue in this way than in others. Taxes on alcohol were raised very sharply during and immediately after the First World War, and those on tobacco during and just after the Second World War, in periods when such moralistic sentiments were particularly easily aroused.

Table 8.3: *The incidence of tax on various commodities, 1985*

	Cigarettes	Whisky	Beer	Petrol	Wine
Factor cost	22.0	1.42	51	83	105
Specific duties	53.9	4.45	14	82	69
Ad valorem tax	24.1	—	—	—	—
VAT	15.0	88	10	25	26
Retail price	115.0	6.75	75	190	200
Tax as % of factor cost	423%	375%	47%	129%	90%

Notes: Cigarettes: pence per packet king-size tipped.
Whisky: £ per bottle blended whisky.
Beer: pence per pint of bitter.
Petrol: pence per gallon four star.
Wine: pence per bottle.
Sources: Reports of Customs and Excise; own estimates.

The adverse consequences of smoking on health have drawn attention to the tobacco tax. A common view is that the government 'cannot afford' to discourage smoking because of the loss of tax revenue which would result. A reduction in smoking would affect the government budget in a rather wide range of ways. The most immediate secondary consequence would be a reduction in medical costs and in claims for sickness benefit. These savings would grow, but over time a number of other factors would become important. Because reduced consumption of cigarettes would significantly increase life expectancy, there would be a rise in revenue from income tax, but an increase also in the cost of retirement pensions and medical treatment for larger numbers of elderly people, partly offset by a reduction in widows' pensions and benefits. Atkinson and Townsend (1977) have quantified a number of these items, which are substantial, and the effects on revenue from tobacco duties are not the only, or necessarily the dominant, element in the calculation of the effects of changes in smoking habits on the government budget.

But as this discussion should make clear, to evaluate these factors simply from the standpoint of their effect on government revenue and expenditure is to take an extremely—indeed offensively—narrow view-point. What is required is a much wider cost-benefit analysis, and the framework of this has been set out by Atkinson and Meade (1974). Estimates by Atkinson and Townsend (1977) leave little doubt that an increase in the tax on tobacco would yield an increase in both government revenue and social welfare. But the force of these arguments has not influenced policy sufficiently to prevent a substantial cut being made in the real burden of the tax. On the (low) estimate of demand elasticity cited above, simple indexation of the tobacco tax over the period in which the relationship between smoking and lung cancer has been known would have reduced deaths from this cause by between 1,500 and 2,000 per year.

The structure of tobacco tax has been revised as a result of EEC harmonization proposals. A duty based on weight of tobacco has been replaced by a specific tax of 2·7p per cigarette and *ad valorem* tax of 21 per cent of the retail price. Because the overall incidence of tobacco taxation is so high, the structure of the tax regime has major effects on the structure of the cigarette market. Cigarette coupons have disappeared (because they are now effectively subject to the 21 per cent tax). Britain used to have shorter cigarettes than other countries, because the weight-based regime gave a strong incentive to reduce tobacco content; now king-size cigarettes dominate the market. The predominantly *ad valorem* tax regimes of France and Italy mean that a saving of 1 centime in manufacturing cost may reduce the retail price by 5 centimes, and hence give an artificial incentive to the use of low quality tobacco and packaging which are characteristic of French and Italian tobacco products. Kay and Keen (1982) show that, in general, specific commodity taxation creates less distortion of consumer choice per pound of revenue.

Expenditure on alcohol and tobacco as recorded in the Family Expenditure Survey (FES) is substantially below the estimates of consumption based on output data. One reason for this is probably the embarrassment some respondents feel about revealing their true consumption, but it is also possible that people with high alcohol consumption and high incomes have a lower response rate in such surveys. Figure 8.1 shows the available data on expenditure on tobacco and alcohol as a percentage of average household expenditure. It appears that the tobacco tax is regressive (that is, it takes a higher fraction of income from the poor than from the rich), and there is some indication that this regressivity has increased over a period of time because tobacco consumption seems to have fallen more among high-income groups. This tendency is strongly confirmed by evidence on smoking trends in different social classes (see Table 8.4). By contrast, the tax on alcohol appears to be progressive. Figure 8.1 shows that expenditure on alcohol increases more rapidly than income, and higher-income groups consume relatively more wines and spirits which are more heavily taxed.

Table 8.4:   *Percentage of cigarette smokers by sex and social class*

	Social class	Men 1958	Men 1978	Women 1958	Women 1978
I	Professional	54	25	43	23
II	Intermediate	48	38	43	33
III	Skilled	60	49	42	42
IV	Partly skilled	54	53	42	41
V	Unskilled	61	60	42	41

Source: Tobacco Advisory Council.

It is much less easy to see why petrol should be considered a suitable subject for especially heavy taxation, though there are arguments for a somewhat higher tax than that on other commodities. Some rationale can be derived from the second-best and external effects arguments described above. Motorists impose disutility on each other and on the population at large; and since road space is costly to provide but can be used free of charge, provision will be excessive if all demands at a zero price are met. In addition, the imposition of a tariff on oil may be a rational response to the OPEC cartel by OECD countries acting collectively. To the extent that the case for petrol tax rests on these arguments, the usual objections to the taxation of intermediate goods do not apply: the demands of industry for road transport are clearly not less offensive or less pressing than those of private motorists. But it is difficult to decide what levels of tax would be justified by these considerations.

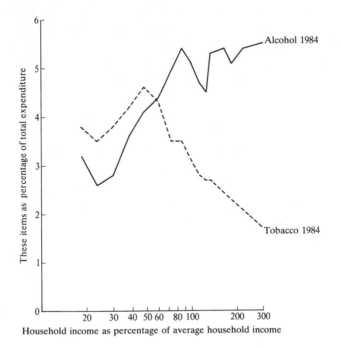

Fig. 8.1. Spending on alcohol and tobacco related to household income

We have already noted that the structure of indirect taxation occasions much less criticism than do the present direct taxes, and we share this view. But we do not consider that the weaknesses of the present direct tax system would be significantly alleviated by a shift from direct to indirect taxes, and we think that the proper balance between the two is actually one of the less important questions facing current British tax policy. The prominence of this issue in current debate is, we suspect, the product of a failure to understand fully the implications of one of the basic principles of public finance which we described in Chapter 1—the irrelevance of the formal incidence of a tax to its effective incidence. It follows from this that one cannot make major improvements, or indeed large changes, simply by changing the identity of the payer of a tax. Nevertheless, there are reasons for supposing that the UK would do better to rely rather more on indirect taxes than it does at present. The most important of these is the problem of enforcement. Any tax is subject to difficulties of defining the base, of policing, or preventing avoidance and evasion. These problems increase more than proportionately with the rates of any particular tax, and indeed we have seen how at very high rates of tax they become overwhelming. If this is so, then if we are to have two broadly based taxes it is better to have two 'medium' taxes rather than one high and one low tax.

9

Local taxation

Rates and local authority finance

Local authorities levy rates on immovable property—houses, shops, offices, factories (though not farms)—within their area of jurisdiction. The basis of the tax is the 'net annual value' of the property. This figure is assessed from time to time and is intended to be the amount for which the property might be let if the tenant were responsible for all repairs. The rate is then fixed as a poundage, so that with a rate of 120p in the £ the owner of a property assessed at an annual value of £500 would pay £600 each year in rates. Although in general there is more than one local authority exercising functions in any area, a system of 'precepting' means that the lower tier authority is responsible for all rate collection.

We distinguish domestic rates—levied on houses—from industrial and commercial rates. In 1983 the total yield from rates was £12,456 million of which 60 per cent came from industrial and commercial property. Only 40 per cent of local authorities' receipts of rates consisted of domestic rates, although these represent a substantial tax on housing. The yield of domestic rates in 1983 was £5,089 million, and consumers' expenditure on housing in the same year was estimated by the CSO to be £27,326 million including rates. This is a rather arbitrary and unreliable figure but it suggests an effective tax rate on housing (rates divided by expenditure on housing excluding rates) of 23 per cent. A tax of this magnitude is greater than the standard rate of VAT, thus providing some justification for not imposing VAT on housing. But this is only part of the story because the disincentive effect of rates is offset by subsidies to all major forms of tenure—tax concessions to owner-occupation, subsidies to local authority tenants, and rent controls in the private rented sector. Although the total value of these subsidies and their effect on the demand for housing are unclear, they certainly exceed domestic rates in their amount.

Since no free market in rented housing has existed for many years, it is difficult to measure satisfactorily the rental values that are supposed to be the basis of the tax. Two post-war revaluations have been conducted (in 1963 and 1973). In these, assessed values for house property have in practice been determined in relation to other assessed values, and it is obscure how the process ever got started; it is clear that any future domestic revaluations will have to be based on the capital value, rather than the rental value, of the house, and a divisor might be specified to produce comparability between domestic and non-domestic valuations. As an economy measure, the next revaluation has been postponed indefinitely. Revaluations change, often rather radically, the relative tax burden on different ratepayers; and both revaluations have led to extensive discontent with the rating system and the establishment of committees of inquiry. The Allen Committee, reporting in 1965, identified the regressive impact of the rating system. This arises at the lower end of the distribution largely because many people (especially pensioners) live in houses that reflect their past, rather than their current, income; while at the upper end rateable values increase less rapidly than either the capital value of houses or the incomes of those who live in them. As a result of the Allen Report, a system of rate rebates was instituted. This was much extended in 1974, and by 1985 housing benefit, providing support for rent and rate payments for those on low incomes, was paid to around 7 million households. The Layfield Committee, which reported in 1976 (Cmnd. 6453), had a broader brief which enabled it to investigate local government finance as a whole.

Table 9.1:   *Sources of local authority finance, 1983*

	£ million	Per cent
Government grants	18,495	60
Non-domestic rates	7,367	24
Domestic rates	5,089	16
	30,951	

Source: CSO *National Accounts*, Tables 4.10, 8.2.

Many people think of rates only as domestic rates, and it is not widely realized that domestic rates are not the most important component of the total rate burden nor rates the most important source of finance for local authorities. Industrial and commercial rates are not paid by the buildings themselves, though this impression is sometimes given; thus one commentator on local government finance has written 'industry and business will have to pay more. This is right and proper; such hereditaments can obviously afford to contribute more to the public purse' (Ilersic, 1973, p. 104). The formal incidence of rates falls on the occupiers of property, the businesses that make use of it; the effective incidence is much less certain. Rates are borne by the owners of commercial and industrial property to the extent that they are capitalized, i.e. reflected in a lower capital value for the rated property (see Chapter 1). Where land prices are a principal element in property values, this is likely to be the case; thus if the rates were removed from central London office property, competition could be expected to bid rents up to very nearly the present level set by rent and rates together, and the main effect would be an increase in property prices. This will be partly true for commercial property in other city centres. Outside these areas, however, rates primarily represent an addition to the cost of one factor of production—buildings. The result of this will be that offices and factories will tend to be more cramped, less well fitted, and less well located than they would otherwise be, and since the tax is an extremely heavy one (averaging around 150 per cent of 1973 rental values) this effect is likely to be substantial. The incidence of the tax will largely fall on final consumers, in these cases, but since they will not be willing to pay more for goods produced in highly rated areas, deviations from the overall average level of rates will be reflected in different local levels of profits, earnings, and employment opportunities. Industrial and commercial rates are a worse tax, not a better one, for being a poorly perceived and understood tax on intermediate goods. The incidence of rates on a factory will fall partly on those who buy the products it makes, partly on those who work in it, and partly on those who own shares in the companies that own and operate the factory. The proportion of the total rate burden that falls on people living within the boundaries of the authority that levies the rate will vary widely from case to case, but will on average be small.

The purposes of the grant system

We have seen that the bulk of local authority revenue comes not from rates but from central government grants. It is therefore impossible to understand the development of the rating system in isolation from the grant system. Why should central government support local services in this way? There are four major reasons. 'Spill-overs' are benefits of local expenditure which arise outside the area of the authority that undertakes the expenditure. Local governments that are principally concerned for their constituents will not undertake enough of such activities, and those that do extend them will impose an 'unfair' burden on local residents. This problem can be dealt with by specific central government subsidies to certain activities, and in the UK government grants to local authorities originated in this way with payments towards the cost of 'national services' such as main roads and education which were thought to generate 'spill-overs'.

A second function of central grants is to alleviate 'fiscal imbalance'. If taxes are raised by that level of government which is able to levy them most efficiently, while expenditures are determined at the level of government which is able to administer *them* most effectively, there is no reason to suppose that the resources and needs of any particular tier of government will match. It is the experience of the UK and of most other countries that tax collection has become more centralized than expenditure decisions, and there is therefore a need for offsetting grants from the centre to local units (revenue-sharing).

Grants can also be used to redistribute revenue among local authorities. We might ask why it is necessary or desirable to redistribute among governments rather than directly to persons. Local authorities differ in terms of resources; some represent poor areas, while others—such as the City of London—have a large local tax base because they contain concentrations of commercial property which yield far more in terms of rateable value than they demand in local services. Local authorities also differ in their needs. Some may have large numbers of children or old people who make extensive use of the facilities that local government provide. It may be more expensive to provide the same frequency of refuse collection or to keep the roads clear of snow in a scattered rural area than in a densely populated urban environment (although it is not obvious why town-dwellers should pay for this). An individual who lives in an area with low resources, or extensive needs, will need to pay more in order to secure the same level of local services as someone who is more favourably located. This is not only inequitable, but may lead to movements between areas which exacerbate the initial problem (as may have happened in the USA).

Designing an equalization scheme to deal with these problems is by no means easy. If resources are measured by rateable value, then areas such as London will appear to have greater than average resources not because Londoners are especially rich but because property in London is relatively expensive. Although the Layfield Committee clearly identified the problem, successive governments appear not to have understood. Nor can the needs of a local authority be objectively determined. Although there is now extensive statistical analysis of the spending patterns of local authorities, the choice of explanatory variables and the legitimacy of particular needs is inevitably a matter of subjective judgement and ultimately of political whim. And what exactly is it that a redistribution scheme should equalize? Perhaps local authorities should each be able to provide the same level of services at the same cost to local residents. But what level of services should be chosen? How much of any increase or shortfall should be borne locally and how much should be reflected in changes in grant? What is meant by cost to local residents?

Yet another objective—and one which has acquired increasing importance—is control over the overall level of local authority spending. This can be achieved by offering carrots and sticks to induce local government to conform to central government wishes. But why should the national government be concerned to control the level of local spending, as distinct from the level of its own contribution to that spending? The difference, after all, is something that local authorities will have to raise for themselves. It is natural that I should monitor carefully my own donation to the Red Cross; less clear why I should want to restrict the amount that the Red Cross obtains from other people. If there were some rigid limit to taxable capacity, then every pound a local authority raised would reduce the revenue available to central government by a pound; and hence central and local expenditures would be directly competitive. But while it is true that the higher the level of taxation the greater is the cost of raising additional taxation, the magnitude of this effect is small. The burden of taxation rises steadily with its level, rather than reaching some fixed ceiling. If local authorities are required to raise the revenue for additional expenditure from their own resources, there is really no more reason for central government to be concerned with their expenditure levels than for it to be concerned with the expenditure levels of any other agents in the economy.

The development of the grant system

Grants were initially related mainly to 'spill-overs'—to encourage the provision of services that benefited the population at large rather than the residents of a particular authority. For this reason, they were 'hypothecated' grants—the government met a proportion of expenditure on specific approved items. As time progressed, fiscal imbalance became a more important rationale for government grants. In the 1960s local revenue sources were much less buoyant than local expenditures and the government greatly increased the proportion of local spending that was met from central funds. As the level of local authority spending rose, so did the need for re-distribution of resources between authorities. Specific grants were substantially replaced by an unhypothecated general grant, which contained elements related to both the needs and the resources of particular authorities.

The Layfield Committee reported in the mid-1970s. It identified incompatible demands on the British local government system. On the one hand, local autonomy and control of local services is jealously asserted; and on the other, we want central government to procure appropriate service levels, to restrain both local and national tax demands, and to achieve equity between different local authorities and between different groups that receive services from local authorities or finance them. We cannot achieve all these objectives simultaneously; and if we insist on trying to do so we move, as we have, to an even more irrational and incoherent system of local authority finance. Layfield therefore proposed that the system should move either in the direction of greater central control of local services, or towards more real independence of local government. The second alternative—which was clearly preferred—required new sources of local revenue in order to increase the financial autonomy of local authorities. A local income tax was proposed as a means of achieving this.

The government buried the Layfield Report under a mountain of platitudes, favouring instead a 'middle way' between the Scylla of central control and the Charybdis of local autonomy. Subsequent events have confirmed the Layfield analysis, and demonstrated that there is no middle way. Either you drive a car yourself, or you allow someone else to do it, possibly under instructions as to the general direction he is to take. If you appoint a driver but insist on dictating every change of gear or steering to him, you will end up off the road; and this is what has in fact occurred. Relations between central and local government have deteriorated rapidly. This has followed from the introduction in 1980 of a new block grant system and from increasing—and generally unsuccessful—attempts to plan the levels of spending both of individual authorities and of local government in aggregate. Under block grant, a grant-related expenditure (GRE) is defined for each authority. This is based on a central government assessment of its spending needs. The basic principle is that each local authority should be able to fund its GRE from its block grant and the notional rate income which it derives from a standard rate poundage. If an authority's expenditure is equal to its GRE, then it has a notional rate income equal to its rateable value times the standard rate poundage. Its block grant will then be equal to the difference between the GRE and the notional rate income.

If block grant were fixed at this level, then local authorities which spent more than their GRE would have to find the balance from their local resources, and those who spent less would be able to refund the difference to their residents. However, block grant varies as actual expenditure differs from the centrally determined GRE. This variation has two purposes. Central government acts to some degree as ratepayer for councils with low rateable resources of their own, and hence makes some contribution to overspending and retains some of the benefit of underspending. At the same time, the government seeks to penalize high spending and discourage low spending. These two objectives are directly contradictory. It follows that deviations from the GRE may be either taxed or subsidized depending on how the balance of them chances to fall, and additional expenditure of £1 may cost local residents more or less than £1.

The basis of grant for an authority whose spending differs from its GRE is fixed by a 'poundage schedule'. The poundage schedule defines the rate which should be levied to fund any specified excess or short-fall from the GRE. Once the relationship between GRE and actual expenditure is known, a 'grant-related poundage' (GRP) can be determined from the poundage schedule. The GRP increases, and at an increasing rate, as expenditure above the GRE increases. The notional rate income—the amount the authority is expected to raise from its own resources—is now equal to the GRP times the rateable value. Block grant is once more equal to the difference between actual expenditure and notional rate income. It follows that if the system operates as it should, two different authorities with actual expenditures that are the same proportion of their GRE would each be charging the same rate poundage, if their other resources were the same. By varying the poundage schedule the government can vary the inducement or penalty for under or overspending.

If the reader finds this difficult to understand then his bewilderment is certainly shared by many local councillors. This very complexity can lead to perverse incentives. If an authority is overspending its GRE modestly, then additional expenditure may be very costly because it leads to substantial loss of block grant. Once grant has been lost altogether, however, the penalty disappears, since you cannot get less than zero grant. The cost to ratepayers of *further* spending falls. It follows that if you overspend at all it may make sense to overspend hugely, and a number of major authorities—such as the Inner London Education Authority—are in precisely this position. The problem is compounded because the inevitable arbitrariness of the expenditure assessment leads to GRE figures that are in many cases quite unrealistic.

Thus these attempts to limit local authority spending have proved ineffectual as well as complex; and have finally been supplemented by direct power to prescribe local authority expenditure levels, 'rate-capping'. The Audit Commission, an independent body established by the Government to assess the over-all efficiency of local government activity, concluded that there was a negligible relationship between expenditure changes and rate increases (Audit Commission, 1984). They concluded that

The present system is being used to try to secure at least four different objectives which are not mutually compatible: to distribute grant in a way some of which reflects local needs and resources, to control aggregate local government expenditure, to ensure that individual authorities do not exceed their spending targets *and* to limit rate rises from year to year for individual ratepayers. Moreover, this review shows that the system which now exists is producing information on current expenditure levels that is misleading to policy makers in both central and local government.

Alternatives to domestic rates

The Government's rather surprising response to the crisis in local government finance has been to conclude that what is needed is a substitute for domestic rates, and a Green Paper 'Alternatives to

Domestic Rates' was published in 1981. Domestic rates occasion much criticism. Often this criticism is less than coherent, and it sometimes seems that a principal reason for the volume of protest is simply that rates are an unusually transparent tax; there are few other cases where individual taxpayers are personally and directly responsible for making payments. The major objections expressed are that the burden of rates is independent of the number of earners in a household; that they bear heavily on people (such as pensioners) who live in property that is large relative to their incomes; and that they are inequitable as between individuals who live in different parts of the country with different property prices. The essence of all these criticisms is that domestic rates are not an income tax; and any attempt to modify domestic rates to respond to these criticisms would have the effect of turning them into something close to an income tax. If this is the basis of the argument on which domestic rates are to be replaced, then there is one and only one alternative tax that meets the bill, and that is local income tax.

These arguments against the rating system are not as strong as they might at first sight appear. Income is a measure of taxable capacity, but it is not the only one or necessarily the best. Income, supplemented by information about housing consumption, may well give a better guide to a household's standard of living than either of these variables alone, and this is what a tax system that includes both national income tax and domestic rates achieves. The argument stresses the importance of looking at the impact of local authority taxation as part of the tax system as a whole, and not in isolation.

Local income taxes are used to finance local services in many other countries. There are, however, peculiar administrative difficulties in implementing a local income tax in Britain. The reason is that while almost all other countries make rough-and-ready deductions of income tax from pay and assess liability by means of an end-year tax return and assessment, the British system attempts to secure exact deductions of the tax due and exempts most taxpayers from an annual return. It is easy in other countries to incorporate the assessment and collection of local income tax in the annual return; in Britain it would be necessary to establish place of residence in a separate inquiry and notify this to employers for each one of their employees individually. Even on the modest proposals of the Layfield Committee, it was estimated that this would require a 15 per cent increase in Inland Revenue staff and expenditure.

There is an obvious alternative, which is for Britain to move over to collecting its income tax in the same way as everyone else. The Green Paper notes this possibility, but observes that 'Major issues of tax policy and administration would be raised which would need to be examined thoroughly and in detail on their own merits before any change of this kind could be made' (para. 6.23). If this statement was intended to be a preliminary to such a thorough examination, it would have been one of the most encouraging statements in the Green Paper; but there is no indication that it is anything of the kind. The reference to thoroughness and detail appears not as a prelude to action, but as a reason for inaction. The best test of the sincerity of the government's intention to seek alternative sources of finance for local authorities is the date and speed with which it begins detailed consideration of the implications of a universal end-year assessment system.

The second alternative to domestic rates is a poll tax. A poll tax could not replace rates, unless levied at unimaginably high levels, but it could supplement existing sources of local authority finance. There are two major objections to it. The first is that it is regressive. This could be overcome by adjusting the national tax and benefit system by increasing income tax allowances and benefit rates. What matters from the point of view of social and economic policy is not the progressive or regressive impact of every individual element of the tax system, but the impact of that system as a whole. It is perfectly possible, and may be necessary, to have a regressive local authority tax system within an overall progressive tax structure.

The second problem follows closely from the first. A general poll tax could be a cheaply administered revenue-raiser for local authorities. But would it be possible to implement such a tax while resisting pressure to exempt old-age pensioners, low income earners, pregnant women, and so on? If not, we could easily end up with a tax system that presented all the administrative burden of a separately administered local income tax with none of the advantages of equity and flexibility that an income tax itself would offer.

The reform of local government finance

It is odd that the subject of reform of domestic rates should have been pushed to the front of the stage. Each of the three main sources of local government finance—domestic rates, industrial and commercial rates, and government grants—is properly the subject of considerable criticism; but the case against the present structure of domestic rates is the weakest of the three. A more urgent reform is one which would make local authorities more effectively responsible for raising their own revenue from their own constituents. This would, as Layfield argued, both restore local autonomy and secure more effective financial control over local authority spending. The grant system and the structure of non-domestic rates require more immediate attention.

A programme of this kind demands substantial reductions in the average level of block grant. Non-domestic rates have little merit as a tax and less as a local tax. There are enormous disparities between authorities in the size of the commercial and industrial rate base, and it is clear that many councils have—perhaps mistakenly—seen it as a milch cow which can be exploited indefinitely without detriment to the local economy. If non-domestic rates are to be retained—and any sudden abolition would create extensive and arbitrary disruption in the property market—then these deficiencies would be removed by transforming them into a national tax at a fixed poundage.

These two changes—reducing grants to local authorities, and transforming industrial and commercial rates into a national tax—would lead to the loss of most existing local authority revenue, and its transfer to the national exchequer. Assuming no major change in the range or level of local authority services, the only possible source of finance on the required scale would be a local income tax at a high average rate. This could be offset by corresponding reductions in the level of national income tax, so that no over-all increase in the burden of income taxation need be implied. If local income tax were to finance most local authority expenditure, it is likely that the typical rate of local income tax would be higher than the residual national income tax. We might see local tax rates of 15 to 20 per cent and a national tax of 10 to 15 per cent. This programme sounds a revolutionary one; but the revolution it requires is mostly the revolution of established arrangements in Whitehall, and the impact of these changes on the man in the street would actually be quite small. By far the most important implication for him is that he would become aware of the scale of local authority expenditure and its potential impact on his standard of living, and conscious of the implications of its control. That is the objective of the change.

10

Principles of company taxation

In the UK, taxes on companies are more recent than personal income taxes. In the US a corporate income tax first appeared in 1909, but the separate taxation of companies began in Britain only in 1947. Before then the taxation of corporate profits was integrated with the personal income tax, and special taxes on profits were used only as war-time measures to raise extra revenue. In 1947 the system was rationalized by raising the rate of profits tax and, exempting individuals and partnerships from the tax altogether. In effect, in addition to income tax there was a separate tax on corporate profits. The system of corporation tax has changed at regular intervals, with major changes occurring in 1958, 1965, and 1973.

The most recent upheaval was in 1984 when the chancellor announced the end of accelerated depreciation together with a number of other changes to the corporate tax base in order to finance a substantial reduction in the rate of corporation tax—from 52 to 35 per cent. These changes took full effect from 1986. They also influenced the US Treasury which, in November 1984, published a plan (US Treasury, 1984) for a major reform of the US tax system. The two sets of reforms have much in common. They aimed to broaden the tax base by moving away from the existing *ad hoc* mix of income and expenditure tax bases in the direction of a comprehensive income tax. In this way some of the striking disparities in effective tax rates on different kinds of saving and investment would be eliminated. Fiscal neutrality was the guiding principle behind the reforms. Such a move reverses the direction of policy over the last thirty years, during which period successive governments tried to raise the growth rate of productivity by providing increasingly generous investment incentives in order to stimulate higher levels of capital formation. But by 1984 reform of corporation tax was urgent following a decade of disarray.

In 1974, following a corporate liquidity crisis in which the tax payments due in 1975 would have led to serious financial difficulties for a number of major firms, a temporary scheme of 'stock relief' was introduced. It eliminated most of the corporation tax liability of UK manufacturing industry. In the corporate sector as a whole the real value of tax payments fell throughout the 1970s. Although the scheme was described as temporary, successive chancellors procrastinated and nothing was done by way of permanent reform. Another liquidity crisis appeared imminent following a massive rundown of stocks during 1980 and it was clear that action could no longer be delayed. Modifications to stock relief were introduced in the 1981 Finance Act, but again these were simply tacked on to the existing system rather than integrated into a coherent reform of corporate taxation. The prolonged debate over the future of stock relief had demonstrated that a rethink of the basis of corporation tax was necessary. After the 1983 General Election, with a new and radical chancellor, the way was open for a major reform to be implemented. The implications of the 1984 changes are discussed in Chapter 11. First, however, we consider some basic questions that must be answered before a satisfactory corporate tax system can be designed.

Perhaps the most obvious question is 'Why tax companies at all?' A common reply, and indeed one that was used in the US to justify the introduction of a corporate income tax, is that corporate status conveys certain privileges, and companies should pay for these privileges. In particular, companies have limited liability status, thus protecting their shareholders in the event of bankruptcy. At first sight this argument has some appeal, but on closer inspection it becomes less attractive. There is no reason to believe that the benefits of incorporation are proportional to profits (indeed, the reverse might be the case) and one might as well argue for a licence fee for companies. More fundamentally, although limited liability is a very convenient form of contractual arrangement between shareholders and creditors, it is a voluntary agreement entered into by both sides. Before lending to the company the creditors know full well that the shareholders' liability is limited, and can adjust the terms on which they are willing to lend accordingly. There is no reason to tax one party more than the other.

Why then do firms incorporate? For large firms the most important reason is that the existence of shares enables the ownership of the company to be divided among, and transferred between, individuals without affecting the scale of control of the firm. The process of management can continue while the ownership of the company is changing. There are two main tax inducements for small businesses to incorporate. The first is that if money is ploughed back into the business the owner of an incorporated business can avoid paying income tax at the cost of paying corporation tax plus, eventually, also capital gains tax. If his personal income tax rate is high enough, incorporation might be worth while. The second reason is that there are generous tax concessions for contributions to company pension funds, which are not available to a self-employed business man on anything like the same scale. If the latter wanted to save for retirement he might well find it profitable to incorporate simply to take advantage of the tax privileges of a company pension. For large firms, however, taxation is not a significant factor because incorporation is necessary for other reasons.

The mere fact that some firms are incorporated is not a very strong argument for imposing a separate tax on them. Indeed, insistence on treating companies as entities distinct from the individuals who own them has provided a tax shelter for retained earnings. Another argument which has been used is that companies can afford to shoulder an extra burden, and that companies, as well as persons, should pay their fair share of taxes. Surprisingly, this view-point has carried a good deal of weight in the USA in the recent debate on tax reform, and has led to a minimum corporate tax. The argument is completely mistaken. The effect of a tax is to reduce either leisure or consumption (whether this year or in the future via a reduction in savings) or both below the levels that would have been chosen in the absence of the tax. Whether any given tax burden is distributed fairly can only be discussed by reference to the effects on the different individuals in society. Companies are owned by individuals and it is meaningless to talk about the 'welfare' of ICI. The fact that a company has a *legal* personality of its own quite distinct from that of its managers, shareholders, and employees cannot change the fact that a tax can only affect the well-being of those who work for or own the company, or consume its products.

The incidence of company taxes

Who then actually pays the corporation tax? Corporation tax is normally levied on company profits, but it is important to distinguish two components which make up the figures that companies report as their profits. One is a return on the capital that companies use in conducting their business—the money they have borrowed to buy fixed assets, stock, etc. In order to attract funds—either from lenders or from those who might wish to buy their shares—companies must offer a return on those funds comparable to that which investors could obtain elsewhere. Companies typically report their gross trading profits—the return they have made before deducting any of these financing costs—and their net profits, which are computed after subtracting the cost of interest payments on the money that they have borrowed but before deducting the cost of servicing the capital that they have obtained from shareholders (the dividends that they have had to promise in order to secure these funds).

Many companies make a return on capital employed that appears to exceed, often by a great deal, the amount that they need to attract funds from investors. For example, in 1975 Rank Xerox reported a return on capital employed of 41·1 per cent, and Marks and Spencer a return of 36·1 per cent (figures drawn from the *Times 1000*), while the Monopolies Commission (1975) discovered that LRC International had obtained a return on capital employed in the manufacture of contraceptive sheaths which exceeded 100 per cent over the period 1969–73. These returns are much greater than these companies would appear to have needed to make, or to promise, to obtain finance for their business. In a competitive economy, it would be difficult for firms to earn such high profit rates, since other people would be attracted into the same line of business by the prospect of these enormous returns; and although many companies seem to earn profits greater than the cost of capital there are few which are as profitable as these. But as these examples suggest, there are at least three reasons why companies might make above-normal profits. Rank Xerox is a company that exists to exploit a highly successful invention, and its profits represent the rewards of being first in the field with a new product (aided by patent protection). Marks and Spencer does not have any single invention that distinguishes it from other companies, but it is an exceptionally successful and efficient firm, which by virtue of effective management and carefully cultivated customer goodwill is able to earn higher profits than other retailers with whom it is competing. We might regard its profits as returns to successful organization. LRC's profits appear to be the rewards of the successful creation and maintenance of a near-monopoly in its products.

Economists describe the amount by which profits such as these exceed the cost of capital as 'pure profits'. Such profits can of course be negative for foolhardy ventures or badly managed firms. At any time some firms will be more successful than the average and others less successful, so that there will be a dispersion of realized rates of return around the cost of capital: lager producers will earn more when the summer is hot, and umbrella manufacturers more when it is wet. But the major sources of pure profits are invention, organization, and monopoly, and we shall broadly describe them as returns to entrepreneurship, noting that in this title we are including activities that we should view with approbation—like successful invention—and others that we would wish to discourage—like the creation of monopolies. Real 'profits taxes' are normally partly a tax on pure profits and partly a tax on capital employed. We shall see that the British corporation tax is a combination of a tax on pure profits and a tax on capital.

We can therefore identify three main groups which may bear part of the burden of corporation tax. One is the people who supply entrepreneurship—Mr Marks and Mr Spencer and others who helped build up their organization, Mr Carlson who invented the Xerox machine, and the owners of the Xerox Corporation which helped him develop it. A second is the people who supply capital to companies. This group overlaps somewhat with the first—the people who supplied capital to Marks and Spencer or Xerox in the early days of their development did very well out of it, though we might argue that by choosing to support these operations rather than others at a time when their potential was not universally recognized these individuals were themselves supplying entrepreneurship as well as capital. It is clear, however, that the people who own shares in Marks and Spencer now are not entrepreneurs in this or any other sense, and there is no reason to suppose that the return they earn on their investment will be higher than they would expect from any other shares they might buy.

This point is important. The present shareholders in this company are not growing fat on its above-average rate of return on capital. This return has been capitalized; the present owners of Marks and Spencer have bought the right to it from the founders, who were thus able to sell their shares and obtain the proceeds of their entrepreneurial activities. Similarly, the present stockholders in the Xerox Corporation are those who have bought the right to Mr Carlson's invention from him and his original backers at a price that reflected the expectation of the profits which the company is currently earning. We have so far only looked at the production side of these activities. The third group of people who may share the burden of corporation tax are those who buy goods and services which are produced by companies. If there is a tax on capital employed in the company sector, and people require a certain rate of return before they will invest in companies (because, for example, they can obtain that return by buying government bonds or investing overseas), then the tax will have to be paid by those who buy goods which are produced by companies. Part of it may also fall on those who form companies to exploit their entrepreneurial activities.

It should be clear from this that the incidence of corporation tax depends in part on the structure of the tax. If it is a tax on pure profits only, then it falls in the first instance on those who supply entrepreneurship to companies—inventors, successful organizers, would-be monopolists. If, as we might suspect, the supply of such entrepreneurship is not too sensitive to its rewards, then these entrepreneurs will pay the tax and that will be the end of the matter; but if they abandon entrepreneurship and enter routine employment instead then consumers will have to bear the burden of the tax, partly in higher prices to induce a little more entrepreneurship and more importantly through the loss of the ideas and efficiency that those people might otherwise have promoted (this is the 'excess burden' of the tax). Moreover, because of capitalization we can tax *past* entrepreneurship at rates as high as we like without the tax being shifted forward to consumers in this way or producing economic inefficiency of any kind. It is possible that if Mr Marks had known that profits would be taxed at 52 per cent, or even 35 per cent, he would not have bothered to think up Marks and Spencer, or that the current shareholders would have been less willing to pay so much to him for his business, but they have made their decisions and there is nothing that they can do about it now.

We should note that similar disincentives apply to entrepreneurship in the unincorporated sector; but there they arise from the effect of the personal income tax rather than the corporation tax. Since the rates of this will very likely be higher (and certainly will be if the invention is a successful one), the disincentive brought about by the corporation tax may be less than that which exists in the economy generally from the effects of other taxes; so that although all activities of this kind are penalized, the use of the corporate form as a means of exploiting invention reduces the tax burden imposed.

We can therefore see that a tax on pure profits is not without economic attractions—though these depend on the belief that desirable entrepreneurship will be inelastically supplied. (If people are deterred from seeking monopolies by the knowledge that the proceeds will be taxed, that is all to the good.) We shall describe a corporation tax that falls only on pure profits as a neutral tax. If a corporation tax is not neutral, it will fall also on those who supply capital to companies. The incidence of this part of the tax then depends on the response of firms and financiers to this change. If there are profitable investment opportunities elsewhere—and foreign investment is probably available to domestic investors and certainly to overseas investors—then firms will be unable to pass the burden of the tax back to investors. They will then try to substitute other factors of production for the now more expensive capital. To the extent that this raises costs and to the extent that they cannot substitute successfully they will have to share the tax between a reduction in any pure profits they may be making (which may be small or zero for many companies) and a higher price charged to the consumers of their products. If this happens, corporation tax will act as a general sales tax on the goods which companies produce (though at different rates on different goods). We may note that the openness of the economy to capital flows will be an important factor in determining the incidence of corporation tax. The greater this is, the greater the proportion of the tax that is likely to fall on consumers.

We have seen that the analysis of the incidence of corporation tax is a complicated issue—and indeed we have underestimated its complexity because we have examined only the most immediate consequences of the tax. There are likely to be further repercussions from the effects on income distribution of whatever the incidence may turn out to be. Nor have we considered adequately the problems we raised in Chapter 1—what is the alternative tax with which we are implicitly comparing the corporation tax? But in this simple framework it seems that incidence depends on empirical questions that are not easily answered, and it is not surprising that the subject has been in long-standing dispute. What we have suggested—and what has perhaps not received sufficient attention in that dispute— is that incidence is likely to be rather sensitive to the structure of the tax; and that the issue of whether the tax is or is not neutral is critical to this. We therefore turn to analyses of alternative tax structures, focusing on this issue.

But before doing so, we should notice that although corporation taxes do not emerge in a very satisfactory light from this discussion, and non-neutral corporation taxes particularly badly, the analysis suggests one argument for such a tax. This is that we have one already. To the extent that the tax falls on pure profits, and stays there, it will be capitalized in share prices; the value of Marks and Spencer is lower than it would be if there were no corporation tax, and this expectation has been reflected in the price at which shares in this company have changed hands in the past. To abolish the tax now would be to confer a windfall gain on these present shareholders.

Systems of company taxation

If a separate corporation tax is to be retained, it is important to choose a tax that does not conflict with the objectives of the personal direct tax system. There are two sorts of questions about company taxes we could ask. What are the different types of company tax systems? What are the economic effects of a tax on companies? It is clear that we cannot answer the second question until we know exactly what type of company tax we are talking about, and so we shall describe some of the main corporate tax systems which could be employed. It is useful to classify corporate tax systems in terms of how they tax distributed profits relative to their taxation of un-distributed profits. When the corporate tax system in Britain was changed in 1965 and 1973, on both occasions the idea behind the change was to alter the relative tax burden on dividends and reten-tions. We shall follow this method of classifying company tax sys-tems. An alternative approach is to look at systems in terms of their effects on the investment decisions of firms by asking the question 'How does the tax system affect the pre-tax rate of return on an investment project required to induce firms to go ahead with the project?' This is a question to which we shall return after describing the different systems of corporation tax.

If there are no taxes, the cost of capital is simply the rate of return demanded by the supplier of finance—the rate of interest at which the firm can borrow, for example. In a competitive economy this cost of capital is independent of the particular method of finance that is chosen. While it may appear, for example, that borrowing secured on particular assets is 'cheaper' than other ways of raising new capital, such activities increase the risk, and hence the cost, attached to other financial instruments, such as unsecured loans or equity shares. Since there must be a lender for each borrower, the outcome will be one in which the 'price' of each kind of capital that the firm has will reflect the degree of risk attached to that particular asset, and the over-all cost of capital cannot be reduced by resorting to so-called 'cheap capital'. It follows from this that there is little to choose between alternative methods of financing when there are no tax considerations, and that such decisions will be very sensitive to tax systems that favour one method rather than another. When tax considerations do apply, a firm will use the cheapest source of finance first, though there are practical limits to this, especially when this source is debt or retained earnings.

Between 1947 and 1965 companies in Britain paid tax at the standard rate of income tax plus an additional rate of profits tax which, until 1958, was charged at a different rate on distributed profits from on retained profits. The differential rates were abolished in 1958 and profits tax was imposed at a uniform rate on all profits. In 1965 corporation tax was introduced and the UK adopted the *classical system*. This is perhaps the simplest system to understand and is often represented as embodying the principle that the tax liability of the company should be completely independent of that of its shareholders. It is the system employed in the USA and in Holland amongst other countries, and was in force in Britain until 1973. Under the classical system the company pays a flat rate of corporation tax on its taxable profits, and then the shareholders pay income tax on their dividends and capital gains tax on the gains that arise from corporate retentions. A company wishing to raise a given amount of finance may either retain profits, or distribute the profits as dividends and issue new shares, or borrow the money and pay interest charges on the loan. The classical system discriminates between the first two sources of funds unless capital gains are taxed at the same rate as unearned income, and it favours debt finance if, as is almost always the case, interest payments may be deducted against profits in assessing liability to corporation tax.

It is precisely this discrimination between dividends and retentions which, so it is claimed, constitutes the major objection to the classical system because it involves the 'double taxation of dividends'. The double taxation arises because dividends are subject to both corporation tax and income tax, whereas retentions are liable only to corporation tax. This argument ignores the fact that capital gains tax is payable on gains arising from retentions although of course it is perfectly true that the effective tax rate on capital gains is much less than the rate of income tax. Nevertheless, in 1973 the classical system was replaced by the *imputation system* in order to alleviate part of the double taxation of dividends. The imputation system gives shareholders credit for tax paid by the company, and this credit may be used to offset their income tax liability on dividends. Part of the company's tax liability is 'imputed' to the shareholders and regarded as a prepayment of their income tax on dividends.

The company pays tax on its profits at the rate of corporation tax, and any profits that are subsequently distributed are regarded as having already paid income tax at a certain rate, which we may call the 'rate of imputation'. In Britain the rate of imputation is always set equal to the basic rate of income tax. Shareholders only have to pay additional income tax on their dividends if their marginal rates of income tax exceed the basic rate, while if their marginal rates are less than the basic rate they actually receive a refund from the Revenue. For example, a charity or pension fund will receive a refund of tax deemed to have been paid on their behalf by the company. Another method of alleviating the double taxation of dividends is to charge a lower rate of corporation tax on distributed profits than on undistributed profits. This is called the *two-rate* system.

An alternative system is simply to integrate the personal and corporate tax systems and, for tax purposes, to regard shareholders as partners in a business. Under the *integrated system*, as it is called, each shareholder is deemed to have earned a fraction of the company's profits equal to the fraction of its shares which he owns. The effect of this is that the company's profits, both distributed *and* undistributed, constitute part of the shareholders' personal taxable income. Once a year each shareholder would receive a piece of paper from the company showing his taxable profits for the last year together with a tax credit for the tax paid by the company on his behalf. The taxable profits would be added to his personal income. A reform along these lines was suggested by the Carter Commission in Canada and was seriously considered in West Germany. In neither country, however, was it adopted, partly on administrative grounds and partly on the irrelevant legal argument that a company is distinct from its shareholders.

Taxes and investment

We shall consider first a project financed entirely by borrowing. Imagine a firm contemplating investing in a project which involves buying a piece of machinery and then using it together with labour and raw materials to produce output which is then sold. If the receipts from the sale of output more than cover *all* the costs involved, then the project will earn profits for the firm and will be given the go-ahead. What do the costs include? Obviously, they include the payments made for raw materials, fuel, and labour, but they also include the capital costs incurred. These will consist of two parts. The first is the interest payment on the loan taken out to finance the purchase of the machinery, and the second is the deterioration in the value of the machinery itself due to wear and tear caused by use, or to obsolescence caused by the invention of better machinery. This second element is the depreciation charge, and is called 'true economic depreciation'. It is important to note that it consists of the change in the value of the machinery during the firm's accounting period regardless of the way the value has changed. Since firms rarely sell machinery it is extremely difficult to value second-hand plant, and so depreciation charges usually follow rather arbitrary rules, such as writing off the cost of an asset in equal instalments over some assumed average life for assets of that particular type, and only approximate true economic depreciation.

If the receipts from the project exceed all its costs, including capital costs as defined above, then the project will earn a surplus for the shareholders of the firm and will be a desirable investment. What matters is not the size of the surplus, but the fact that it *is* a surplus. A proportional tax on this surplus will still leave a positive surplus for the shareholders, and therefore will not affect investment decisions. In the case we examined, investment was financed by borrowing and in that case capital costs consisted of interest payments on the borrowed money and depreciation of the capital equipment. As far as investment financed by borrowing is concerned, a corporation tax that allows as deductions both interest payments and true economic depreciation will be neutral.

What happens if the project is not entirely financed by borrowing? The argument remains valid if the costs of different forms of finance can be fully deducted from profits for corporation tax purposes. For financing by new share issues this has never been true, since dividends are not a 'cost' for corporation tax purposes. Under the classical system, no part of dividends can be offset against liability to corporation tax; hence the discrimination against financing projects this way is very heavy, and to the extent that such finance is necessary the required rate of return from the project is increased. With the imputation system, dividends are partially deductible for corporation tax purposes; £100 paid out as gross dividends reduces the final corporation tax liability by £30, while £100 paid out in interest or any other cost would reduce it by £35. Thus there is some increase in the required rate of return, but the effect is much smaller than under the classical system, especially when the rate of imputation is close to the corporate tax rate. This has been true since April 1986 when dividends became almost fully deductible for corporation tax purposes.

If the investment is undertaken from retained profits, the position is more complex. The cost of internal finance depends on the personal tax rates of the owners of the company because they can avoid paying income tax on their returns by sheltering behind the combined burden of corporation tax and capital gains tax. It is possible that for some wealthy investors this double burden is less than their marginal rate of income tax, which actually lowers the required rate of return on investment projects financed from retained earnings.

We shall now apply these principles to an analysis of how company taxes operate in Britain today.

11

Company taxation in the UK

In 1984 the structure of corporation tax in the UK was radically reformed. The direction of the reforms of the previous two decades, which introduced increasingly generous incentives to investments, were reversed. This overhaul followed a decade in which the inconsistencies in the corporate tax system became only too evident. The interaction between the imputation treatment of dividends (see below) and large tax reliefs for investment led to a situation in which many companies paid no tax. This led, on the one hand, to falling real revenues from corporation tax, and, on the other, to serious distortions in the incentive to invest that varied significantly not only from one company to the next but also between different investment projects.

To overcome these difficulties, the chancellor decided to adopt a system that was more neutral as between different methods of financing a company's operations and between different types of investment. The 1984 changes, which came into full effect in 1986, reduced the rate of corporation tax from 52 per cent to 35 per cent, and at the same time eliminated the very generous treatment of investment in plant, equipment, and industrial buildings that had developed in the 1970s. We examine the effects of these changes in more detail below. But we start with a review of how the tax system affects the way in which a company chooses to finance its investment. We then examine how taxes affect the incentive to invest.

The financing of investment

One of the major financial decisions facing a company is its choice of capital structure. What fraction of its investment should it finance by equity and what fraction by debt? We saw in the previous chapter that a company cannot alter the terms on which it can obtain funds from the capital market by changing its debt–equity ratio. The risk premium demanded by the suppliers of finance depends upon the perceived risk attached to the income earned on the assets of the company, and not upon the way in which those assets were financed.

But the tax system provides an additional incentive to use debt finance because the return on such finance, namely the interest payments paid to the holders of debt, are deductible for the purposes of corporation tax. In contrast, equity investment has to bear at least part of the burden of corporation tax. To offset some of the disincentive to equity finance implied by this, the current UK corporate tax system allows dividends to be partially deductible. This is achieved by the imputation system which has been in operation in the UK since 1973.

To illustrate how the system works, consider a shareholder who has received a cheque for £100 as his annual dividend. With a corporate tax rate of 35 per cent, the pre-tax profits that are required to finance this dividend amount to £154, with the difference of £54 going to the Revenue in corporation tax. Part of this corporate tax bill is in fact prepayment of income tax at the basic rate on dividends which is deducted at source, and this component is paid directly to the Revenue when dividends are distributed. This is usually before the date when companies are normally required to pay corporation tax on profits for the year, and so this prepayment of tax is called advance corporation tax (ACT). In fact this description is somewhat misleading because the payment is more properly regarded as a deduction at source of basic rate income tax on dividends and not corporation tax at all. The remaining corporation tax payments to the Revenue are described as 'mainstream' corporation tax. They constitute the effective corporate tax burden since the amounts which are described as ACT would be paid, as income tax, even if corporation tax were completely abolished.

The essence of the imputation system is that when the shareholder receives his dividend cheque for £100 he is deemed to have already paid income tax at the basic rate on that dividend. If all shareholders paid income tax at the basic rate the matter would end there. But some shareholders have marginal tax rates higher than the basic rate and others lower, and this complicates matters somewhat because we have to calculate the amount of extra tax that is due. To do this we must ask the question 'What dividend before tax would I need in order to finish up with £100 after payment of basic rate income tax?' Suppose the basic rate of income tax is 30 per cent. Then to end up with £100 after tax I would need £143 before tax. This is the notional pre-tax dividend that the shareholder received—the 'grossed-up' dividend—and £43 is the notional tax that he has paid.

Although this may seem rather abstract, the shareholder will in fact find that with his dividend cheque for £100 will come a piece of paper representing a tax credit of £43 exactly equal to the notional tax that we have just described. On his tax return the shareholder must enter the notional pre-tax dividend of £143 (equivalent to the value of his dividend of £100 plus the tax credit of £43) which will then be added to his other income in order to calculate his total taxable income, but since he is deemed to have already paid the notional tax he can use the credit as an offset against his income tax liability. If he pays tax at the basic rate, the credit eliminates the liability, and he can forget about the imputation system of corporation tax. If his marginal income tax rate is, however, 60 per cent, then his tax liability on the dividend is £86 minus the tax credit of £43. He will therefore have to send a cheque for the balance of £43 to the Revenue. But if the recipient of the dividend cheque were either a charity or a pension fund, and hence not liable to tax, the boot would be on the other foot and the Revenue would have to refund the tax credit of £43 to the shareholder. Of the pre-tax profit of £154, a basic rate taxpayer would receive £100 (an effective tax rate of 35 per cent), a charity would receive £143 (a tax rate of 7 per cent), and an individual with an income tax rate of 60 per cent would receive £57 (an effective tax rate of 63 per cent).

The example has been discussed at length so that the reader should understand the principles of the system and not be confused by the terminology used in the actual operation of the imputation system in Britain. The reason for its complexity is that imputation is granted at the basic rate of tax, and because of the progressive marginal rate structure of income tax some shareholders are required to pay additional tax on dividends whereas others are refunded the tax credit. The system of tax credits is needed to ensure that the correct amounts are paid. In the UK the rate of imputation has always been set equal to the basic rate of income tax. This is done on administrative grounds because the large majority of shareholders pay tax at the basic rate, and hence for a large number of dividend recipients no net payments or refunds are required. Although this is convenient, it is in fact a rather restrictive feature of the tax system. There is no obvious reason for setting the rate of imputation equal to the basic rate of income tax, and there are in fact two objections to it. Firstly, it has the consequence that an increase (decrease) in the basic rate of income tax increases (decreases) the tax burden on earned income, but has no effect on the tax burden on the dividend income of shareholders paying the basic rate. This is because the tax credit rises (falls) in line with the increased (decreased) income tax liability, and if the credit has risen this will actually benefit exempt shareholders such as pension funds.

Secondly, the imputation system was introduced to reduce the fiscal discrimination between dividends and retentions, and hence between the different methods of raising finance. But the basic difficulty with the system is that it can lead to a neutral tax position only for those shareholders paying one particular rate of income tax. If we ignore capital gains tax this neutral position exists only for shareholders paying the basic rate. For other shareholders there will be discrimination in one direction or another. But the neutral tax rate does not coincide with a weighted average of the marginal income tax rates of shareholders, which is somewhat below the basic rate of tax and has been falling rapidly over the last two decades (see King, 1977, Appendix A; King and Fullerton, 1984, Chapter 3). The two factors responsible for this fall have been the rapid growth in the share-holdings of tax-exempt institutions—mainly pension funds—and the reduction in personal tax rates on high-income individuals in the 1979 Budget.

An additional complexity in the system is advance corporation tax. The Revenue does not wish to pay to shareholders any refunds of tax that it has not received from the company in the first place, and this is why each company is required to pay ACT before any refunds can be made. The value of ACT is equal to the total value of the tax credits received by the company's shareholders. The rate of credit (and hence also ACT) is defined as the ratio of the notional tax paid by the company on behalf of its shareholders to the dividends distributed, and so is always expressed in the rather strange form of 30/70, for example, if the basic rate of income tax is 30 per cent.

ACT may be offset against the company's eventual liability to corporation tax. But in the 1970s and early 1980s there were many companies with small or zero tax liabilities, and for these companies the ACT was unrelieved. Surplus ACT may be offset against the corporation tax payments of the two previous years or carried forward. But in the early 1980s a great deal of concern was expressed about the problem of unrelieved ACT. The principle of the imputation system is that part of the company's tax bill is regarded as a credit against the shareholders' income tax liabilities on dividends, but if the company has paid no tax then there is no reason to give the shareholders credit. If the company turns out to have a zero tax liability, then ACT is simply unrelieved. There are two things to note about this outcome. The first is that an imputation system does not rest easily with a corporate tax base under which many companies have no tax liability. This was the position before the 1984 tax reform. Secondly, because the imputation system is effectively withdrawn when companies have no mainstream tax liability, the incentive to use different sources of finance vary not only from company to company, but even from year to year for the same company. This is a bizarre outcome which gives firms yet more incentives to devote talented manpower to planning their financial structure rather than to the quality and range of their products.

Fiscal neutrality

By 1984 it was clear that corporation tax distorted the incentives facing companies with respect both to their financial decisions and to their investment plans. Moreover, these incentives varied from company to company. The attractions of a more neutral system were apparent, and the concept of 'fiscal neutrality' became the cliché of the day. To see why this was so it is instructive to consider the history of changes in the tax treatment of corporate finance in the UK.

The tax treatment of dividends and retentions has oscillated since the last war, first favouring one and then the other. After the introduction of corporation tax in 1965 debt finance was very attractive, but new equity finance reappeared after the change in 1973. Issues of preference shares (a security with a fixed rate of interest which may if necessary be reduced, thus giving some of the flexibility of equity finance) were virtually killed off in 1965, and yet this sort of finance would have helped some companies with their liquidity problems in 1974.

The main effect of the many changes in the corporate tax system has been to introduce fiscal considerations into decisions which there is every reason to believe are best left to companies themselves. The capital structure of a company and the method by which it finances its investment are matters which the tax system ought not to try to influence, and if it does it will create difficulties for itself. Divergences from a neutral tax system give rise to the need for complex legislation to prevent abuse and avoidance through the conversion of income into whatever legal form happens to be taxed most lightly. It is very difficult to distinguish clearly between capital and income, and yet that is what is required if the present system is to work smoothly. Complaints by companies about the losses they have made on foreign currency loans illustrate how income and changes in capital values are not easy to separate. By repurchasing their own debt at below its nominal value companies can substitute tax-deductible interest payments for repayment of capital, with favourable tax consequences. Even the difference between debt and equity can be blurred, and in the 1960s there was extensive import of the American device of the convertible loan stock, which is debt to the taxman and equity to the holder. The partial indexation of capital gains tax in 1982 increased further the discrepancies between the treatment of debt and equity.

Any deviation from a neutral tax system will provide someone with an opportunity to invent methods of avoiding tax. The authorities then respond with legislation to prevent such abuse, and effort then goes into devising even more ingenious financial operations to save the company and its shareholders tax. A pound in tax saved is worth as much to the company as a pound earned by productive activity. Most of these side-effects of a non-neutral tax system were unintended and, if perhaps not enormously harmful to the economy, nevertheless constitute a diversion of resources of time and skilled manpower to pointless activities. The frequency of the changes in the tax system aggravates the situation.

Similar considerations apply to the tax treatment of investment. Throughout the post-war period governments of all persuasions tried to encourage investment by providing more and more generous incentives for such expenditure. To limit the revenue costs these incentives were not given uniformly but limited to those types of investment which were thought to be especially meritorious. As a result by 1984 there were enormous disparities in the treatment of different investment projects. Investment in plant and machinery could be depreciated in the first year (a 100 per cent first-year allowance or 'free depreciation'). Industrial buildings qualified for a first-year allowance of 75 per cent as well as 4 per cent per annum allowances on the balance on the cost of the asset. In addition, there were, and remain, special cash grants to certain kinds of investment in the assisted regions, and also discretionary grants under Sections 7 and 8 of the 1972 Industry Act. No depreciation allowances, however, were given for investment in land or commercial buildings (except for hotels which received an initial allowance of 20 per cent plus further depreciation allowances) because such assets are expected to retain their value. There was a special form of relief for investment in stocks, which is discussed below in the context of inflation accounting.

The net result of these provisions was that the system as it stood in 1984 introduced significant discrimination between investment in different types of asset and between investment in different sectors. Plant and machinery received favourable treatment whereas commercial buildings did not. Stocks of both raw materials and finished goods received unfavourable treatment until 1974, generous treatment thereafter until the stock relief scheme was modified in 1981, and less highly favoured treatment after that date. The rationale for these differences is unclear, and the 1984 reforms attempted to reduce their importance.

The 1984 reform

There were two main components to the 1984 reform of corporation tax. The first was a significant reduction in the rate of corporation tax from 52 per cent to 35 per cent (staggered over a transitional period that was completed in 1986), and the second was the elimination of 100 per cent first-year allowances and their replacement by depreciation allowances more closely related to true economic depreciation. The reduction in the rate of corporation tax reduced the attractiveness of debt finance. Under the post-1986 regime the rate at which interest payments are tax-deductible—the corporate tax rate of 35 per cent—is very close to the rate at which dividends are effectively deductible under the imputation system—the basic income tax rate of 30 per cent. The adoption of depreciation allowances closer to some measure of true economic depreciation also reduced the variation in tax rates between different types of asset. Although these reforms did reduce the variability in tax rates on different types of investment, this was achieved at the cost of an increase in the overall tax rate on new investment. This is shown in Table 11.1. From a value close to zero the average marginal tax rate on corporate investment in the UK has risen to a level of between 35 and 40 per cent.

Table 11.1: *Effective marginal tax rates on corporate investment*

	Pre-1984 (%)	1986 (%)
Type of asset		
Plant and machinery	−35.6	19.8
Buildings	24.2	53.8
Stocks	41.7	51.2
Method of finance		
Debt	−61.1	20.8
New share issues	−0.8	22.6
Retained earnings	15.2	42.4
Overall	−0.1	37.4

Table 11.1 shows effective marginal tax rates on corporate investment in different assets and financed by different means for both the pre-1984 position and the new regime following the reforms announced in 1984 and implemented in full in 1986. The total wedge between the rate of return on investment and the rate of return received by savers depends upon both personal and corporate taxes. The figures in Table 11.1 include the effects of both sets of taxes. They are calculated under the assumption that investment projects earn a pre-tax rate of return of 10 per cent per annum and that the inflation rate is 5 per cent. It can be seen that before 1984 investment in plant and machinery and investment financed by borrowing were both subsidized by taxpayers at large. Tax rates on these projects were actually negative. In contrast, equity investment and investment in less highly favoured assets paid high marginal tax rates. The current position is that a much greater degree of uniformity has been introduced into the pattern of effective tax rates. The difference between equity and debt finance is now much smaller than before, and although machinery retains some tax advantage its magnitude has been reduced. The gains in terms of greater fiscal neutrality have been achieved at the expense of an increase in the overall marginal tax rate on new investment in the corporate sector.

The new system purports to be a stable basis for the taxation of companies. But there are two reasons for casting doubts on this proposition. The first is that, as we have seen, the new system provides on average significantly less incentive to invest than the pre-1984 regime. A future government concerned with Britain's investment performance may wish to promote greater investment by a system of accelerated depreciation allowances, and an expectation of higher allowances would lead to a postponement of investment that might in turn justify the eventual change. The second reason concerns the failure of the new system to allow for inflation. With 100 per cent first-year allowances, a company may write off its investment immediately and this reduces the effective cost of an investment by a proportion that is independent of the inflation rate; but when depreciation allowances can be used only gradually over time, the allowances are devalued by inflation. Only if the depreciation allowances are indexed to inflation will the incentive to invest be independent of the inflation rate. No such provision was contained in the 1984 reform. Moreover, current accounting methods include purely book profits on the increase in the value of stocks in taxable income. This became so important in 1973 that the government had to introduce a 'temporary' system of stock relief designed to prevent a serious cash-flow crisis in the corporate sector. By 1984 no permanent method of inflation accounting had been devised and the chancellor simply abolished stock relief altogether. The current position is, therefore, one in which a new inflationary shock would lead to another cash crisis and significantly higher effective marginal tax rates in the corporate sector. Indeed, the system is more vulnerable to an inflationary shock than it was in 1974. Moreover, in the absence of indexation, tax rates can vary significantly with inflation whenever the inflation rate is of the same order of magnitude as the underlying real rate of profit. Since the latter is probably within the range of 5 to 10 per cent then even an inflation rate of 5 per cent is still significant in this context.

For these two reasons—the disincentive to investment inherent in the present system and its vulnerability to an inflationary shock—it is worth asking whether there is an alternative reform that would achieve the objective of fiscal neutrality without the disadvantages of the 1984 reform.

The cash-flow corporation tax

Given the difficulties that have been experienced in designing a satisfactory reform of the corporate tax system, it is tempting to consider abolishing the corporate tax altogether, and if it did not exist then we would not wish to introduce it. Attractive though it might seem, there are problems with this idea. First, if the tax were abolished now there would be windfall gains and losses to individual shareholders. Following the 1984 reform these windfall gains would be significantly positive on average. In addition, the easiest way of extracting tax revenue from British subsidiaries of foreign-owned companies and from those shareholders of British companies who reside overseas is to have an independent corporate tax.

The most desirable reform of the corporate tax system, we believe, would be to convert the present tax into a tax based on cash flows. The existing treatment of depreciation makes no allowance for inflation, and grants depreciation allowances on some estimate of the rate of decline of true economic value. This is 25 per cent per annum for most types of plant and machinery. But in an uncertain world the rate at which assets depreciate can vary enormously not only from one asset to another but from one project to another. Economic depreciation is just as elusive a concept as economic income, and for the same reasons. The tax system cannot be based on subjective evaluation, and so in practice economic depreciation must be defined in terms of rather arbitrary rules. In contrast, a tax based on cash flows would present none of the problems of defining economic profit.

The principle of the cash-flow tax is that no distinction is made between expenditure on current items (labour, materials, etc.) and expenditure on capital goods. The tax base is simply the difference between receipts from the sales of goods and services (including the proceeds from selling assets) and the money spent on acquiring goods and services. For this reason we shall describe such a tax as a *cash-flow corporation tax*. The essence of the tax is that all receipts and payments, whether they correspond to current or to capital items, enter into the tax base and therefore there is no need to define 'true economic depreciation'.

What would the effect of such a tax be? Imagine a firm contemplating a specific investment project which would cost £1 million. With a cash-flow tax it would be able to deduct the £1 million spent on purchasing equipment against its profits on other projects, thus reducing its total tax payments. If the tax rate were 50 per cent the reduction in taxes would be £½ million. The future profits of the project would also be reduced by 50 per cent by such a tax, and so the net effect is that both the initial outlay and the subsequent returns are reduced by the same proportion, a proportion equal to the rate of tax. The tax scales down the size of the project financed by the company, but it does not alter the rate of return on the money invested in the project by the company. With a 50 per cent tax rate, what the government is saying is 'in any project in which you invest we shall compulsorily acquire a 50 per cent stake, and we shall of course provide half the finance in return for half the profits'. The reason this tax system can raise revenue is that it ensures that if firms are in a position to earn pure profits then the government too will get a good share of the excess profits. It is for this reason that the cash-flow tax is well suited to tackling problems such as how to tax the profits on North Sea oil and gas extraction. We believe that it also represents the best way of allowing for inflation in a simple manner without the need for complicated conventions on how to account for inflation. It taxes companies on those flows that are most important to the companies themselves, namely flows of cash.

In the above example it was crucial that the firm had available profits from other projects against which it could deduct investment expenditure on new projects. But a new or expanding firm might not have sufficient profits for this purpose, and such a possibility was an important element in the decision to replace accelerated depreciation allowances with cash investment grants in 1966. The problem can be partly met by allowing companies to carry forward tax losses, not as at present simply at their nominal value, but marked up by an interest factor to allow for the fact that they have to wait to get the benefit of the first-year tax allowances. Alternatively, companies could be allowed to trade unused tax losses so that a company with a tax loss could sell its unused tax credit to a company with positive taxable income.

Because the tax is based on cash flows as and when they occur, there is no need to index for inflation. The distinction between capital and income would be irrelevant, and the effects of inflation would be allowed for automatically without the need for any special adjustment. It is important to stress the simplicity of this system in contrast to the complexity of the alternative methods of calculating taxable profits which have been suggested.

To convert the current tax system into a cash-flow corporation tax would necessitate several changes. The first would be to bring back 100 per cent first-year allowances and extend them to all types of capital expenditure in order to eliminate any distinction between current and capital items for tax purposes. Corporate capital gains would no longer be taxed at concessionary rates, and the proceeds from all sales of assets would be taxed at the full corporate tax rate. The other major set of changes that would be required concern the treatment of payments to the suppliers of finance. In principle, interest payments would no longer be tax-deductible. This means that the effective cost to companies of borrowing would be the gross interest rate and not, as at present, the net-of-tax interest rate. But there is a better way of achieving this than simply disallowing interest payments as a tax deduction. This is to allow interest payments to be tax-deductible as at present but to treat new borrowing as a taxable receipt. This would have the desired effect of making the effective cost of borrowing the gross interest rate, and would allow the cash-flow corporation tax to be applied to financial companies. The taxation of financial companies, primarily banks, raises a number of difficulties. The need to retain the tax deductibility of interest payments exists because the abolition of tax deductibility has as its logical counterpart the abolition of the taxation of interest income. If this were done then any profit made by lending at interest rates higher than those at which money can be borrowed would go untaxed. Yet this is exactly what financial companies do. The reason why they pay lower interest rates than those at which they themselves can lend is because they do not charge market prices for the financial services they provide. For example, banks have only recently started to pay interest on special current accounts, and on most accounts pay no interest and do not charge the full price for the banking services they offer. The logical treatment is to regard an interest-free current account as representing a combination of an interest-bearing deposit and a charge for banking services. The present interest-free account is attractive to the customer because the income he is receiving in the form of free services is not taxed. Hence the tax treatment of banks is a problem for both income tax and value added tax, as well as corporation tax. The problems posed by the measurement of bank profits were recognized in 1981 when a special tax on banks related to the size of their deposits was levied.

The final change required for a cash-flow corporation tax is the elimination of imputation credit paid on dividends. The principle of the cash-flow tax is to allow full deduction of all payments for real goods and services but no deduction of payments to the suppliers of finance. Consequently, the imputation system would be abolished and we would return to a classical system of corporation tax in which dividends distributed would be subject to personal income tax.

This proposal would create transitional difficulties if companies were allowed to engage in financial transactions in anticipation of the change in the tax system. They would have an incentive to increase borrowing before the tax was introduced and to repay this debt by the issue of new equity after the new tax came into force. It is not clear that these transitional incentives are any greater than those experienced in previous tax changes in the UK—notably those in 1965 and 1973—but anti-avoidance provisions would be needed. In the UK context, the simplest solution is for the chancellor to announce that if the proposal were passed by Parliament then the new tax base would apply to transactions in debt or equity from the date of announcement of the tax change. There are precedents for this type of provision, and indeed until very recently the rate of corporation tax in the UK was determined at the end of the tax year rather than in advance.

With satisfactory transitional arrangements, the cash-flow corporation tax offers a means of attaining fiscal neutrality with uniform incentives to invest for all types of investment, and is robust to changes in the inflation rate that are as hard to predict as they are to control.

12

Taxing economic rent

One of the oldest ideas in public finance is that there are advantages in basing tax on economic rent. Most people are familiar with what is meant by the rent of land or buildings, but the concept of rent in economics has a specific technical meaning. It is the amount that a factor of production earns over and above that which it could earn in its next best use. If a singer earns £100,000 a year, and his next best employment would be as a barber at £5,000 per year, then he is obtaining economic rent of £95,000. Two points follow immediately from this example. One is that rent is the result of the scarcity of particular factors of production. If all barbers would make equally good singers, then the earnings of singers would be bid down to the earnings of barbers, and no rent would be derived. The second feature to note is that the rent could be taxed, or otherwise reduced, without any economic distortion resulting. So long as our singer nets more than £5,000 per year, he will continue his present occupation and stay out of the barber's shop.

There is obviously a close association between the concept of economic rent and the everyday notion of rent. Figure 12.1 shows the traditional analysis in a simple economy in which land was mainly used for agricultural purposes. The cost of production is taken to be the same for all land, but land varies greatly in fertility and so does the value of output from it. The economic rent derived from the land is the difference between value and costs, and is positive for all land inside the margin of cultivation—there is some land so poor that it is not worth cultivating. The total rent derived is measured by the shaded triangle.

If the price of the crop were to increase, the value of output would shift outwards and the margin of cultivation would be extended. The economic rent accruing to all the intra-marginal land—which would have been cultivated even at the lower price—will increase. In a competitive market, the rent which farmers will pay to landowners will be equal to the economic rent earned by the land. Because land has no profitable alternative use, the whole of the rent is economic rent. If the farmer is an owner-occupier, then part of the return to his farming activities will be the economic rent derived from his land—and also any economic rent derived from his superior capabilities as a farmer. Economic rents are often internalized in this way, rather than being the subject of explicit transactions.

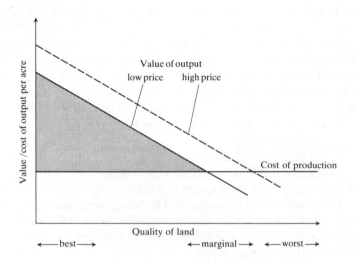

Fig. 12.1. Economic rent in a simple economy

At the end of the nineteenth century, a movement led by Henry George argued, vigorously, that for these reasons land should be the principal tax base. This tradition still survives, although it is apparent that the total of economic rents, of all kinds, is not now a sufficiently large proportion of national income for this to be a practicable means of obtaining the resources needed to finance a modern state.

But the underlying intellectual argument for seeking to tax economic rent retains its force. There are areas in which the argument seems especially strong. Economic rents arise from the existence of scarce factors. Often, the availability and distribution of scarce factors are determined by nature—talents for singing, or outstanding views. But there are other scarce factors where the scarcity is created, or allocated, by the community. Examples might include oil and gas exploration licences, planning permissions, and television franchises.

In this chapter we examine the various ways in which the British tax system attempts to base itself on economic rents. We can generally identify these areas by the existence of special tax regimes on particular activities. We therefore look at property development, at North Sea oil and gas, at television contracting, at gambling, and at banking. In introducing special taxes for these activities, politicians have been motivated less by any sophisticated understanding of the theory of economic rent than by a sense that money was there for the taking. But it is the existence of economic rent which explains why these activities were so profitable and why it might be thought that discriminatorily high taxes could be imposed without inflicting economic damage. An appreciation of the underlying theory will enable us to see when this is possible, and when it is not.

Land and property development

Rent is naturally associated with land and property. But agricultural land is no longer the important source of wealth and income that it was when the economic analysis of rent was conceived. Today, even the best agricultural land is unlikely to be worth more than £3,000 per acre. Land in the south-east of England suitable for housing development may easily sell for £250,000 per acre. Office sites in central London are much more valuable still.

These price differences arise mainly because land that is favourably located for offices or housing is scarce. But this scarcity is greatly increased by the existence of planning controls. By limiting further the availability of land for development, these controls enhance the value of sites that are already built on or for which planning permission can be secured. The consequence is that the decision of a planning authority may determine whether a piece of land commands only its low agricultural use value or its development value. Such a decision will rest, not on the amount of work done by the owner of the land or how socially deserving he is, but on consideration of the balance of amenities attached to development in a particular area.

These windfall gains have always appeared promising subjects for taxation. Moreover, the theory of economic rent suggests that they could be taxed very heavily without inhibiting development. Suppose the award of planning permission increases the value of a plot of land from £3,000 to £250,000. Then even if the resulting gain were taxed at 90 per cent, the developer would still be better off by almost £25,000 using the land for housing than retaining it for agricultural purposes. Substantial incentives to bring projects forward would remain.

There is, however, a weakness in this argument. It supposes that the tax is expected to be permanent. If the developer sees the only alternatives as agricultural use or immediate development, it is obvious that he will prefer immediate development. He may, however, believe that there is another alternative—that of retaining the land and delaying his application for planning permission or his sale of the land until the tax regime is more favourable. If this were to happen, the supply of land for development would be reduced and the price of that land which was available would increase. Contrary to the expectations suggested by the theory of economic rent, a tax on gains from development levied in these circumstances would raise land prices, increase the scarcity of housing and housing land, and inhibit property development generally.

Frequent attempts have been made to implement special taxes on development gains—on three separate occasions since the Second World War. In each case, landowners and developers have believed the tax would not be permanent, and in each case they have been right. The first cycle began with the introduction of planning controls in 1947. This was accompanied by a betterment levy, designed to secure that—eventually—all gains from the grant of planning permissions accrued to the public. The measure raised little revenue and was abolished by the incoming Conservative government. Rather similar provisions were reintroduced by the next Labour government in 1966, and again they were repealed.

The most recent tax on development gains was introduced in 1973—by a Conservative government. Before the tax was announced, property prices had been rising very sharply, and the size and scale of development programmes were growing rapidly. The tax was introduced in response to feelings right across the political spectrum that the magnitude and profitability of this activity were quite out of proportion to its economic significance. The announcement of the new tax more or less coincided, however, with a variety of other political and economic events—war in the Middle East, the oil price rise, the miners' strike, and the defeat of the government—which brought an abrupt end to the property boom. Property developers were more concerned to stay in business than with how notional gains would be taxed. The charge remained, was recast as development land tax in 1976, but finally abolished in 1985. Gains that arise from the granting of planning permission or from development are now treated in the same way as other capital gains.

Oil and gas

The production of minerals is an activity that generates economic rent. In Figure 12.1, we might read 'most easily worked reserves' in place of 'best land' and 'hardest to work deposits' in place of 'worst land', and our discussion would follow more or less unchanged. By far the most important source of economic rent of this type for Britain is North Sea oil production. This is true not only because of the significance of the output; it is also important to note that the activities of OPEC have raised oil prices far above the costs of production even of relatively expensive North Sea reserves. For these reasons, taxes on rents from North Sea oil have become a major source of revenue for the UK exchequer.

A special tax regime has been constructed for North Sea activities. A royalty is payable of $12\frac{1}{2}$ per cent of the value of the oil extracted. Petroleum revenue tax (PRT), at 75 per cent, is due on the receipts from selling North Sea oil less the costs of finding it, extracting it, and bringing it ashore. The costs are those incurred in the field from which the oil comes—thus PRT is levied on a 'field basis'. Royalties can be treated as a cost in computing PRT. An 'uplift' provision allows 135 per cent of initial capital expenditures to be offset against PRT. There is an oil allowance of 500,000 tonnes of oil a year which is free of PRT, subject to a cumulative total for each field of 5 million tonnes. There is also a 'safeguard provision' for rebating PRT if the historic cost profitability of a field becomes too low. In 1983 a number of concessions, including the abolition of royalties, were made for new discoveries.

Companies are also liable to corporation tax (CT) on their profits. A 'ring-fence' is drawn round the North Sea, so that only expenses or allowances relating to North Sea activities can be deducted in computing liabilities. Before North Sea production began, many oil companies had no liability to mainstream corporation tax. They typically had unused relief from capital allowances, stock relief, double tax relief, and advance corporation tax from their activities on the UK mainland and in the rest of the world. The ring-fence

arrangement prevents tax losses and double tax relief derived elsewhere being used against North Sea profits and restricts the capacity
of the companies to obtain relief for advance corporation tax.

A fourth tax—supplementary petroleum duty (SPD)—was introduced in 1980. It is a hybrid between royalties and PRT. It is
based on 20 per cent of gross revenues less the oil allowance. In
1982 it was renamed advance petroleum revenue tax (APRT), and
payments of APRT can be offset against future payments of PRT.
The law provides that any APRT that has not been relieved after
five years will be refunded.

Table 12.1: *North Sea oil tax revenues* (£ million, current)

Actual

	Royalties	SPD	PRT	APRT	CT	Total
1977	200	—	—	—	—	200
1980	900	—	1,600	—	600	3,000
1983	1,800	300	3,900	2,300	900	9,200
1984	2,200	—	5,200	2,200	2,100	11,700
1985	2,200	—	6,900	1,500	2,800	13,300

Prospective

	4% inflation, oil price per barrel of:		
	$30	$20	$10
1986	9,900	6,500	3,600
1987	9,200	4,600	800
1990	6,300	3,500	1,200
1993	2,800	1,900	600

Source: IFS estimates.

One additional complication concerns gas production. Until 1983,
any company discovering gas in the North Sea was obliged to offer
it to the British Gas Corporation. With the power that this restriction
gave it, British Gas was able to drive hard bargains and in particular
was able to make long-term contracts for gas supplies that were
discovered before the 1973/4 oil crisis at prices which were, in the

light of subsequent developments, extremely low. These contracts are now very profitable to British Gas, and can be seen, depending on your point of view, either as a public share of the rents from North Sea gas production or as an economic rent attributable to the conferment and exercise of monopsony buying power. In either event, the rent is substantial and a special tax—the gas levy—is imposed to recoup the proceeds directly for the exchequer. This tax raises a number of wider issues which we discuss below under privatization.

One might conclude from the complexity of the North Sea tax system that it was a finely tuned instrument in which each element made a contribution to some carefully conceived overall design. This conclusion would be entirely mistaken. The planning period for investing in offshore oil exploration and development is a very long one, and one of the most important objectives of a tax regime for these activities is to provide a stable environment in which such plans can be made. The government has been spectacularly unsuccessful in achieving this objective, and the tax structure and rates have been subject to substantial modifications every year since they were introduced, and have often been changed several times in a year.

Worse than that, the interaction of the taxes is riddled with anomalies. On the one hand, there is a North Sea 'poverty trap', in which tax may take more than 100 per cent of additional revenue from a marginal field; on the other, there is the possibility of 'gold-plating', where more than 100 per cent of additional capital expenditure may be deductible against tax. The potential tax charge on the same discovery, or potential deduction for the same expenditure, varies widely across the North Sea according to the company that undertakes it and the field in which it occurs. The combination of the height of the tax rates imposed, uncertainty about their future, and the random relationship of tax to profitability has now reduced the rate of exploration and development to low levels.

The cash-flow principle is particularly well suited to the taxation of this type of activity. The mechanics of applying a progressive tax on cumulative profitability were described by the Part Committee (1982), and the merits of the approach are very clear. Such a tax is relatively simple, robust to changing circumstances, and because it is directly related to economic rent and the measures that oil companies use in appraising investment—expected cash flow—it secures a substantial share of the revenues of highly successful ventures while minimizing the disincentive to marginal ones.

It is often said that in attempting to reform the tax system we are constrained by history. If only we could start from scratch, things would be very different. The sorry history of the taxation of North Sea oil demonstrates that this is not true. We had a chance to invent a new tax system in the 1970s, with a clean slate; and we invented something which in its complexity, anomalies, inequities, and disincentives has all the characteristics of the British tax system as a whole. The fault lies not with our ancestors, but with the ways in which we determine tax policy. Half-baked measures are hastily devised, and then quickly and repeatedly modified to deal with some immediately pressing problem, all without any sense of long-term strategy or of how proposals fit into some overall picture. This book describes the consequences.

Other sources of rent

Economic rents arise where individuals or companies have privileged access to scarce factors, and are particularly appropriate subjects for taxation where the government confers access to these scarce factors. It does this when it awards licences to explore and develop in the North Sea. Another example is when it allows the Independent Broadcasting Authority to award television franchises.

When commercial television was introduced in the UK, one contractor was appointed for each region, with a franchise which was subject to regular renewal. Advertising revenue grew rapidly, and these franchises became very profitable. Lord Thomson, who controlled the company that obtained the right to broadcast in central Scotland, was reported to have described it as 'a licence to print money'. In a competitive market, this degree of profitability would have attracted new entrants, and returns would quickly have been bid down to normal levels. The regulatory restrictions on television production prevented this happening. Indeed by severely limiting the amount of advertising that companies could transmit—and hence raising its price—they may even have raised these profit levels still further. The government responded by introducing a special levy on the profits of television contractors.

Gambling is another industry subject to tight restriction. Controls on casinos are particularly severe. It is necessary to establish a board of bishops, retired police officers, or other persons of unimpeachable reputation to satisfy the Gaming Board that a company is of sufficient standing to hold a licence to run a casino, and even with these spiritual and temporal aids several major public companies have failed to win, or retain, their licences. In consequence the business is extremely profitable for those who are successful in obtaining licences, and a special tax regime absorbs some of that profitability.

It is clearly undesirable that there should be a proliferation of industry-specific tax regimes. The results are likely to be inequitable and inefficient and, additionally, associated with an undesirable degree of arbitrary political power. The existence of economic rents provides a particular justification for these *ad hoc* taxes, especially where the rent is conferred by public action. Arguments for other special taxes on profitable industries or activities should be viewed with suspicion. The higher level of profitability is either the product of superior efficiency—in which case it should not be the subject of discriminatory taxation—or of the exercise of market power, which should be tackled directly rather than taxed. Only if this is impossible or undesirable does an argument for taxation remain.

Banking is often suggested as a possible victim for special taxation, and indeed a one-off special levy on banks was imposed in 1981. Some of this simply reflects a primitive distrust of finance. Certainly it is difficult to see how any economic rents accrue in banking. It is true that established banks enjoy an advantage over newcomers to the industry, but this seems no more an appropriate subject for taxation than the good reputation of any other supplier. Entry to banking is easy, and the British clearing-banks have seen their retail market share eroded by building societies and their wholesale activities challenged by the growth of American and other international competition. Perhaps the nearest approach to control of a scarce factor is their dominance of the clearing system—the method by which cheques are returned to be debited to the accounts of those who draw them. But, albeit reluctantly, the banks have given newcomers access to this system.

Banking does, however, raise one special problem. Banks operate largely by financing their costs through differences in their borrowing and lending rates. Because their charges are implicit rather than explicit, there are indirect consequences for revenues from income tax, corporation tax, and VAT. The issue was discussed in Chapter 11. Edwards and Mayer (1983) conclude that services provided by banks and other financial institutions should be unbundled, at least for tax purposes, and that some additional tax payment would be the likely outcome.

Privatization

The possibility of tax on economic rent arises where a firm or individual has exclusive access to scarce factors. It is open to governments to create such limited access, and to tax the resulting revenue; and we have noted how this has been attempted or accomplished in such diverse areas as development gains, television contracting, and gambling. In all these instances, the underlying rationale of the restriction is social rather than fiscal. The fiscal opportunity is simply a by-product.

Governments could, however, create monopolies with the primary motive of taxing the resulting profits. The tobacco monopolies of several European countries—such as France and Italy—originate from this approach, although they do not serve this function now. In general, the creation of a monopoly would seem to have no fiscal advantage over achieving the same result by direct taxation, and some potential disadvantages, particularly on incentives to efficiency in the industry concerned; and in both these countries, revenue is now mainly derived from conventional taxation (which applies both to domestic production and to imports) rather than from monopoly profit. A government particularly desperate for revenue could sell the monopoly; by this means it would derive the capital value of a stream of future profits (or tax revenues) immediately.

In the Middle Ages, disreputable monarchs would raise revenue in this way by the granting of monopolies. Astute merchants would offer to finance the king's expenditure in return for some exclusive trading rights. No modern government would undertake any procedure so crude; but very similar issues arise, in slightly disguised form, in current proposals for privatization. The issue is that a wide range of public sector assets are, in fact, economic rents. Either, because they do represent particular scarce factors, they have not until recently been considered suitable for public ownership; or scarcity and rents have been created by statutory restrictions on competition.

The gas levy discussed above is one example. The rent arises from limitations on competition in favour of a public sector body. At the time of writing it is not clear whether if British Gas is privatized the gas levy will continue, or whether it will be abolished and the proceeds of the sale increased correspondingly. If the latter happens, the effect, if not the intention, will be that the government will have created profits by statutory restriction and sold the capital value of the resulting income to private shareholders.

Other nationalized industries enjoy similar benefit from economic rents. Much of the revenue of British Airways derives from rights to participate in international aviation cartels (Ashworth and Forsyth, 1984). The British Airports Authority derives most of its revenue from two sources, both rents (Starkie and Thompson, 1985). One is landing charges at Heathrow Airport (a scarce factor). The other is the sale of duty-free goods. Not even medieval kings thought of selling the right to sell goods free of taxes imposed on other traders, and it is more than extraordinary that a modern government should plan to do precisely that.

13

Taxation and inflation

Inflation has probably been the most potent influence for change on the structure of the British tax system in the last fifteen years. It raises problems of two distinct kinds. There is the issue of 'bracket indexation' which arises because tax schedules are defined in money terms. Income tax gives a personal allowance of £2,205 for a single person and £3,455 for a married man. Capital transfer tax is imposed on transfers that in total exceed £67,000. It is necessary to register for VAT if your turnover is greater than £19,500. You must pay stamp duty if you buy a house for more than £30,000. There is a tax of 2·7p per cigarette and of 82p per gallon of petrol. With inflation, the meaning of these monetary amounts changes. Fifty years ago, a house costing £30,000 would have been a mansion. Now it is very difficult to find any house in the south of England as cheap as that.

Inflation also poses difficulties for the definition of income itself—the problem of 'capital-income indexation'. When prices are stable, an investor who earns 3 per cent on £100 he deposits in the bank is better off by that amount at the end of the year: £3 is the sum which he can prudently spend while maintaining his capital and his ability to earn a similar sum in future years. When inflation runs at 20 per cent per annum, the man who earns 12 per cent on his bank deposit is in a very different position. The interest he receives is significantly short of what he needs simply to stay as well off as he was when he deposited the money in the first place. Thus when inflation is taken into account his real income is negative, not positive. He cannot spend this £12 except by making himself worse off in future, and hence it is as much part of his capital as is his basic £100. Nevertheless, the taxman will present a demand for 30 per cent (or up to 60 per cent) of his nominal income of £12, so that the amount by which his receipts after tax fall short of what is required to keep pace with inflation is greater still.

Bracket indexation and fiscal drag

What we have called bracket indexation, following the Meade Committee (1978), was first noticed in relation to income tax and was somewhat inelegantly christened 'fiscal drag'. Inflation means that year by year people earn larger and larger amounts of money even though they are not necessarily better off. But a progressive income tax bases liability on their money income, and so demands each year a higher proportion of their rising money income in tax. With tax brackets fixed in nominal terms, someone with a constant real income will find himself paying higher and higher effective rates of tax. Thus the Revenue's take, as a proportion of total personal income, will increase steadily and this is precisely what has happened. Although tax thresholds have frequently been raised in money terms, they have declined relative to earnings. In 1952/3 a married man had to earn almost £800 per year to be liable for standard rate tax. If his salary kept pace with average earnings between 1952 and 1986, it would have risen to almost £15,000 and he would have been on the verge of paying higher rates. At the highest real income levels, however, the burden is now lower than at any time since the war.

Fiscal drag was traditionally a boon for dishonest chancellors of the exchequer. Each year they could announce 'reductions' in income tax while each year they would in fact increase the burden of the tax. Until the mid-1970s, this is exactly what happened in most years. In the course of debate on the 1977 Finance Act, back-bench pressure secured the passage, against government opposition, of what became known as the Rooker-Wise amendment. This required indexation of the basic single and married (and some other) allowances. Initially the government resisted these measures, but more recently the principle of bracket indexation has been accepted and extended. It now applies to the higher rate bands and to thresholds for capital gains tax, investment income surcharge, and capital transfer tax.

When people talk about fiscal drag they usually refer to income tax, but the same problem is relevant to other taxes with a progressive rate structure. Capital transfer tax (CTT) also has a series of rate bands, while capital gains tax is progressive in effect because of its high exemption limit. Indexation of CTT poses a special problem. If prices have risen by 50 per cent in the past five years, then a gift of £40,000 made five years ago is equivalent to a gift of £60,000 made now. This change should be reflected in the threshold for CTT; but it should also be reflected in the cumulative total on which CTT is levied. With thoroughgoing indexation, a gift of £40,000 five years ago and of £60,000 now would lead to a cumulative total equivalent to a gift of £120,000 made today. Possibly because of the complexity of this procedure, the indexation of capital transfer tax is limited to the threshold and does not apply to the various rate bands.

Proportional taxes are largely unaffected by inflation. The yield from VAT increases in line with rising prices. Revenue from national insurance contributions increases at the same rate as earnings. The yield of car tax moves in line with the price of cars. Some peripheral aspects of these taxes do need regular readjustment, such as the threshold of turnover below which it is unnecessary to register for VAT, and the rate bands for national insurance contributions. The VAT threshold has been subject to frequent review, and the national insurance limits move in line with changes in the rate of state pension (and hence with prices).

A final group of taxes includes those that are levied as flat monetary amounts. To use a motor vehicle it is necessary to buy an annual licence at a cost of £100, and we described several other taxes of this kind in Chapter 8. When the value of money falls, so does the burden of these taxes. Table 13.1 shows how this has happened. In this table, we show not only the rates of tax levied at the time but also what they would now be if they had been increased in line with prices generally since then.

Table 13.1:   *Indirect taxes, 1966–85*

Year	Actual rates				At 1985 prices			
	Cigarettes	Whisky	Beer	Petrol	Cigarettes	Whisky	Beer	Petrol
1966	16	1.88	4.3	18	98	11.55	26	111
1972	18	2.20	4.7	23	78	9.58	21	100
1978	39	3.49	10.0	43	74	6.61	19	81
1982	71	4.90	19	82	83	5.71	22	96
Tax, 1985					93	5.33	24	107
Price, 1985					115	6.75	75	190

Notes: Cigarettes: pence per packet king-size tipped.
Whisky: £ per bottle blended whisky.
Beer: pence per pint of bitter.
Petrol: pence per gallon four star.
Wine: pence per bottle.
Sources: Reports of Customs and Excise; own estimates.

If the impact of inflation on the tax system is not recognized, then it can have substantial effects on the structure of taxation. Income tax revenue will rise, relatively, while receipts from specific duties will fall. There will be a switch from indirect to direct taxation. Such a move may or may not be desirable, but it should not simply be an unintended by-product of inflation. Between the mid-1960s and the mid-1970s, this is precisely what did happen. In 1965 income tax (including national insurance contributions) was 45 per cent of total government current receipts; in 1975 it was 53 per cent. At the same time, the share of indirect taxes fell from 29 per cent to 23 per cent. Since then there has been general recognition of the problem. Action has been taken to prevent further unplanned moves in this direction and to restore the proportion of indirect taxes in the total by the 1979 shift from income tax to VAT. Although there is considerable tidying up to be done, bracket indexation is now a general feature of the UK tax system.

Inflation in the capital market

We have noted that inflation raises problems for the definition of income. When prices are changing, people need to have more money in order simply to maintain the value of their wealth. If I had £100 in the building society last year, and have £110 this year, and prices have risen by 10 per cent, then I am no better off than I was a year ago.

One way of securing protection against inflation would be to lend on terms that were indexed. I would hand over £100 and what I would be repaid would have the same value in the money of the day as £100 has now. If prices had doubled, I would get £200. Obviously I would expect a much lower interest rate on such an investment; however, it would be a 'real' interest rate rather than a nominal interest rate and I could go out and spend my annual interest confident that my capital was maintaining its value. I could also quite fairly be taxed on the 'real' interest I received. Notice that there is no economic law that says that real interest rates have to be positive. It is possible that I might have to pay someone who offered to keep my capital intact for me, and in fact in most recent years this would have been quite a good deal for most people—better, at least, than other forms of saving and investment offered them.

Several other countries have experimented at various times with indexation of this kind—it has been pursued furthest in Brazil, Finland, Iceland, and Israel.

The possibility that indexed bonds might exist in Britain was first canvassed in the mid-1970s when inflation topped 25 per cent. Merchant banks prepared prospectuses but the Bank of England indicated that it would intervene to prohibit such issues. The reasons for this prohibition, which survived for several years, were obscure. One argument was that indexation involves accepting, or institutionalizing, inflation; but this is a bit like saying that taking an umbrella with you involves accepting, or institutionalizing, bad weather. It was also argued that Middle Eastern states were so anxious to obtain bonds of this kind that capital would flood into Britain on an unprecedented scale if they were available. This was apparently considered undesirable. It was never clear why the king of Saudi Arabia should wish to link his assets to the price level in Britain and subsequent events have shown that he does not in fact want to do so.

A limited experiment was made in 1975 with 'granny bonds' which allowed pensioners to lend £500 to the government, the sum to be revalued in line with prices before it was repaid with a small bonus in addition. Grannies had to be resident in the UK, thus cunningly excluding the king of Saudi Arabia. Eventually it was realized that protecting your capital against inflation is more important before you have retired than afterwards and 'granny bonds' were opened to all. Attempts to rechristen them 'people's bonds' were not very successful.

Pressure for wider measures of indexation grew from a variety of sources. Governments that annually ran very large deficits felt under pressure to invent imaginative new ways of borrowing money. Critics of official determination to get inflation down pointed out that a policy of raising money for twenty or thirty years at high fixed interest rates made sense only if the government had no real intention of reducing inflation. Many of the problems of pension funds were attributed to their inability to find assets of known and constant real value. In 1981 the government issued the first index-linked government stock; each unit of stock cost £100. It was to be repaid in 1996, and the amount of the repayment would be whatever was needed to buy then what £100 would buy in 1981. In the mean time, a real interest rate of 2 per cent was offered; the interest payment would itself be revalued each year in line with the retail price index. Only tax-exempt pension funds were allowed to buy the bonds; thus the

question of how the interest and capital repayment were to be taxed
did not arise.

A world of indexed bonds would need many fewer actuaries and
investment managers, and it is perhaps understandable that they
did not give the new securities a particularly warm welcome. Since
inflation was falling rapidly at the time, they may even have been
right. In any event, the bond quickly fell to a discount on its issue
price. Partly to stimulate demand, and partly because the predicted
disasters from introducing indexation had not materialized, the
government in 1982 allowed anyone—even foreigners—to buy
index-linked government stock. By 1985 index-linked issues accounted for 9 per cent of the value of marketable government
securities.

Indexation and taxation

The growing importance of index-linked securities raised the question of how they should be taxed. The longest dated of the index-
linked stocks will be repaid in 2020. Even on the most optimistic of
views about the future course of inflation, anyone who holds a bond
till then will be sitting on a substantial capital gain. With an average
inflation rate of only 5 per cent, the maturity value of this stock will
be over £500. But every penny of that capital gain will be the result
of inflation; none of it will be real gain at all.

The fact that most recent capital gains are of this kind has been
recognized for some time. In 1977 the government promised to
'look sympathetically' at the problem. A consultative document was
prepared which presented, and demolished, a ridiculous proposal
for 'tapering' the tax charge on capital gains according to the length
of time for which the asset in question had been held. It is a common
administrative tactic to resist suggested change by dissecting, with
apparent seriousness of purpose, an impractical version of it. In-
experienced observers of Whitehall may be led to think that the
matter has been given careful consideration and that nothing can be
done; there is, of course, no reason whatever to suppose that either
is true. In the event, the only change was that small gains were
exempted from tax. Three years later a further review was undertaken. The outcome was a further increase—to £3,000—in the threshold for capital gains tax.

With the arrival of indexed securities, however, the problem could no longer be evaded. The government announced that it would index capital gains tax. The principle of indexation of capital gains is a reasonably straightforward one. Suppose you buy an asset for £1,000 and sell it some years later for £2,000, by which time prices have risen by 90 per cent. We index your acquisition cost, so that in terms of current purchasing power what you paid for it is not £1,000 but £1,900 and your real gain is £100 not £1,000. If you sell the asset for only £1,500, you have made a real loss of £400, and this is indeed the situation; you would have been able to buy goods worth £400 more, at current prices, if you had spent the money immediately instead of investing it. The scheme introduced in 1982 was a good deal more complex than this, involving the calculation of a con-voluted 'indexation allowance', but in 1985 the government introduced full indexation of capital gains tax.

It is, however, vital to understand that the problems of assessing investment income under inflation are not confined to capital gains. Imagine a world with no inflation. People might earn 3 per cent on investment in bonds and 4 per cent on investment in property (to reflect the greater uncertainty about the capital value of property). Now suppose prices rise each year by a general and predictable 10 per cent. The owner of property makes a 10 per cent capital gain each year. What happens in the bond market? For bonds to remain equally attractive, the yield on them will have to rise also. This could happen as a result of a move to indexed loans; these would offer a real yield of 3 per cent and a capital gain of 10 per cent per year, equal to the rate of inflation. If loans remain unindexed, however—and this is the normal situation—then the interest rate on them will have to rise. If they are to maintain the same relationship with property yields, the nominal interest rate will now have to be 13 per cent. In one case, compensation for inflation takes the form of a capital gain; in the other case, there is a rise in the nominal interest rate. Both the capital gain and the inflationary component in the interest rate are illusory; an equitable tax base would exclude them both.

But if this is true for lenders then just the same is true for borrowers. If I take out a £10,000 mortgage, pay interest at 13 per cent, and repay my £10,000 either at the end of the mortgage or in instalments over life, then the real value of what I repay is much less than I borrowed. Most of my interest payment is not real interest but repayment of capital. Just as the lender should be taxed only on the real component of the interest he receives, so the borrower should obtain tax relief only on the real component of the interest he pays. The prospect of losing this relief must seem very alarming to companies or to households that think that current interest rates are very high. But the reason they seem so high is precisely because borrowing is undertaken in nominal rather than real terms. A mortgage of 13 per cent fixed in money terms imposes a very serious initial burden which declines steadily as inflation progresses. An indexed mortgage at 3 per cent fixed in real terms would impose a much smaller initial cost, but one which would remain constant over its life. If tax relief were given on real interest only, it would be necessary to reconstruct mortgages in this way, and they would then be no more difficult to afford than at present. It was indexation of the capital market which led us to indexation of the tax system; but it seems that indexation of the tax system leads us back to indexation of the capital market.

The extent of indexation

We described a world in which there was no inflation and where bonds yielded 3 per cent and property 4 per cent. With 10 per cent inflation, the return on bonds might rise to 13 per cent. Property would continue to yield 4 per cent but holders could expect an annual 10 per cent capital gain. If the tax system is fully indexed, then the inflation component of 10 per cent is excluded in computing tax liability on bonds, so that holders pay tax on the real return of 3 per cent. Property-owners pay tax only on their real capital gain—the part that exceeds 10 per cent.

Suppose no adjustments whatever are made to the tax system. Then lending is less attractive than before—because the tax burden has increased—and borrowing is more attractive, because the tax burden has declined. Suppose everyone pays tax at 50 per cent. Then the return on bonds would need to rise to 23 per cent before they were equally attractive to lenders. On £100 of loan, tax of £11·50 would be payable on £23 interest. At 10 per cent inflation, the net-of-tax real return on the loan is £1·50: exactly what it would have been with a 3 per cent yield and no inflation. Moreover, the borrower can afford to pay 23 per cent without being any worse off, because the tax deduction he obtains is now so large.

For a variety of reasons, things do not work as smoothly in practice. Not everyone is subject to tax at the same rate, so that lending becomes very attractive to those who do not pay tax, and borrowing is attractive to those who do. Interest rates therefore will not rise as high as 23 per cent. This means that lenders who pay low rates of tax (like pension funds) benefit from inflation; so do borrowers who pay high rates of tax (like people who buy expensive houses). There is therefore redistribution among borrowers and lenders. The interaction of tax and inflation also alters the attractiveness of different kinds of asset. The inflation element of interest payments is taxed as if it were income while the inflation component of the returns from property is treated more favourably as capital gain, so real assets like property become attractive compared with nominal assets like bonds. People may suffer from money illusion, so that they think that 23 per cent is a very high interest rate even if they are told that tax relief and inflation make such borrowing very cheap. And to some extent they are right to think this, since borrowings are structured in such a way that 23 per cent interest is initially very onerous. If the capital market were indexed things might be different but we have not yet reached that stage.

Nevertheless, with no indexation one might reach a sort of equilibrium with a new, much higher level of nominal interest rates. This outcome might not be very different from the position that would be achieved with no inflation. Central to this argument is an element of symmetry in the tax treatment of debt. This means that lenders pay tax on what borrowers are allowed to deduct. If this symmetry exists, and borrowers and lenders are liable to tax at similar rates, then the net effect of inflation on tax receipts and on savings and investment behaviour may be quite small.

Partial indexation—which makes allowance for inflation in some areas but not others, or for certain items but not for others—presents many difficulties, and that is the position we have now reached. With partial indexation, symmetry disappears. This inevitably means that essentially similar transactions receive different tax treatment; that deductions are available for payments that are not taxable when they are received, or conversely; and that there is endless scope for anomalies and abuse. The present degree of partial indexation is the consequence of indexation of capital gains tax but not interest income.

The present position is one in which relief for inflation is allowed if compensation for it takes the form of a capital gain, but not if it takes the form of an enhanced interest rate. If you own a real asset and it rises in value because of inflation, you get an indexation allowance. If you hold a bank deposit and the interest rate rises because of inflation, you pay tax on the full amount of interest received. The distinction between the two types of compensation for inflation has nothing to commend it. It has no economic content. It is inequitable: capital gains are already more lightly taxed than income and generally accrue to better-off people. It is impractical: as we saw in Chapter 4, income and capital gains can readily be interchanged and this will happen if there is some advantage to the switch. For this last reason, if no other, we do not expect the present position to survive unmodified for long.

Unanticipated inflation as a capital tax

It was an important element in the discussion above that inflation was expected. If everyone anticipates that inflation will run at 10 per cent, then this will be reflected in the terms on which they want to lend or borrow and interest rates will rise correspondingly. If inflation is unanticipated, then many people will find themselves locked into contracts which they made at fixed nominal interest rates. In these circumstances, inflation becomes a tax on capital. Suppose prices have been stable, and are expected to remain so, and many people have lent money at a fixed rate of 3 per cent. If inflation now rises to 10 per cent, they earn a real return of -7 per cent: their capital depreciates in value at 7 per cent per year.

Most of the expenditure undertaken by governments is funded from explicit taxes, like income tax and corporation tax, which we describe in other chapters of this book. However, governments do not always match their revenue and expenditure, and meet deficits by printing money or borrowing it. This inflationary finance acquires resources for the government and diverts them from its citizens, in just the same way as other taxes. The form of the tax is a levy on people who hold assets denominated in money terms, such as fixed interest securities or cash itself.

If the tax system is not indexed, then of course the impact of the inflation tax is exaggerated. If your 3 per cent nominal interest is liable to tax at 50 per cent, then the real rate of return that you obtain, after tax, is now −8½ per cent: a net yield of 1½ per cent in money terms, reduced by inflation of 10 per cent. For borrowers, of course, the opposite is true. The burden of their debt has fallen in real terms, and hence unexpected inflation can be seen as a subsidy to debt. It is worth noting that in Britain, as in most modern economies, by far the largest fixed-interest borrower is the government itself.

If we regard unanticipated inflation as a tax, then the picture we painted in Chapter 4 of steadily diminishing yields from capital taxation looks very different. Much of the inflation that occurred in the 1970s was unanticipated, and real returns on investment were frequently negative even for non-taxpayers. Inflation acted as a substantial and redistributive capital tax. But as a tax it has little to commend it. It is a tax on assets and a subsidy on liabilities imposed at a rate that has nothing to do with the circumstances of the individual taxpayer, but that depends solely on the rate of inflation and the extent to which assets are held in money form. This is a very odd state of affairs and does not appear to correspond with the platform of any political party.

Inflation accounting

Concern that company accounts gave a misleading picture of their affairs under inflation rose with the inflation rate itself in the early 1970s. Proposals were produced for a scheme of current purchasing power (CPP) accounting. The government was worried by the wider implications of these ideas—especially for the tax system—and appointed a committee to review them. The Sandilands Committee (1975) rejected CPP and put forward a set of proposals of its own, described as CCA (current cost accounting). After lengthy debate a version of CCA was adopted as an accounting standard (SSAP16) for large companies.

Although the details are complicated, the central difference between CCA and CPP is a simple one. Suppose an oil company holds a large stock of oil, and that the oil price rises while other prices do not. Has the oil company made a profit or not? Proponents of CCA would argue that it has not, since in order to remain an oil company it is necessary for it to go on holding stocks of oil at the new higher prices and the 'profit' is not something that it can effectively realize. Advocates of CPP would claim that nevertheless people who held claims to stocks of oil are now better off than people who did not, and that this gain should be reflected in an assessment of profit and loss. CPP measures gains and losses relative to a general price index, CCA relative to one that reflects the structure of the assets held by the business whose affairs are being considered. The issue is one which has no simple answer and it is really not possible to make a judgement on it independently of the particular circumstances in which the profit is obtained.

CCA involves four main adjustments to published accounts. Depreciation charges should no longer be based on the historic cost of the asset but on the current cost of similar items of equipment. A cost of sales adjustment is required to remove from profits the element attributable to increases in the price of goods held in stock. As well as holding stock, many firms find it necessary to extend trade credit to their customers and a monetary working capital adjustment (MWCA) makes allowance for the effect of inflation on the finance necessary to cover outstanding accounts. These three modifications mostly work in the direction of reducing profits. However, many firms finance these activities—buying fixed assets, holding stocks, or funding trade credit—from borrowed money. Inflation reduces the value of the amount that needs to be repaid. A gearing adjustment reduces the adjustment to historic cost profits by an amount calculated to reflect the ratio of debt to total assets (or gearing) of the company.

In 1973 there was a sharp rise in the price of most primary commodities. The most important and most permanent change was a fourfold increase in the price of oil, but many other raw materials also recorded large price increases. This was associated with a spurt in the general rate of inflation. Many companies recorded large accounting profits on their stocks of commodities. However, these book profits—the result of stock appreciation—had to be reinvested immediately in maintaining stocks at the new price levels. This stimulated an extensive debate on the appropriate measure of profit under inflation. More immediately, companies were faced with tax bills on these profits and many of them lacked the liquid resources needed to meet them.

It is a surprising idea to many people—including some accountants—that you can make a profit but still be short of cash. But there is nothing contradictory about this. Profitability and liquidity are not the same thing, and this is well understood by owner-occupiers who have found it profitable to purchase a home even if this imposed strains on the liquid resources of the household during the first years of a mortgage. The appropriate conclusion is that profitability is not the only, or necessarily the best, measure of the firm's ability to pay dividends or taxes.

The need for a clear view as to what should constitute the tax base for companies is illustrated by the experience of stock relief in the 1970s and 1980s. In 1974 companies were facing severe liquidity problems and the chancellor decided that he could not wait until a permanent method of inflation accounting had been agreed upon before giving some tax concessions to the corporate sector. With most firms using historic cost accounts it was impossible simply to exempt stock appreciation from tax, and an arbitrary form of re-lief—stock relief—was introduced in November 1974, retrospective to 1973. Under this scheme companies could deduct for tax purposes the excess of the change in the book value of stocks over 10 per cent of gross trading profits. The increase in the book value of stocks in any year consists of stock appreciation plus the value of physical investment in stocks. The figure of 10 per cent of gross profits was held to be a rough average for the economy of the value of additions to stocks plus 'normal' stock appreciation, from which it was felt exemption from tax was not justified. This was evidently a rough-and-ready justice which took no account of the circumstances of individual companies.

In Chapter 11 we described the pattern of recent modifications to the structure of corporation tax. It is sometimes suggested that corporation tax should be based on current cost profits, and indeed the need to await the agreement of the accountancy profession on an appropriate inflation accounting standard was often cited as a reason for delaying proposals for more fundamental changes to the corporation tax structure. The scheme of stock relief introduced in 1980/1 bore some resemblance to the cost of sales adjustment, but none of the other adjustments required for current cost accounting have had counterparts in the tax system. Stock relief was abolished altogether in 1984. At the same time 100 per cent first-year al-lowances (which automatically allowed for inflation because there were no depreciation allowances to be carried forward whose value might be eroded by inflation) were abolished, and replaced by stan-dard depreciation allowances more closely related to the likely asset lives. But these allowances are not indexed and inflation reduces the present value of such allowances. With the abolition of stock relief the UK corporate tax system is now totally unindexed, and more vulnerable to an inflationary shock than it was even in the crisis year of 1974 when stock relief was first introduced.

Given that the chancellor has abandoned indexation in the area of corporate taxation, though not in others such as capital gains, it is perhaps not surprising that the accounting profession has also virtually given up the attempt to agree on a uniform standard of accounting for inflation. Current cost accounting has come under fire from backwoodsmen of the accountancy profession who do not see why practices that have served accountants well for the past century should not suffice equally well for the next hundred years. It is more surprising that a chancellor with a reputation for interest in reform should appear to share the same view.

Inflation and tax policy

In this chapter we have described the adaptation of the British tax system to an era of inflation. The changes we have been describing are substantial, far-reaching, and by no means complete. We do not think that the degree of indexation that has now been achieved can possibly be a final resting place. If inflation remains at the low levels experienced in the mid 1980s, it might appear that the need for indexation is not great. But indexation is required when the real rate of return and the inflation rate are of the same order of magnitude. Inflation rates of 3 to 5 per cent are still significant when compared with real rates of return of around 5 per cent. Indexation of the tax system and indexation of the capital market are inextricably linked. We are therefore discussing a series of fundamental changes in the British financial system. We would wish to report that such changes had been extensively debated, carefully considered, and skilfully planned. In reality none of these things are true. The argument has been conducted secretively and, we would judge, superficially; each change has occurred as an isolated response to some immediate problem; most have been forced unwillingly on the institution— Bank of England or Inland Revenue—immediately responsible for their implementation.

Concealment is characteristic of much policy formation in Britain. It is, nevertheless, barely credible that announcement of policy decisions as important as the issue of index-linked stock and the indexation of capital gains tax should have come as a surprise even to well-informed observers. It follows that the views of those who would be most involved with the consequences of these decisions cannot have been taken into account, and it is inevitable that there would be serious technical deficiencies in the formulation of the proposals in both cases, as indeed there were. This might matter less if the quality of the strategic thinking behind the decision were high. In fact there is no evidence of any strategic thinking at all. The decision to move to an indexed income tax system rather than to a regime based on cash flows, or not to move at all, is the product of drift rather than decision. The inevitable interim problems of a partially indexed system are to be dealt with, in so far as they are dealt with at all, on a trial and error basis.

In other chapters, we have presented what we believe are strong arguments for moving to a tax base that avoids the use of income concepts—by relating personal taxation to expenditure, and company tax to cash flows. But perhaps the most important argument for such a move is that the problems of capital-income indexation we have described in this chapter are entirely avoided. Indexation of income tax is not undesirable—indeed we think it an inescapable part of an efficient and equitable tax system. But it is inevitably rather complicated, poses awkward transitional problems, and has ramifications that extend far beyond the tax system. If any reader needs persuading that there must be a better alternative he should read the clauses and schedules that implemented the indexation provisions of the 1982 Finance Act.

14

The distribution of the tax burden

Our concern in this chapter is with the way in which the tax burden is distributed between individuals. We have noted in particular contexts that all taxes are ultimately taxes on individuals, and it is in this connection and only in this connection that considerations of equity enter the analysis of taxation. It simply makes no sense to talk about 'fairness' between sectors of the economy, or industries, or between the personal and corporate sectors. But these aspects of distribution may be very relevant to the effects of the tax system on efficiency and to the way in which the tax burden is distributed between people with different tastes or between wage-earners and the owners of capital.

The theory of public finance has traditionally distinguished between *vertical* and *horizontal* equity in taxation. Vertical equity is concerned with how tax liabilities are arranged among people whose circumstances are acknowledged to be different: with the distributive and redistributive implications of taxation, with the 'rich' and the 'poor'. Horizontal equity is derived from the application of the axiom that similar individuals should be treated similarly. This axiom seems compelling, though it may conflict with other objectives. (Two men are in a lifeboat with only enough water for one. The only horizontally equitable outcome is that both die.)

In practice, horizontal equity is most frequently violated when administrative arrangements are unsatisfactory; when tax impinges heavily on some transactions but can be avoided on others; when tax is paid principally by the honest, or those without effective tax advisers or the readiness to reorganize their affairs so as to minimize their liabilities; when border-lines between activities or commodities cannot be satisfactorily defined. A high proportion of popular complaints about the tax system result from inequities of this kind. We have seen serious difficulties here in the UK income tax. They arose to a scandalous extent with the old estate duty and are beginning to do so with capital transfer tax also.

The difficulty of principle in applying horizontal equity is that the identification of 'similar circumstances' raises awkward problems of fact and of values. In general, most people seem to take the view that the tax (and benefit) system should recognize differences where they are involuntary but not where they are a matter of choice. We want to take account of differences in endowments of wealth or skill but would resist more favourable treatment of those who are unlucky enough to have expensive tastes, although the approach is not (and cannot be) pushed very far. The most pressing problem of horizontal equity is to decide how the tax system should take account of household composition and arrangements in defining 'similar circumstances'. This is difficult because these matters involve both choice and necessity. Is having children more akin to losing a leg (which it is agreed should reduce the contribution one is expected to make to national revenue) or to buying a Rolls-Royce (which it is agreed should not)? We shall not attempt to answer this question.

In fact the principle of horizontal equity has practical import only in so far as it places constraints on the sorts of taxes that may be used. No two individuals are ever likely to be in exactly similar circumstances, and the real issue is how we should treat people in dissimilar circumstances. For example, should married couples face the same schedule as two single people? Of course, we could postulate hypothetical cases in which there is no difficulty in defining 'similar circumstances'. If in our previous example the two men in the lifeboat had tossed a coin to see who survived, some people might claim that horizontal equity had been achieved. But the introduction of the random element in taxation would generally be regarded as unacceptable. More realistically, horizontal equity limits the way in which taxes are determined. Taxes are not a function of race or colour, nor even the football team one supports (though the supporters of more successful teams undoubtedly experience more 'utility' than those of repeatedly unsuccessful teams). In practice, a major practical problem raised by the concept of horizontal equity concerns the definition of the tax unit. We shall therefore examine the relationship between the tax treatment of individuals and that of households. We then look at some empirical evidence on the effects of the tax system on vertical equity, and consider what economic analysis can contribute to the definition and resolution of the issues involved.

The tax unit

The problem of the tax unit is to decide how households should be taxed relative to individuals. This issue arises for all direct personal taxes, but we shall discuss it with primary reference to an income tax. The present British tax and social security system encourages the poor to cohabit, those on average incomes to marry, and the rich to get divorced. It is difficult to imagine any social philosophy that would intend this combination of outcomes. A Green Paper was produced in 1980 but no proposals for action followed until 1985, when the government declared its support for a system of transferable allowances, a system described further below.

The British tax system operates on the dependency principle. The income of a married woman is simply treated as if it were her husband's, and in recognition of the burden she imposes on him he receives a specially enhanced married man's allowance. Social pressures have led to two important modifications of this principle. A wife is entitled to a single personal allowance against her own earnings. The household can opt for separate taxation of husband's and wife's earnings (but because this involves the loss of the married man's allowance it is rarely advantageous, see p. 26). The underlying principle is self-evidently anachronistic; it dates from a time when Soames Forsyte was the representative taxpayer.

One widely felt objection to it is the elements of sex discrimination that are involved. Many women find it offensive that their husbands are required to prepare, sign, and answer for a return of their income. Some men may resent being expected to proffer details of, and be liable for tax on, income to which they may have no legal, and feel no moral, right. It should be noted, however, that a couple can choose to make separate returns and be separately assessed (an option distinct from separate taxation, since separate assessment has no effect on the couple's aggregate tax liability). But if Mrs T earns £30,000 a year as prime minister while Mr T stays at home and minds 10 Downing Street, and the couple have no other income, they are liable for tax of around £8,400; if Mr T is prime minister and Mrs T does the washing up their tax bill rises by £1,100. There are other instances where liability to tax is a function of the sex of the earner, and it is certainly paradoxical that a Parliament that has outlawed sex discrimination in general should sustain a tax system with these properties.

A more important, if less controversial, failing of the present system is that it is far too generous to working couples without dependent children. A couple in this position receives a married man's allowance (MMA) of £3,455 and a personal allowance of £2,205, so that its first £5,660 of joint income is free of tax. Two single people receive joint allowances of £4,410, and a married couple with a dependent child who prevents the wife from working receives tax allowances of £3,455 and child benefit of £364, equivalent to total tax allowances of around £4,700. It is difficult to see any reason why the tax and benefit system should treat the first of these couples so much more favourably than the other two.

A final problem is that aggregation of investment income may lead to a substantial increase in the tax bill on marriage. If Charles with £25,000 of investment income marries Diana who has the same, their joint tax bill will rise by £5,000 per annum. While the plight of this couple will not bring many tears to the eyes, the irrationality of the marriage penalty is evident.

The Green Paper proposed a number of cosmetic changes to reduce the force of these objections but almost all the submissions examined by Kay and Sandler (1982) supported more radical measures which involved the abolition of the married man's allowance. This would yield around £5 billion and it is hardly surprising that there are sharp divisions on how this revenue should be used. There are two main possibilities. One is to adopt an *individual* basis, which 'looks through' the household and taxes each member of it as an individual in his or her own right. The other is a *unit* basis, under which husband and wife or perhaps the complete household are taxed together by reference to their joint—or collective—income. The case for the individual basis rests on the view—which many people hold strongly—that they are individuals and their tax position should depend on their own earnings and circumstances and not on the earnings and circumstances of others, even those others with whom they may choose to live. But it is difficult to overlook the fact that in many cases the interdependence of these factors is absolutely fundamental. It is clear that we would wish to discriminate between the millionaire's wife who has no income because she stays at home to oversee the servants and the inebriate woman who sleeps under the arches at Charing Cross, even though on paper their personal financial circumstances may appear to be identical. There is a tension between our desire to respect the rights of an individual to independent treatment, and the desire to relate liabilities and benefits to the whole of that individual's circumstances.

The individual basis has the further disadvantage that the way in which partners choose to arrange their financial affairs within marriage may have important consequences for their joint tax liability. It is easy to reduce tax liabilities by transferring investment income from a high-income spouse to a low-income spouse. This will cost a lot of tax revenue; nor does it seem desirable that tax avoidance should become a part of everyday family life. It is only necessary to envisage the conversation that runs ' "Why don't you transfer your property to me, darling, and we shall pay less tax", "I love you, darling, but not as much as that" ' to see some of the difficulties. There is a fundamental conflict between the principle that marriage should affect tax payments little, if at all, and the principle that arrangements within marriage should affect tax payments little, if at all.

A unit basis supposes that the living standard of a couple is determined by its joint income, but the underlying premiss is not really valid. A couple in which the husband earns £15,000 per year and the wife nothing is typically much better off than two spouses each earning £7,500 per year. This is partly because there are costs to earning income—not only the cost of bus fares to work and leisure forgone, but also costs attributable to the need to eat convenience foods and to tolerate more dust on the furniture. These are costs that rise quite rapidly if there are dependent children. The unit basis is extremely favourable to households where the wife does not work.

This difference of principle between an individual and a unit basis for taxation is reflected in two main proposals for using the revenue gained from the abolition of the married man's allowance. Supporters of the individual basis would favour an increase in child benefit, leaving in the tax system only a single personal allowance which each individual could use against his or her own income. Supporters of the unit basis favour a scheme of transferable tax allowances, under which each couple would have two allowances available against the income of either. It is interesting that many of those who support transferable allowances begin by saying they favour an individual basis for taxation, a tribute to the fact that the emancipation of women has had more impact on the language people use than on the attitudes that they adopt.

Both proposals would leave two-earner couples without children worse off. Transferable allowances would protect the position of women who do not work, but hit working wives with children. Increased child benefit would protect women with children (whether or not they worked), but hit wives who do not have children and do not work.

In our judgement, neither the individual basis nor the unit basis can reasonably command unqualified support; and we observe that no country has adopted a purely individual tax system and few have employed a completely unit based structure. Both systems are the expression of objectives that have some merit, and hence we see no alternative to a compromise that involves elements of each, recognizing that the nature of the compromise may change as social attitudes do. We have equally little doubt that current social attitudes point towards a largely individual system for earnings, but less clearly for investment income.

Similar principles seem appropriate for taxing the income of children. Their earnings might be taxed on an individual basis, which means that in practice they would not be taxed; there is no feasible alternative. The tax treatment of the investment income of children has become a political football, kicked from one end of the pitch to the other depending on which party has the ball. Both convenience and common sense suggest that until children are old enough to achieve independent economic status their investment income should be treated as the income of their parents.

If a shift is made in the direction of an expenditure tax, then the individual basis loses some of its appeal, and Kaldor (1955) has argued that a quotient system would then be the most appropriate. After all, a natural way to define a household is as a group of people who incur expenditure on a unit rather than an individual basis, and it is very reasonable to apply the same principle in taxation. And it is even easier for spouses taxed as individuals to arrange their savings and dissavings so as to minimize their joint liability than it is for them to organize their investment income. But the objections to the quotient system apply with equal force under expenditure-based taxation. A couple's standard of living is not related to its joint expenditure alone, but will depend on whether that expenditure is derived from the income of only one of them or equally from both; and the strong discouragement to wives to work which results from the over-generous treatment of non-working wives and which applies under a quotient-based income tax arises equally well with a quotient-based expenditure tax.

Indeed the arguments and conclusions that we have rehearsed in the income tax case are not modified much if expenditure taxes are used instead. Earned income might be taxed on an individual basis, savings and dissavings on a unit principle. It may seem somewhat odd to have an expenditure tax that discriminates between types of income, but if we think of the lifetime expenditure tax as a tax on lifetime receipts (as we know we can) the logic becomes more apparent. It poses no practical problems either; the reader who turns back to the expenditure tax form (Figure 6.2) will see that some items (earnings, pensions) would require that an individual should enter his own receipts, while others (gifts, dividends, sales of securities, etc.) would ask for half the joint total to be entered. The most difficult case is trading receipts, where the distinction between earned and investment income is blurred; this is a familiar difficulty under the present tax system (which is not to say that it is easily or satisfactorily solved).

Any treatment of the tax unit must be related to the social habits of a particular time, and must change as those social habits change. A unit basis supposes that units can be identified and are fairly stable. Adopting marriage as the basis of definition works well in the UK at present. If large numbers of couples live together in continuing household units—as is the case in Sweden—or a high proportion of marriages end in divorce—as in the USA—then a unit basis, of any kind, becomes harder to sustain. Both these trends are increasing in Britain; if this continues an individual basis is likely to be the final outcome and it would then be a desirable outcome.

The progressivity of the tax system

How should the tax burden be distributed between different individuals and households? We shall discuss this question as if the only tax in the economy were an income tax, but this is simply for expository convenience. An income tax schedule relates tax liability to income received, but as we saw in our discussion of empirical evidence on tax incidence the relevant question is the way in which the burden of all taxes is related to a somewhat broader concept of the individual's resources than his taxable income.[1] But the income tax is for those in work the most important and most flexible influence on the distribution of tax liabilities.

We have defined a progressive tax schedule as one in which the proportion of income that is taken in tax increases with income. This definition implies that the *average* rate of tax should increase with income. It is a common error to think that this means that the *marginal* rate of tax should also increase with income (as it in fact does in the UK and most other countries), but this is not the case. A tax system is progressive if, and only if, the marginal rate of tax is higher than the average rate of tax: if you pay a higher rate of tax on any *additional* earnings than you do on your current earnings. Figure 14.1(*a*) illustrates one possible relationship between average and marginal rates of tax. On incomes less than OA, both marginal and average rates of tax are increasing. At incomes above OA, the marginal rate of tax begins to fall, but because it is so high the average rate of tax continues to rise. Only at incomes above OB, where the marginal tax rate falls below the average rate, does the average rate start to fall; this tax schedule is progressive throughout the range OB.

The schedule shown in Figure 14.1(*a*) is not a very likely one, but the case illustrated in Figure 14.1(*b*) is important. This shows a tax schedule in which a certain amount of income, OX, is exempt from tax, and earnings in excess of that are taxed at a rate of OY. Someone whose income barely exceeds OX pays virtually no tax, and hence his average tax rate is very low (although his marginal rate is OY). As income increases, the fraction of it that is taxed becomes larger and larger, until for those with very substantial incomes the allowance OX is hardly significant and their average rate of tax is nearly equal to OY. If the personal allowance is paid as a 'tax credit' to those with incomes too low to make full use of it (i.e. those with incomes below OX), then the schedules of average and marginal rates are extended as shown by the dotted lines. This is a *linear tax schedule*, and it is completely described by two parameters—the basic allowance OX (which we shall assume is greater than zero) and the tax rate OY.

---

[1] Readers of recent literature on 'optimal income taxes' will realize that the lifetime expenditure tax discussed in Chapters 5 and 6 is much closer to the taxes analysed there than are real-life income taxes.

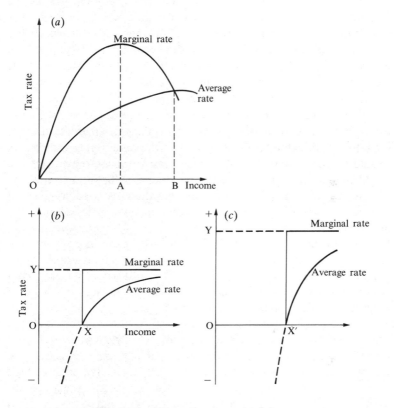

Fig. 14.1. Alternative tax schedules

A linear tax system is progressive, since the average tax rate increases steadily with income. The slope of the schedule of average rates gives the rate at which the average rate rises, and is an indication of the degree of progressivity of the schedule. If OX and OY are both increased, as to OX′ and OY′ in Figure 14.1(c), then the curve of average rates becomes steeper and the rate structure is more progressive. For most taxpayers the present British tax system with its personal allowance and wide basic rate band is a linear one (if we ignore its interaction with national insurance contributions and means-tested benefits).

Designing a tax schedule

The appropriate structure for a tax schedule was extensively discussed in the nineteenth century, in an era when the view was widely held that the utilities enjoyed by different individuals could be measured and compared in much the same way as their heights. Debate raged between the principle of equal sacrifice (by which tax should be computed so as to impose equal utility losses on all), the principle of equiproportional sacrifice (everyone should lose the same fraction of their utility), and the principle of minimum aggregate sacrifice (the total utility loss of the community as a whole should be minimized). The objective of minimum aggregate sacrifice might have won the day, were it not rather easy to show that if one adds the assumptions (i) that everyone has the same capacity to enjoy income, (ii) that utility increases with income but at a decreasing rate, and (iii) that the tax schedule does not modify behaviour in ways that would change incomes before tax (there are no disincentive effects), the conclusion is that everyone should have the same income, net of tax: 'the crowning height of the utilitarian principle, from which the steps of a sublime deduction lead to the high tableland of equality' as Edgeworth put it (1897, p. 553).

Since neither the objective nor the assumptions are very plausible, this analysis received as little attention as it deserved; and until recently economists had little constructive to say about tax schedules. But this ignores an important problem. Progressivity requires high marginal tax rates, but as we saw in Chapter 3 it is precisely this aspect of the tax system which generates disincentive effects. Thus there is a basic conflict between equity and efficiency considerations in the design of tax schedules, and it is important to understand the interrelationships and the empirical information that is needed to determine these issues. While few people now happily accept the utilitarian objective or the assumption of identical tastes, it is nevertheless necessary to express some view on the consequences of drawing tax revenue from people at one income level rather than another. We might start by characterizing two extreme positions. In one, the government is simply indifferent to the source of its tax revenue; a pound is a pound and valued equally whether it is in the wallet of a rich man or a poor man. The other extreme, often attributed to Rawls (1971), only looks at the welfare of the least advantaged; the fate of others matters only in so far as their activities have effects on him (which mainly take the form of generating tax revenue for his benefit). In effect, one position ignores considerations of income distribution altogether; the other thinks of nothing else. It is possible to go beyond either of these extreme view-points: to argue that inequality built Versailles and commissioned Beethoven's late string quartets and is desirable for its own sake, or that inequality is so offensive that the rich should be made worse off even if no one else's standard of living rises as a result. But many people might be willing to agree that an appropriate stance was somewhere between these two.

Even the Rawlsian view, however, implies less than perfect egalitarianism. Under it, public policy is concerned with the interests of the rich only in their function as milch cows for the poor, valued only for the tax revenue they provide. But the interests of the poor require that tax revenue from the rich be maximized, and this is not achieved by 100 per cent rates. People who find themselves paying 100 per cent of income, or additional income, in tax are unlikely to trouble to earn much of it; and we would obtain more tax revenue if we retained some incentive by allowing them to keep part of their earnings for themselves. In fact it is possible to go beyond this and show that the marginal tax rate faced by the man with the highest income should, under an optimal rate schedule, be zero. The argument hinges on the point that tax revenue depends on average rates of tax but disincentives on marginal rates. If we lower the *marginal* tax rate on the richest man, we reduce disincentive effects on him without reducing the amount of tax that he (or any one else) pays. So if these disincentives are of any significance, earnings will increase and so will tax revenue. It does not matter if we attach no value to the welfare of this man, so that we give no weight to the increase in his post-tax income. So long as we do not actually wish to see him made worse off, whether any one else benefits or not, the increase in tax revenue allows lower average tax rates on everyone else and an unequivocal all-round gain. This argument should not be taken absolutely literally. We cannot have different tax rates for each individual, and it tells us nothing even about the appropriate tax rate on the second-richest man. But it does show that even a firm belief in progressive taxation does not imply that marginal, as distinct from average, rates should increase with income.

A rather similar argument may be applied at the opposite end of the distribution: the marginal tax rate faced by the lowest income group should also be very low. This is not the same as saying that the average tax rate on the lowest income group should be very low—as most people would agree it should—since it is quite possible to have low (or negative) average rates of tax on low incomes but high marginal rates. We saw in Chapter 7 that this is precisely what the 'poverty trap' and a number of proposed social security reforms entail. The case for low marginal rates is different, and derived from efficiency rather than distributional considerations. The problem with reducing marginal tax rates on low incomes, as chancellors have discovered, is that it reduces the average tax rate faced by absolutely everyone, and so is extremely costly in revenue. The re-introduction of the 'reduced rate band' had to face this difficulty. We can offset the cost by lowering the tax threshold, so that the lower rate is payable from a lower level of income; the problem with this is that while it has desirable effects on incentives and reduces the 'poverty trap' it raises the amount of tax payable by people with low incomes who are now brought into the system as a result of the reduction in the basic allowance. But at the lowest levels of income there is no one 'below' who will be caught up in the tax net; and it is therefore possible to reduce marginal rates of tax without compromising distributional objectives.

The principles that emerge—that marginal tax rates should be low at both the highest and the lowest levels of income—contrast sharply with what most people have previously believed (ourselves included). They also suggest a pattern different from that observed in the UK and most other countries—where, as we saw in Chapter 3, the *highest* marginal rates are found at the top and bottom of the income distribution (because of higher rates in one case and the poverty trap in the other). But the arguments that lie behind them are in fact rather familiar, and we have only focused rather sharply on points that have been widely if indistinctly appreciated. High marginal tax rates on the largest incomes bring in very little revenue, and are not worth pursuing if they have any adverse consequences. Measures of support for low-income families achieve rather less than nothing if their receipts are recouped by high marginal rates of tax. But it is of particular interest that the conclusions reached remain valid over a rather catholic range of views about the ethical importance and empirical significance of distributional factors and tax disincentives—for any, in fact, between the extreme Rawlsian and extreme output maximization positions we have described.

But this is not quite as encouraging as it might appear. A major difficulty with these arguments is that although they tell us about marginal tax rates at the very top and very bottom of the income scale they tell us little about the rates in between, even at income levels rather close to these extremes. In answering this question, the relative weights that are given to disincentives and to distribution are absolutely crucial. But it is important to see that the answer is likely to go in the same direction at both ends of the scale. If we think disincentive effects are probably not too substantial, or that equality of after-tax incomes is very important, then we would want to select rather high *marginal* tax rates throughout the intermediate range. We would be anxious to narrow the gap between the poor and the very poor, the rich and the very rich, and would not be unduly concerned by the disincentive effects that stem from the high marginal tax rates necessary to do it. We would in this way compress the whole distribution of income after tax. If, on the other hand, we attach a lot of emphasis to incentives and are not much worried about the resulting distribution, then we would choose low marginal rates throughout. It does not follow from this that the marginal rate would, in either case, be the same throughout the distribution, and in general the appropriate tax structure is a rather complicated function of the two underlying objectives—distribution and incentives—and the distribution of earning capacities in the population. But since this information is not easily obtained, and a linear tax schedule has obvious administrative advantages, it is worth examining further the properties of such a system.

Linear tax systems

One of the commonest criticisms of the British tax system is that too wide a range of income is taxed at the basic rate. It is often suggested that it is unfair that a married man with an income of £15,000 should pay the same basic rate of tax as one with an income of only £3,500; or that someone who is only just paying tax should be charged at a rate as high as 30 per cent.

Much of this criticism results from a simple confusion between average and marginal rates of tax. It is true that someone who earns £3,500 is liable to tax at the basic rate of 30 per cent, and so is someone who earns £15,000. However, the man on £3,500 pays annual tax of £13·50—equivalent to an average rate of tax of 0·4 per cent. His counterpart on £15,000 has to pay £3,463·50, an average tax rate of 23·1 per cent. The fact that they are both in the basic rate band does not prevent the man with the higher income from paying a much higher proportion of his income in tax.

But isn't the marginal rate too high on those with low incomes? It is clear that equity demands a lower *average* rate of tax on the poor than the rich. It is much less clear that it demands a lower *marginal* rate. Marginal rates are relevant to individuals because they determine their incentive or disincentive to work, and there is no obvious reason why it is either just or efficient to impose a greater disincentive on high-income earners than on people whose incomes are low. It is possible that disincentives have a greater impact on the work effort of poor households, but we know of no convincing evidence.

The British tax system could certainly be made more progressive if the existing basic rate band were replaced by a more graduated pattern of marginal rates. Very similar results could be achieved, however, by simply increasing the threshold and the basic rate. Low-income households would pay less, high-income households more, in just the same way. Thus there is no inconsistency between a linear tax schedule and substantial progressivity—indeed we can have a completely egalitarian outcome if the basic allowance is equal to average income and the marginal tax rate is 100 per cent, though it is not likely that this is a good idea.

The fact that someone is paying a marginal rate of tax of 60 per cent demonstrates that he is facing a substantial disincentive to work, a strong temptation to convert his income into other forms, and that he is likely to be rather disenchanted with the way the tax system affects him; but it does not necessarily mean that he is paying a lot of tax, because that is a function of his average rather than his marginal rate. The mathematical properties of rate schedules imply that this average rate an individual pays depends not on his own marginal rate, but on the marginal tax rates of everyone below him in the income distribution. This was illustrated most clearly by the tax system as it stood before the reforms of 1979. In 1976/7, a household with net income of around £7,500 faced a marginal tax rate of 50 per cent; to pay an average rate of tax of 50 per cent it was necessary to have an income around £20,000. Over one million households came into the former category; 60,000 households were in the latter group (*Inland Revenue Statistics 1978*). A system with escalating marginal rates imposes high marginal rates on relatively many, and high average rates on relatively few.

Other constraints on progressivity

There are two other important constraints on the progressivity of a tax system. The first of these relates to administrative feasibility. We have shown in Chapters 3 and 4 that the highest rates of tax in the UK did not work, and it is very improbable that they could have been made to work. This might not be too important if they were uniformly ineffective, but this is not the case; the result of this (and the general result of procedures that are administratively impracticable) is that the outcome is erratically and unfairly effective. But it is difficult to assess what the maximum marginal tax rate that can work reasonably well in practice is likely to be. The top rates in most developed countries lie in the range from 50 per cent to 70 per cent. Britain has historically been outside this range but has now moved within it.

The second constraint is the possibility of migration. Very rich individuals may choose tax exile; less affluent households may put taxation in the balance when they decide whether to accept a job overseas or to return to this country. Some countries, indeed, act as tax havens: they set low tax rates but derive substantial revenues because they become attractive to rich immigrants. The Channel Islands have prospered on this basis. They are well placed to adopt this policy because the number of potential residents is large relative to their native population. Even for large countries, however, very high marginal tax rates at the upper end of the income distribution may prove counterproductive if taxpayers depart and take part of the tax base with them.

We must now bring out explicitly two assumptions that have been underlying our analysis. We have assumed that all income is earned. At high levels of income this is only the case to a very limited extent, though the discussion of incentives applies equally to earnings that although classed as investment income are in fact the return to business activities. While incentives—of a different kind—also affect investment incomes, it is clear that the factors which should influence the taxation of income or expenditure from inherited wealth are rather different, and the reasons for limiting top marginal rates are less compelling. We should note, however, that the arguments on migration and on feasibility apply to unearned incomes also; and that it is probably on employment incomes that the present top rates of tax are less easily avoided and come closest to working as intended.

The second assumption is that the value of people's work is approximated by what they are paid. If they are paid more than their work is worth, there will be losses to everyone else if they are induced to do more such work; if they are paid less than their work is worth, then the argument operates in the reverse direction. At low and medium ranges of income, our assumption is not too bad, but for high-income earners the position is more complicated, and the relationship between the value of work and the way in which it is remunerated becomes much more tenuous. We should also note that the work they do will often be intrinsically attractive, and disincentive effects consequently less serious. These groups will include people in the City who occupy sinecures or perform services of no social value; they will also include people in positions where the competent exercise of their functions can generate benefits far greater than any one would consider paying them. If under Lord Weinstock the productivity of GEC is $\frac{1}{2}$ per cent higher than it would be under the best alternative manager, then the benefits of this are £30 million per year and one such individual can compensate for the entire boards of several merchant banks. The direction of bias in this area is therefore unclear.

One conclusion to emerge from our discussion in earlier chapters is that the definition of the tax base may be more important in determining the effective progressivity of taxation, especially at high income and expenditure levels, than the shape of the rate structure. The difficulty in constructing rate schedules is that substantial progressivity requires that average rates should be much higher at high-income levels than at lower ones; but this requires high *marginal* rates on those in between. If the majority of income-earners are concentrated in a rather narrow range—and 95 per cent of all units have incomes below £20,000 per year—then these marginal rates may have to be distinctly high and will have to be imposed on people who are not the primary target of redistributive taxation. High marginal rates at the top lead to many of the adverse consequences of progressive taxation without having much real effect on distribution, because the number of people who face correspondingly high *average* rates as a result is very small.

Tax and distribution: evidence

The concept of a linear tax system provides us with a simple means of assessing the progressivity of the tax structure taken as a whole. Figure 14.2 represents the linear tax schedules of Figures 14.1(*b*) and (*c*) in a slightly different way: we illustrate the relationship between income and total tax payment. With an allowance of OX, someone with that income pays no tax, and liability increases proportionally thereafter. If we project the tax line back to zero income, someone with zero income would receive a rebate of OZ. Of course, this is a purely hypothetical calculation. People do not have zero incomes, and if they did they would not receive such a rebate—they would simply escape liability for any tax. (Although under the tax credit scheme, which we describe in Chapter 7, they would have received such a rebate. For this reason, we call the intercept OZ the tax credit.)

Thus any linear tax system can be described by reference to its tax

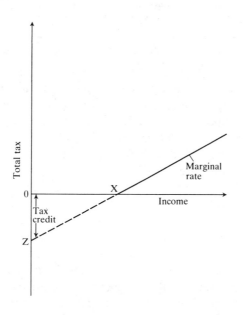

Fig. 14.2. A linear tax schedule

credit and its marginal rate. Moreover, these parameters illustrate the degree of progressivity of the system. A higher marginal rate or a higher tax credit would both increase progressivity, and it is obvious that any progressive linear tax will have a positive credit (treating OZ as positive) and any regressive one a negative credit.

The two largest revenue-raisers among British taxes—income tax and national insurance contributions—are both linear taxes over a very broad range. Other taxes, such as VAT, are not levied on income; but by assessing expenditure patterns we can measure their relationship to income. This will not necessarily be a linear relationship, but in practice a linear function represents the incidence of most indirect taxes relatively well.

Table 14.1 shows the incidence of taxation in 1985/6 as measured by this approach. The British tax system, as a whole, is substantially progressive. The overall marginal rate for the household in Table 14.1 is 53 per cent. This means that when the incidence of all taxes is taken into account, most people will find that more than half of any additional sum they earn goes to the government. This marginal rate is higher than the average rate, which would be 41 per cent for someone earning £10,000 per year. At £5,000 this would have fallen to 30 per cent and at £15,000 the average rate is 45 per cent.

The whole of this progressivity results from income tax. National insurance contributions are broadly proportional to income, and indirect taxes taken as a whole are also more or less proportional. This overall impression conceals substantial variation in the impact of individual taxes. VAT is decidedly progressive, reflecting the effects of zero-rating food and fuel. So is petrol duty, but most other indirect taxes are regressive.

It is worth observing that an indirect tax that was simply proportional to overall expenditure would appear regressive, if it were paid out of income that had already been subject to a progressive income tax. The reason for this is that expenditure, and hence tax payment, would necessarily be a lower proportion of the incomes of those who had already paid relatively more in taxes on their income.

Thus the measures of the progressivity of individual taxes which are derived from Table 14.1 are interdependent, and this illustrates an important economic lesson from this approach. The distributional impact of the tax system is best seen as a whole, and not by reference to its individual components. It would be erroneous to conclude from these figures, for example, that a good way of achieving greater equality would necessarily be to increase income tax and reduce indirect taxes. The same result could equally well be achieved by adjusting the structure of income tax, and perhaps better achieved in that way, because the progressivity of VAT is bought at a high price, in both administrative costs and the resulting narrowness of the base.

Table 14.1:   *The tax system as a whole in 1985/6 for a married couple with two children*

	Tax credit (£)	Marginal rate (%)
Income tax	1,265	23.6
National insurance	—	17.6
Total direct	1,265	41.2
VAT	92	4.7
Petrol	116	1.6
Drink	−43	0.6
Tobacco	−66	1.4
Housing	−77	0.4
Licences	−110	0.1
Intermediate	−7	3.0
Total indirect	−95	11.8
TOTAL	1,170	53.0

Note: Only head works, not contracted-out of SERPS, earning less than national insurance ceiling, paying basic rate income tax.

In Table 14.2 we examine how the figures in Table 14.1 have changed over the post-war period. It shows that the tax system is now substantially more progressive than in the earlier years examined, and that the change principally occurred in the 1970s. Two main factors are at work. One is that national insurance contributions—which were initially levied as a flat sum per week, to be paid regardless of earnings (above the floor)—have been transformed into a proportional tax. Since 1985 they have even become a slightly progressive one. The second element is that indirect taxes have

diminished in importance relative to direct taxes, and at the same
time have become more progressive in nature. This reflects a shift
from reliance on staples like tobacco and alcoholic drinks to VAT.
The changes shown in Table 14.2 are startling, and not widely recognized. They illustrate the importance of viewing the system as a
whole, and it is to this we turn in Chapter 15.

Table 14.2:   *The tax system as a whole, 1948–85*

	Tax credit (£)	Marginal rate (%)
1948	−340	43.4
1953	54	43.1
1958	−400	39.7
1963	−505	41.4
1968	−608	44.7
1973	265	43.4
1978	1,133	50.7
1982	1,200	53.2
1985	1,170	53.0

Note: Household as in Table 14.1.
Source: Derived from Dilnot, Kay, and Morris, 1984,
and Table 14.1.

15

The tax system as a whole

Is Britain overtaxed?

We have devoted a good deal of attention to the structural deficiencies of the British tax system. We have not, however, considered explicitly the view that these structural deficiencies would not be very important if the rates of tax were not so high. This argument has considerable validity. The base of the American income tax, for example, is probably more defective than that of the UK, but because tax rates are much lower at all income levels the anomalies, loopholes, and distortions which result are less significant. Is the real problem that the British are simply overtaxed?

Since there are few people who do not believe that they personally are overtaxed, we must search for some more objective yardstick. A natural one to use is an international comparison: is the tax system required to raise more revenue in Britain than in similar countries overseas? Table 15.1 sets out what figures we have on this matter. It shows the ratio of total tax revenue to GNP in 1983 for 15 major OECD countries. The highest tax ratios are to be found, not surprisingly, in the Scandinavian countries and the Netherlands, followed by several other European economies—Belgium, France, Italy, and Ireland. In this league table Britain comes ninth out of the 15 countries. Nor was 1983 an atypical year. If we examine the UK's position in the league table of tax ratios of the same 15 countries for each year since 1965 we find that the UK never came higher than fifth and never lower than ninth.

International comparisons can be misleading, and all we can do is to point to some of the difficulties which arise. The decision as to whether a certain payment is or is not a tax is often an arbitrary one. For example, help to families may take the form either of extra tax allowances, which reduce taxation, or of cash payments, as with child benefits in Britain. The latter are often regarded as government expenditure rather than negative taxation, thus making it difficult to compare tax ratios in cases when countries adopt different forms of family support. The same argument applies to investment incentives which may be given either as tax allowances or as investment grants. A less obvious, but probably more important, source of difficulty is the treatment of pension contributions. In many continental countries state pensions are much higher (relative to average earnings) than in Britain, and occupational pensions correspondingly less developed. Contributions to these state schemes are financed by social security contributions and not by payments to private schemes. In Table 15.1 the former are regarded as taxation and the latter not. If social security contributions were excluded the UK would move from ninth to sixth place in the league table of tax ratios. On the other hand, there are very good reasons for regarding social security contributions as equivalent to a tax on earned income, as we have argued in Chapter 3. Contributions to health insurance may take the form of voluntary, semi-compulsory, or compulsory contributions to private or state schemes, or may simply be incorporated in general taxation: such payments may sometimes count as taxes and at other times not, but the practical difference is often very slight.

It is possible to quibble endlessly about these problems of definition (in a way which suggests that the underlying question has not been carefully formulated), and some people are willing to do so (Bracewell-Milnes, 1976, and the references therein). But it is difficult to avoid an impression that there are three main groups of developed countries for these purposes: Holland and the Scandinavian countries, other Western European countries, and a somewhat disparate group containing Japan, Switzerland, and the USA. These groupings reflect different attitudes to the value of public services and the role of the state in promoting social welfare, and Britain's placing in the second group seems an appropriate reflection of prevailing ideologies. It is true that if Britain were to move into the first or third of these divisions (and we shall not say which we think is which) the problems confronting the tax system would be rather different; but it is clear that such a decision should be taken on the basis of a much wider assessment of gains and losses than those that result from dissatisfaction with the tax system. Nor do we think it probable that either of these shifts will occur.

Although the UK tax ratio can only be described as average, the sources of the revenue it produces are superficially somewhat different. The most striking feature of Table 15.1 is the small dependence of the British system on social security contributions, but if one believes that it is more appropriate to include these with taxes on income then the only difference between Britain and other countries is the slightly smaller reliance in this country on taxes levied on consumption spending. Even this difference was diminished by the increase in VAT in 1979.

Table 15.1:   *Level of taxation in selected countries, 1983*
(Tax revenues including social security contributions as % of GNP at market prices)

	All taxes	Taxes on spending	Taxes on income	Social security contributions	Other
Sweden	50.5	12.3	21.4	13.6	3.2
Netherlands	47.3	11.4	13.0	21.3	1.6
Norway	46.6	16.8	18.6	10.1	1.1
Denmark	46.2	16.5	25.4	1.8	2.5
Belgium	45.4	12.0	18.6	13.9	0.8
France	44.6	12.9	7.9	19.6	4.1
Italy	40.6	9.5	14.9	14.6	1.6
Ireland	39.2	18.1	13.0	5.8	2.3
UNITED KINGDOM	37.8	11.3	14.6	6.7	5.3
Germany	37.4	10.3	12.5	13.3	1.4
Canada	33.0	10.8	14.4	4.3	3.5
Switzerland	31.6	6.1	13.2	9.9	2.5
Australia	30.0	9.9	15.8	—	4.3
US	29.0	5.2	12.4	8.3	3.1
Japan	27.7	4.2	12.5	8.3	2.7

Note: Individual figures may not sum to totals because of rounding errors.
Source: *Revenue Statistics of OECD Member Countries,* OECD, Paris.

A broader tax base?

We have seen that the revenue raised from the British tax system is not out of line with that raised in other European countries. We have argued, however, that most of the undesirable effects of taxation are the result of high marginal rates of tax, and we should consider whether it might be possible to effect substantial reductions in *marginal* rates without correspondingly large reductions in average rates and hence in total tax revenue.

It is often suggested that if only all allowances could be swept away we could be happy with a single low rate of tax on all income. In 1976 *The Economist* suggested that this would allow a tax rate of only 15%. Similar proposals have recently been widely canvassed in the USA. But they do not survive careful scrutiny. The most important allowances are the basic personal allowances. If these were removed, the result would be a very substantial redistribution to those with above-average incomes from those below. We saw above how the degree of progressivity of a tax system could be altered by varying the parameters of a linear tax schedule; the proposal for a single rate of tax eliminates all such progressivity by abolishing the personal allowances altogether. The most important untaxed components of incomes are listed in Table 15.2. The table does not include contributions to pension funds because the chancellor in 1985 stated that there was no intention of imposing a tax on such funds for the foreseeable future.

Table 15.2: *The cost of principal tax allowances and expenditures, 1984/5* (£m)

Married man's allowance	11,700	Mortgage interest relief	3,500
Single person's allowance	6,750	Interest on national savings	
Wife's earned income relief	3,100	certificates	350
Age allowance	420	Exemption for charities	270
Relief for approved pension		Exemption of first slice	
schemes	1,250	of capital gains	230
Self-employment retirement			
annuities	500		

Source: *Inland Revenue Statistics 1985*, Table 1.6.

The most serious possibilities for broadening the income tax base are to modify the present favourable treatment of owner-occupied housing, and to tax capital gains as ordinary income. The first of these is certainly capable of producing substantial revenue. Tax relief on mortgage payments cost £3·5 billion in 1985/6, and to tax the 'imputed income' from owner-occupied property (see p. 55) could easily raise £4 billion, depending upon the level at which the notional 'rents' for such property were set. But these figures should be viewed sceptically. We have suggested that, given the capitalization of these tax benefits, the case in equity for withdrawing them has little merit; that considerable hardship would be caused to many people; and that we would hesitate to make such changes except in the context of a general review of housing policy. And if the objective of change is to rearrange the tax burden in a way that is likely to provoke less public hostility, we need spend little time considering this particular alternative.

Although it is certainly true that capital gains could be taxed more heavily, and in fact for most individual investors the tax has effectively been abolished, it is unlikely that taxing indexed capital gains as income would do more than raise a few hundred million pounds, which would allow a reduction in the basic rate of income tax of only a fraction of one percentage point.

If we turn to VAT, the two most important categories of exemption are housing and food. It would be possible to bring housing within the scope of VAT by imposing it on rents and on new construction. But as we have seen, there is already a very heavy indirect tax on housing (rates), and our usual caveats about piecemeal changes in the housing market apply. There is a long tradition in Britain of slightly hysterical opposition to the taxation of food; the origins of these sentiments lie in controversies over the relative political roles of agriculture and commerce and the desirability and effects of Imperial Preference in tariff policy which have no contemporary relevance. It is now suggested that food is a necessity; but very little of the food that would not be eaten if it were 15 per cent dearer is in the least necessary, and other taxed goods such as clothing are 'necessary' in exactly the same (limited) sense. The substantive argument for exempting food is that such exemption is progressive in its distributional effects; the rich spend a smaller proportion of their incomes on food than the poor. (The main category for which this is not true—meals away from home—is subject to VAT.)

This is not a particularly effective means of achieving these distributional objectives, as we observed in our general discussion of indirect taxes. The distributional effect of the tax system is best viewed as a whole, and there are more sensitive instruments than discriminatory rates of VAT. Davis and Kay (1985) have suggested that the British tax system could be made *more* progressive if VAT were extended to food and fuel, and the proceeds used to increase social security benefits and tax thresholds. Table 15.3 illustrates the

impact on different household types. This example does illustrate
how a broader tax base offers both equity and efficiency advantages
over the present system. But it does not allow any substantial reduction in marginal rates of tax, because most of the proceeds must
be used on tax thresholds (the tax credit in terms of Chapter 14)
rather than on rates, if distributional neutrality is to be maintained.

Table 15.3: *Effects of VAT base extension and increased benefits and
thresholds on different types of household, 1984* (Gain or loss in £ per week)

By type of household		By range of household income (£ p.w.)	
Single person	−0.75	<55	+1.28
One-parent family	+1.54	55–85	+1.60
Childless couple	−1.34	85–125	+1.31
Couple + 2 children	−1.18	125–175	−0.30
Couple + 4 children	+1.29	175–250	−0.96
Single pensioner	+1.12	250–400	−1.13
Pensioner couple	+1.80	>400	−3.35
All	−0.01	All	−0.01

Source: Davis and Kay, 1985.

It is clear that the main possibilities for broadening the tax base
would allow a negligible reduction in the basic rate of tax. Major
improvements in the tax system must come from more fundamental
structural reforms. In 1984 it appeared that the chancellor was em-
barked upon a programme of reform that might lead in this direction. Tax relief for premiums on life insurance policies was abolished,
and the generous accelerated depreciation available to companies
was also eliminated. The Budget was greeted with great enthusiasm
as the first step along the road to real tax reform. An attempt had
been made to broaden the tax base, to move back toward the idea
of a tax on true economic income, and the prospect was one of lower
tax rates as the reward. But these dreams faded with the reality of
the 1985 Budget. In this the chancellor had the opportunity to continue down the same road but decided not to take the opportunity.

The reason was that he had taken the easiest steps down his chosen road, and the logical next steps involved taxing either the contributions to or the investment income of pension funds, together with the reduction in or abolition of mortgage interest relief to home-owners. On both counts not only did he take no measure but he announced that in neither case would additional taxes be levied in the lifetime of the current Parliament. Following the 1985 Budget, it is clear that tax reform in the sense of going back to a coherent income tax has run out of steam, and future changes are likely to involve a return to the tinkering of the past.

Another lesson that confirms this depressing experience comes from the USA. In November 1984 the US Treasury published a very imaginative plan for tax reform that would have implied the return to a comprehensive income tax. Many tax allowances and concessions would have been eliminated, and indexation on a comprehensive scale introduced. The report was welcomed with even more enthusiasm than the 1984 UK Budget, but within months it was clear that the plan could not succeed. This was due in some part to pressure groups wishing to maintain their special exemptions, but also to two economic problems with the proposals. The first was simply the technical difficulty of designing a comprehensive package of indexation including not only capital gains and depreciation allowances for companies, but also interest income. Once problems had been found with the proposals for indexation of interest income the whole scheme started to unravel. The second problem was that there was significant pressure to retain the cash-flow elements in the existing system. Tax relief for individual savings and corporate investment is seen as an important incentive to capital formation. Our conclusion is that any significant change to the size of the tax base will require a structural shift toward the taxation of expenditure rather than income.

Harmonization and the internal market

Harmonization of taxation within the European Community is a dull and difficult subject, but one of central importance if a real common market within Europe is to be achieved. The object of full harmonization of European tax laws is Utopian, and probably not desirable; it is hard to imagine that exactly the same tax system will ever fully meet the needs of both Germany and Portugal. Integrated federal states such as Switzerland and the USA retain quite significant differences in both direct and indirect taxes between jurisdictions while retaining unimpeded trade and having fully unified economies. It is therefore important to distinguish those differences between states that must be eliminated or reduced and those that are of no great practical importance. There are several different, and largely independent, objectives that require attention.

It is desirable to remove tax differences between countries that distort or disrupt the pattern of trade. If an activity is more heavily taxed in one country than another, the pattern of production across the Community will reflect these fiscal differences rather than the most efficient outcome for the Common Market as a whole. What matters here is principally those taxes that are paid by producers. It may be observed that among many factors that continue to inhibit free trade in this way, fiscal differences are probably well down the list in significance. The most important of these fiscal factors lie in the area of the different treatment of investment under the company tax regimes of member states. Precisely because this is an important element in the economic policies of individual governments, it is an issue on which little progress has been made. A draft directive on the form of corporation tax has been issued—which requires an imputation system—but its influence on what member states actually do is small. The commission had at an earlier stage favoured a two-rate system, and then a classical structure of corporation tax. Throughout it has been swimming with the tide rather than setting the pace.

Another object of common policies should be to remove 'tax jungle'. Most of the fifty American states impose corporate income taxes, with somewhat different rules and rates. There are, however, very substantial common elements in the rules applied in different states. If there were not, the system could not possibly work. Small business operating in several states would be driven into bankruptcy by the burden of compliance costs, and interstate trading would be severely inhibited. We should therefore aim to establish greater uniformity of detailed rules for calculation and compliance.

A third aim is to remove fiscal frontiers—the border checks between countries which irritate personal travellers and impose costs and delays on commercial transactions. The psychological boost to a common market which could be achieved if these frontiers could be removed would be enormous, quite apart from possible economic advantages. The European Commission has recently presented a report outlining proposals for removing border controls (European Commission, 1985). But its treatment of taxation issues is weak because it does not distinguish carefully between those changes that require administrative integration and those that demand substantive harmonization (Cnossen, 1986). Until there is a Europe-wide budget, countries will wish to collect taxation on goods sold within their boundaries and this means that records of imports and exports would be necessary even if all countries had identical tax rates. The issue is whether these adjustments could be carried out by internal procedures rather than at frontiers—as, substantially, they are already. By linking approximation of tax rates with the elimination of border controls, the commission's approach makes it unlikely that either will happen.

Conclusions

We have tried to ask of each part of the tax system 'What are the underlying principles here?' This may appear to conflict with the typical administrator's motto 'We start from where we are'. It is often believed that this 'practical' approach removes the need to give thought to where, in the long run, we are aiming to go. It is true that the practical man who knows where he is, and has not given any thought to where he is going, may appear more in command of his situation than the academic theorist who knows where he wants to go but is unsure of how to get there; but both of them end up comprehensively lost. It is in this way that we have finished up where we are.

The mess into which the present British tax system has drifted has been documented in earlier chapters. Anyone who came to it for the first time would regard the present system with some incredulity. There is a maze of taxes on different kinds of income, each tax with its own rules for determining taxable income and liability. The interaction between these taxes is difficult to comprehend, and, because of this, is rarely brought out into the open when tax changes are discussed. We have noted at various points the absurdity of the interrelationship—or rather the lack of interrelationship—between income tax and national insurance. At one time, there were separate surcharges on each of employment income, investment income, and earnings from self-employment. Investment income, once more heavily taxed than earnings, is now taxed more lightly—by historical accident, not design. The overall system is one which no one would have designed on purpose, and no one did.

There are more important examples than this one, but it illustrates how pragmatism that is not motivated by an overall view of the principles and operation of the tax system as a whole is not a principle of good administration, but a recipe for unnecessary complexity and excessive administrative costs. We expect that some readers of this book will think that the objections to the existing British tax system we have made carry some weight, but might be more appropriately met by measures that stop short of any radical reappraisal of the principles of taxation. The idea of a lifetime expenditure tax may seem appealing but perhaps many of the benefits of such a reform might be obtained by some further concessions to savings within the context of the existing income tax. If they think this, they have completely misunderstood our whole argument. It is true that some of the deficiencies we have noted could be ameliorated by further *ad hoc* modifications of the shambles we have portrayed. It is certain, however, that these modifications would lead to still greater complexity in the tax system and to further abuses, anomalies, and loopholes, few of which will be anticipated.

The only prospect for an efficient tax system, whether efficiency refers to its economic effect or to the cost-effectiveness of its administration, is to adopt one which is based on a small set of clear principles, and which departs from them only in a number of limited and clearly recognized ways. The alternative to this course is to devise particular rules for each situation as and when it arises, and since we cannot define or anticipate all possible situations or even fully appreciate the consequences of our last decision, these rules are bound to proliferate indefinitely.

'Income Tax', ruled Lord Macnaghten, 'is a tax on income', and this has been the principle, if one may call it that, underlying direct taxation in the UK since the days of Pitt. But, as we saw in Chapter 5, it is not a very useful principle for practical purposes, because income is not an easy concept to define precisely nor to measure objectively. The fact is that in many circumstances there is only a tenuous relationship between monetary transactions and whatever it is that one means by income, and any attempt to pretend otherwise leads either to the kinds of difficulties we have described in earlier chapters, or to the forced adoption of cash flows as the measure of taxable income.

The case against the existing structure of the UK tax system and for the kind of reforms we have proposed rests on an accumulation of arguments rather than on a single decisive argument, and we are reluctant to summarize the main points of our thesis. Nevertheless, there are three points to which we would give special emphasis.

First, there has been enormous misdirection of the redistributive elements of the tax system. These have rested mainly on high tax rates on individuals with large incomes from employment. But high earnings are not an important source of wealth inequality in the UK, so that these taxes fall heavily on those engaged in productive sectors of the economy without achieving much in the way of redistribution. The tax system has been—rightly—criticized on both counts; the conflict between equity and efficiency in tax policy has appeared very acute. Although this trade-off is a real one, preoccupation with rates of tax and with the appearance of the tax system rather than the reality have led to excessive emphasis on it; and to a futile process in which political parties have sought to compensate for deficiencies in the structure of taxation by changes in the rates. The expenditure tax proposal is capable of achieving both greater equity and greater efficiency by imposing lower rates on a tax base which is more closely related to taxable capacity.

The second argument for an expenditure tax rests on the deficiencies of the present methods of taxing savings and investment income. They are not simple, they are not fair, they are not effective, and they have been characterized by rates of tax which are tolerable only because they are not intended seriously. It is difficult to believe that at least some objectives could not be achieved better in other ways. The logic of the income-based approach suggests that a comprehensive income tax, which would remove existing savings concessions and integrate the tax treatment of income and capital gains, is the way forward. We analysed this proposal in Chapter 5, and found it unattractive. It is not an accident that we have the income tax we do, and not a comprehensive income tax; and it is only to a limited extent true that this result is attributable to the frailties of politicians in the face of pressure from particular interest groups. Most of the changes that are required to transform the existing income tax into a comprehensive one either involve acute administrative difficulty (such as the taxation of pension fund income) or require the introduction of charges that would be widely perceived as unfair—and not just by those involved in paying them (such as the taxation of imputed income from durable ownership and housing). The logical approach is to adopt the expenditure tax proposal. Not only does this not suffer from these difficulties but it is probably closer to the reality of what we in fact do.

The third argument for an expenditure tax is administrative. It is only gradually being realized how many of the avoidance opportunities intrinsic in the income tax and how much of the complexity of income tax codes are the result of the difficulty of applying an income concept in a modern economy with a sophisticated financial system. Hicks wrote that income and capital 'are bad tools, which break in our hands', and they have broken. It is a common thread of the proposals we have made for reform that they abandon the use of an income concept and adopt a tax base that is closely related to identifiable and measurable flows of cash.

Is it possible that our proposals are in fact more radical than necessary, and that a shift of emphasis towards existing—indirect—taxes on expenditure would achieve the same results as a shift towards a direct expenditure tax more simply and less controversially? We might examine this suggestion in the light of the three principal arguments we have set out above. We suggested that an expenditure tax could achieve desired redistribution with less damage to incentives. Because this argument requires that the *progressive* elements of the tax system should be expenditure-based, it is only a direct expenditure tax which can achieve it, and a switch to existing indirect taxes is of no assistance. Our second argument concerned the tax treatment of savings and investment. A broadly based expenditure tax such as VAT does avoid the distortions and anomalies that income tax introduces. But to eliminate these distortions it would be necessary to eliminate income tax, and to reduce them substantially it would be necessary to reduce income tax substantially. Neither of these can be achieved with the existing limited VAT base, although marginal gains are possible.

Our third argument concerned administration. It is only possible to get rid of the administrative costs and complexity of income tax by getting rid of income tax. It is true that some gains can be achieved by reductions in the rates; there are some avoidance schemes that are not worth undertaking when tax rates are lower, and some inequities or problems that are more readily tolerable. There are some minor benefits from a shift from the basic rate of income tax to the standard rate of VAT, and more substantial benefits from reductions in the top rates of income tax. On balance, there are small advantages to be derived from a shift from income tax to indirect taxes, and we do, in the absence of substantial reform, favour some such shift. The main benefit is some easing of the pressure of capital market distortions. But the central problem remains. Income tax is a deplorable tax, whether one examines its administration or its economic effects. It is highly desirable to be rid of it. Of course, this is not possible next year, or even in five years' time. But the long-term transformation of the existing income tax into a direct expenditure tax is the only serious scheme for abolishing income tax that has been proposed.

Our long-run objective is, therefore, a lifetime expenditure tax. To achieve this objective a number of steps ought to be taken now. The first is the abolition of cumulative PAYE and a move towards a non-cumulative system with annual returns from all taxpayers. This would enable us to begin the process of rationalizing the tax and social security systems and to sort out the present unsystematic reliefs to savings, and to envisage the wider changes of abolishing capital gains tax and extending the range of registered assets described in Chapter 6. Such a reform would also allow serious consideration to be given to local taxation and the financing of devolution. The second immediate change would be the transformation of the existing corporation tax into a cash-flow tax on the lines set out in Chapter 11. This would involve transitional problems, but these would be no more acute than those experienced in the many previous changes of corporation tax.

We should end with a plea for realism in expectations of what can be achieved by tax reform. The changes we have advocated can only be implemented over a long period of time. They will not transform the British tax system into an instrument of economic progress or social change, though we believe that they will make it simpler, fairer, and more efficient, and reduce the number and extent of its unintended ramifications. They will not satisfy those who are looking for measures which can be adopted in the next Budget which will revive small business, restore incentives, effect irreversible change in the distribution of wealth and power, or achieve whatever else was featured on last week's 'Money Programme'. The ill-considered expedients that are constructed to meet the demands of those with large ambitions and little time will leave their objectives as far from realization as ever, and the tax system a little more complicated than it was before. We see the British tax system as a chronically diseased patient; but one who, obsessed by the last symptom he happened to observe, disregards considered medical advice and insists on being completely cured by next week. There is never any shortage of quacks willing to minister to his needs; and he never gets even slightly better.

Further reading

We have not given individual references for the rates of tax and benefit which we have reported frequently in the text. There is a wide variety of commercial guides to the tax system, which range from those designed to give useful advice on how to complete your tax return to handbooks for tax lawyers and accountants. The publishers Tolley produce manuals covering not only the principal taxes but also national insurance and social security, and the information they provide is comprehensive.

Chapter 1

The two classic texts on the theory of public finance remain those of Musgrave (1959) and Shoup (1969). The best modern survey is that of Atkinson and Stiglitz (1980), but this is a good deal more advanced in approach.

Chapter 2

Statistics about the tax system can be found in the annual publication *Inland Revenue Statistics* and in the Reports of the Commissioners of Inland Revenue. Johnston (1965) provides a now somewhat outdated account of the functioning of the Inland Revenue. Good international comparative material is surprisingly hard to come by; some help can be obtained from OECD reports (particularly OECD, 1986), from the publications of some of the leading accountancy firms, and from the evidence provided for the Treasury and Civil Service Committee's enquiry into the structure of personal income taxation and support. Smith (1986) provides a comprehensive review of evidence on the black economy.

Chapters 3 and 4

On the incentive effects of taxation there is a helpful introduction by Break in the Brookings Institution volume (1974). More technical surveys of the disincentive effect of income tax on work decisions have been written by Stern (1976) and Godfrey (1975). For a detailed analysis of the American evidence, including an account of the results of the New Jersey negative income tax experiment, see the volumes by Cain and Watts (1973) and Pechman and Timpane (1975). Some econometric results for Britain based on a research project at Stirling University are discussed in Brown, Levin, and Ulph (1976). The redistributive role of taxation and the determinants of the distributions of income and wealth are analysed in Atkinson (1983). Much less has been written on the taxation of savings and investment income: the Meade Report (1978) is a good discussion of general principles, and Kay (1986) explains the most recent developments in the system. King and Fullerton (1984) compare the effects of different treatments in several Western countries.

Chapter 5

The best-known and most detailed proposals for a comprehensive income tax are those put forward in Canada by the Carter Commission (1966). A more recent analysis is US Treasury (1984). The concept of income is discussed by Hicks (1939) and Simons (1938), but the best survey is that by Kaldor (1955, Appendix). A collection of some of the more important contributions on the subject has been edited by Parker and Harcourt (1969).

Chapter 6

The two most cogent cases for an expenditure tax are the classic exposition of Kaldor (1955), arguing from the theoretical view-point, and the case put by Andrews (1974) on practical grounds. Official reports explaining how an expenditure tax would work have been produced abroad, in the USA (US Treasury, 1977), in Sweden (Lodin, 1978), and in Ireland (Irish Tax Commission, 1982). A survey of the issues is Pechman (1980).

Chapter 7

An introduction to the British social security system and its possible reform is Dilnot, Kay, and Morris (1984). Recent studies of the causes and characteristics of poverty are those of Beckerman and Clark (1982) and Townsend (1979).

Chapter 8

Statistics on the collection of indirect taxes are contained in Customs and Excise Reports. The distinction between direct and indirect taxes is at best an arbitrary one, and for further reading on the theoretical issues contained in this chapter the reader is referred to the notes on Chapters 3 and 14. An introduction to the theory of optimal indirect taxation is Sandmo (1976).

Chapter 9

The broad issues of the relationship between central and local taxation are discussed in the paper by Netzer in Brookings Institution (1974). In the UK context helpful sources are the Layfield Committee Report (HMSO, 1976), the 1981 Green Paper, Travers (1982), and Foster *et al.* (1980).

Chapters 10 and 11

A detailed analysis of corporate tax systems and their effects on firms' financing and investment decisions may be found in King (1977). The Green Paper on corporation tax (1982) provides a good survey of the issues involved in reform of the UK system.

Chapter 12

The taxation of rent is a topic that attracts no more than brief attention in most public finance texts; but the influence of George (1879) continues. Oil taxation is the subject of much more extensive discussion—see, for example, Devereux and Morris (1983).

Chapter 13

An excellent discussion of the impact of inflation in the tax system is contained in Chapter 6 of the Meade Report (1978); a wider discussion is in Liesner and King (1975). A survey of progress towards indexation in other countries is OECD (1976). The issues raised by inflation accounting are discussed by Whittington (1983); one of the few discussions of the general issues raised by indexation is Mukherjee and Orlans (1975).

Chapter 14

The theoretical literature on the distribution of the tax burden is extremely technical. The pioneering contribution was that by Mirrlees (1971). A less technical but still demanding paper is Atkinson (1973b); for the theory of the measurement of inequality see Atkinson (1973a) which contains a very useful non-mathematical discussion of the main concepts. Annual discussions of the distributional impact of the tax system are to be found in *Economic Trends* and *Fiscal Studies*.

Chapter 15

Discussions of how the tax systems should be changed are not difficult to find. The most comprehensive survey of the British tax system and possibilities for reform is the Meade Report (1978). The Reports of the Irish Commission on Taxation have considerable relevance for the UK. US Treasury (1984) is an important contribution to the literature on tax reform; so too are a variety of documents associated with recent major tax changes in New Zealand

References

Allen Report (1965). *Committee of Inquiry into the Impact of Rates on Households*, Cmnd. 2582, HMSO, London.

Andrews, W. D. (1974). 'A Consumption-Type or Cash Flow Personal Income Tax', *Harvard Law Review*, 87.

Ashworth, M. H. and Forsyth, P. J. (1984). *British Airways: Civil Aviation Policy and the Privatisation of British Airways*, IFS Report Series No. 12, London.

―― and Dilnot, A. W. (1986). *Company Car Taxation in the UK*, IFS Report Series, forthcoming.

Atkinson, A. B. (1972). *Unequal Shares*, Allen Lane, London.

―― (1973a). 'On the Measurement of Inequality', reprinted with non-mathematical summary in A. B. Atkinson (ed.), *Wealth, Income and Inequality*, Penguin, London. (Originally published in *Journal of Economic Theory*, 2, 1970.)

―― (1973b). 'How Progressive Should Income Tax Be?' in M. Parkin (ed.), *Essays on Modern Economics*, Longman, London.

―― (1973c). *The Tax Credit Scheme and Redistribution of Income*, IFS, London.

―― (1983). *The Economics of Inequality*, Oxford Univ. Press, London.

―― and Harrison, A. J. (1978). *The Distribution of Personal Wealth in Britain*, Cambridge Univ. Press, London.

―― and Meade, T. W. (1974). 'Methods and Preliminary Findings in Assessing the Economic and Health Services Consequences of Smoking, with Particular Reference to Lung Cancer', *Journal of the Royal Statistical Society*, Ser. A, 137.

―― and Stiglitz, J. E. (1980). *Lectures on Public Economics*, McGraw-Hill, London.

―― and Townsend, J. L. (1977). 'Economic Aspects of Reduced Smoking', *Lancet 3* Sept. 1977, No. 8036, Vol. 2 for 1977.

Audit Commission (1984). *The Impact on Local Authorities' Economy, Efficiency and Effectiveness of the Block Grant Distribution System*.

Barr, N. A., James, S. R., and Prest, A. R. (1977). *Self Assessment for Income Tax*, Heinemann, London.

242   *References*

Baumol, W. J. and Bradford, D. F. (1970). 'Optimal Departures from Marginal Cost Pricing', *American Economic Review*, **60**.

Beckerman, W. and Clark, S. (1982). *Poverty and Social Security in Britain since 1961*, Oxford Univ. Press.

Beveridge, W. (1942). *Social Insurance and Allied Services*, Cmnd. 6404, HMSO, London.

Blundell, R. W., Meghir, C., Symons, E., and Walker, I. (1984). 'On the Reform of the Taxation of Husband and Wife: Are Incentives Important?', *Fiscal Studies*, Vol. 5, No. 4.

Bolton Committee (1971). *Small Firms: Report of the Committee of Inquiry on Small Firms*, Cmnd. 4811, HMSO, London.

Boskin, M. J. (1977). 'Taxation, Saving and the Rate of Interest', *Journal of Political Economy*, **86**, No. 2, S3–S28.

Boswell, J. (1973). *The Rise and Decline of Small Firms*, Allen & Unwin, London.

Bracewell-Milnes, B. (1976). *The Camel's Back*, Centre for Policy Studies, London.

Break, G. F. (1957). 'Income Taxes and Incentives to Work: An Empirical Study', *American Economic Review*, **47**.

Brookings Institution (1974). *The Economics of Public Finance*, Brookings Institution, Washington, DC.

Brown, C. V. (1968). 'Misconceptions about Income Tax and Incentives', *Scottish Journal of Political Economy*, **15**.

——, Levin, E., and Ulph, D. T. (1976). 'Estimates of Labour Hours Supplied by Married Male Workers in Great Britain', *Scottish Journal of Political Economy*, **23**.

Cain, C. and Watts, H. (1973). *Income Maintenance and Labour Supply*, Markham, New York.

Carter Commission (1966). *Report of the Royal Commission on Taxation*, Ottawa.

Chawla, O. P. (1972). *Personal Taxation in India*, Somaiya Publications, Bombay.

CIPFA (Annual). *Return of Rates*, Chartered Institute of Public Finance and Accountancy, London.

CIR (1979). '121st Report of the Commissioners of Inland Revenue', Cmnd. 7473, HMSO, London.

Cnossen, S. (ed.) (1986). *Tax Coordination in the European Community*, Kluwer, Deventer.

Cripps, T. F. and Godley, W. (1976). *Local Government Finance and its Reform*, Department of Applied Economics, Cambridge.

Customs and Excise (1976). *Report of the Commissioners*, HMSO, London.

Davis, E. H. and Kay, J. A. (1985). 'Extending the VAT Base: Problems and Possibilities', *Fiscal Studies*, Vol. 6, No. 1.

Deaton, A. S. (1975). *Models and Projections of Demand in Post-War Britain*, Chapman & Hall, London.

Devereux, M. P. and Morris, C. N. (1983). *North Sea Oil Taxation: The Development of the North Sea Tax System*, IFS Report Series No. 6, London.

Diamond, P. A. and Mirrlees, J. A. (1971) 'Optimal Taxation and Public Production', *American Economic Review*, **41**.

Diamond Commission (1977). *Royal Commission on the Distribution of Income and Wealth, Report No. 4*, Cmnd. 6626, HMSO, London.

Dilnot, A. W., Kay, J. A., and Morris, C. N. (1984). 'The UK Tax System, Structure and Progressivity, 1948–82', *Scandinavian Journal of Economics*, **86**, 2.

―― and Morris, C. N. (1981). 'What Do We Know About the Black Economy?' *Fiscal Studies*, Vol. 2, No. 1.

―― ―― (1982). 'The Tax System and Distribution, 1979–82' in J. A. Kay (ed.), *The 1982 Budget*, Blackwell, Oxford.

―― ―― (1983). 'The Private Costs and Benefits of Unemployment', *Oxford Economic Papers*, Nov.

Edgeworth, F. Y. (1897). 'The Pure Theory of Taxation (III)', *Economic Journal*, **3**.

Edwards, J. S. S. and Mayer, C. P. (1983). *Issues in Bank Taxation*, IFS Report Series No. 5, London.

Erritt, M. J. and Alexander, J. C. D. (1977). 'Ownership of Company Shares: A New Survey', *Economic Trends*.

European Commission (1985). *Completing the Internal Market*, 7674/85, COM(85)310.

Feige, E. (1979). 'How Big is the Irregular Economy?', *Challenge* 22.

FES Report (1975). *Report on the Family Expenditure Survey*, HMSO, London.

Fiegehen, G. C., Lansley, P. S., and Smith, A. D. (1977). *Poverty and Progress in Britain 1953–73*, National Institute of Economic and Social Research Occasional Paper xxix, Cambridge Univ. Press, London.

―― and Reddaway, W. B. (1981). *Companies, Incentives and Senior Managers*, Oxford Univ. Press.

Fields, D. B. and Stanbury, W. T. (1971). 'Income Taxes and Incentives to Work: Some Additional Empirical Evidence', *American Economic Review*, **41**.

Flemming, J. S. and Little, I. M. D. (1974). *Why We Need a Wealth Tax*, Methuen, London.

Foster, C. D., Jackman, R. A., and Perlman, M. (1980). *Local Government Finance in a Unitary State*, Allen & Unwin, London.

George, H. (1879). *Poverty and Progress*.

Godfrey, L. (1975). *Theoretical and Empirical Aspects of the Effects of Taxation on the Supply of Labour*, OECD, Paris.

Goldthorpe, J., Lockwood, D., Beckhofer, F., and Platt, J. (1970). *The Affluent Worker. Industrial Attitudes and Behaviour*, Cambridge Univ. Press, London.

Goode, R. (1976). *The Individual Income Tax*, Brookings Institution, Washington, DC.

Government Actuary (1983). *National Insurance Fund: Long-Term Financial Estimates*, HC 451, HMSO, London.

Hannah, L. and Kay, J. A. (1977). *Concentration in Modern Industry*, Macmillan, London.

Harbury, C. D. (1979). *Inheritance and Wealth Inequality in Britain*, Allen & Unwin, London.

—— and Hitchens, D. M. (1976). 'The Inheritances of Top Wealth Leavers', *Economic Journal*, **86**.

—— and McMahon, P. C. (1973). 'Inheritance and the Characteristics of Top Wealth Leavers in Britain', *Economic Journal*, Sept.

Hausman, J. A. (1981). 'Labour Supply' in H. J. Aaron and J. A. Pechman (eds.), *How Taxes Affect Economic Behaviour*, Brookings Institution, Washington, DC.

Hemming, R. and Kay, J. A. (1982). 'The Costs of the State Earnings Related Pension Scheme', *Economics Journal*, **92**.

Hicks, J. R. (1939). *Value and Capital. An Inquiry into some Fundamental Principles of Economic Theory*, Clarendon Press, Oxford.

HMSO (1942). *The Taxation of Weekly Wage Earners*, Cmd. 6348, London.

—— (1972a). *Taxation of Capital on Death* (Green Paper), Cmnd. 4930, London.

—— (1972b). *Proposals for a Tax-Credit System*, Cmnd. 5116, London.

—— (1974). *Wealth Tax* (Green Paper), Cmnd. 5704, London.

—— (1975). *Report of the Select Committee of the House of Commons on Wealth Tax*, HC 696, London.

—— (1976). *Local Government Finance*, Report of the Committee of Inquiry (Chairman F. Layfield), Cmnd. 6453, London.

—— (1977). *Local Government Finance*, presented to Parliament by the Secretary of State for the Environment and the Secretary of State for Wales, Cmnd. 6813, London.

—— (1980). *The Taxation of Husband and Wife* (Green Paper), Cmnd. 8093, London.

—— (1981). *Alternatives to Domestic Rates* (Green Paper), Cmnd. 8449, London.

—— (1982). *Corporation Tax* (Green Paper), Cmnd. 8456, London.

—— (1985). *Reform of Social Security*, Cmnd. 9691, HMSO, London.

Hobbes, T. (1651). *Leviathan or, the Matter, Forme and Power of a Commonwealth Ecclesiasticall and Civil*, Andrew Crooke, London.

Horsman, E. G. (1975). 'The Avoidance of Estate Duty by Gifts *Inter Vivos*', *Economic Journal*, **85**.

Howrey, E. P. and Hymans, S. (1978). 'The Measurement and Determination of Loanable Funds Saving', *Brookings Papers on Economic Activity*, No. 3, 655–85.

Ilersic, A. (1973). 'Grant Determination and its Distribution' in Institute for Fiscal Studies, *Proceedings of a Conference on Local Government Finance*, IFS, London.

Institute for Fiscal Studies (1973). *Proceedings of a Conference on Local Government Finance*, IFS, London.

Irish Commission on Taxation (1982). First Report, *Direct Taxation*, The Stationery Office, Dublin.

IRS (1979). *Estimates of Income Unreported on Individual Income Tax Returns*, US Internal Revenue Service, Washington.

Johnston, A. (1965). *The Inland Revenue*, Allen & Unwin, London.

Kaldor, N. (1955). *An Expenditure Tax*, Allen & Unwin, London.

—— (1956). *Indian Tax Reform*, Ministry of Finance, India.

—— (1980). *Reports on Taxation, I*, Duckworth, London.

Kay, J. A. (1977). 'Inflation Accounting—A Review Article', *Economic Journal*, **87**, 300–11.

—— (1982). 'The Taxation of Life Insurance in the UK', IFS working paper.

—— (1984). 'The Effect of Increasing Tax Thresholds on the Poverty and Unemployment Traps', *Fiscal Studies*, Vol. 5, No. 1.

—— (1986). 'Approaching an Expenditure Tax?', *Fiscal Studies*, Vol. 7, No. 2.

—— and Keen, M. J. (1982). *The Structure of Tobacco Taxes in the European Community*, IFS Report Series No. 1, London.

—— and Morris, C. N. (1979). 'Direct and Indirect Taxes', *Fiscal Studies*, Vol. 1, No. 1.

—— and Sandler, C. J. (1982). 'The Taxation of Husband and Wife', *Fiscal Studies*, Vol. 3, No. 3.

King, M. A. (1977). *Public Policy and the Corporation*, Chapman & Hall, London.

—— and Fullerton, D. (eds.) (1984). *The Taxation of Income from Capital*, Chicago Univ. Press.

Layfield Report, *see* HMSO (1976).

Lewis, A. (1978). 'Perceptions of Tax Rates', *British Tax Review*, No. 6.

Liesner, T. and King, M. A. (1975). *Indexing for Inflation*, Heinemann Educational Books, London.

Life Offices Association (1982). *Life Assurance in the United Kingdom*, London.

Lodin, S. O. (1978). *Progressive Expenditure Tax—An Alternative*, Liber Forlag, Stockholm.

MacAfee, K. (1980). 'A Glimpse of the Hidden Economy in the National Accounts', *Economic Trends*, No. 316.

Meade, J. E. (1972). 'Poverty in the Welfare State', *Oxford Economic Papers*, **24**.

Meade Committee (1978). *The Structure and Reform of Direct Taxation*, Allen & Unwin, London.

Merrett-Cyriax Associates (1971). *Dynamics of Small Firms*, Research Report for the Bolton Committee, HMSO, London.

Mill, J. S. (1865). *Principles of Political Economy* (6th edn.), Longman, London.

Minford, A. P. L. (1982a). 'The Development of Monetary Strategy' in J. A. Kay (ed.) (1982), *The 1982 Budget*, Blackwell, Oxford.

—— (1982b). *Unemployment: Cause and Cure*, Martin Robertson, Oxford.

Mirrlees, J. A. (1971). 'An Exploration in the Theory of Optimum Income Taxation', *Review of Economic Studies*, **38**.

Monopolies Commission (1975). *Contraceptive Sheaths*, HC 135, HMSO, London.

Morris, C. N. (1982). 'The Structure of Personal Income Taxation and Income Support', *Fiscal Studies*, Vol. 3, No. 3.
—— and Warren, N. A. (1982). 'Taxation of the Family', *Fiscal Studies*, Vol. 2, No. 1.
Mukherjee, S. and Orlans, C. (1975). *Indexation in an Inflationary Economy*, PEP, London.
Musgrave, R. A. (1959). *The Theory of Public Finance*, McGraw-Hill, New York.
—— and Musgrave, P. B. (1976). *Public Finance in Theory and Practice* (2nd edn.), McGraw-Hill, New York.
Newbery, D. (1970). 'A Theorem on the Measurement of Inequality', *Journal of Economic Theory*, 2.
Nicholson, J. L. (1974). 'The Distribution and Redistribution of Income in the UK' in D. Wedderburn (ed.), *Poverty, Inequality and Class Structure*, Cambridge Univ. Press, London.
Nordhaus, W. D. (1975). 'The Political Business Cycle', *Review of Economic Studies*, **42**.
OECD (1976). *The Adjustment of Personal Income Tax Systems for Inflation*, Paris.
—— (1986). *Personal Income Tax Systems Under Changing Economic Conditions*, Paris.
Okner, B. A. and Pechman, J. A. (1974). *Who Bears the Tax Burden?*, Brookings Institution, Washington, DC.
Opinion Research Centre (1977). 'A Survey of the Motivation of British Management', London.
Parker, R. H. and Harcourt, G. C. (eds.) (1969). *Readings in the Concept and Measurement of Income*, Cambridge Univ. Press, London.
Part, A. (1982). *The Taxation of North Sea Oil: Report of a Committee*, Institute for Fiscal Studies, London.
Pechman, J. A. (ed.) (1980). *What Should be Taxed: Income or Expenditure?*, Brookings Institution, Washington, DC.
—— and Timpane, P. M. (eds.) (1975). *Work Incentives and Income Guarantees: The New Jersey Negative Income Tax Experiment*, Brookings Institution, Washington, DC.
Prais, S. J. (1976). *The Evolution of Giant Firms in Britain*, Cambridge Univ. Press, London.
Public Accounts Committee (1977-8). *Sixth Report of the Public Accounts Committee*, HC 574, HMSO, London.

Radcliffe Report (1954). *Report of the Royal Commission on Taxation of Profits and Income*, No. 2, Cmnd. 9105, HMSO, London.

Ramsey, F. A. (1928). 'A Mathematical Theory of Savings', *Economic Journal*, **38**.

Rawls, J. (1971). *A Theory of Justice*, Clarendon Press, Oxford.

Revell, J. (1965). 'Changes in the Social Distribution of Property in Britain during the Twentieth Century', paper given to Third International Conference of Economic History, Munich, 1965.

—— (1967). *The Wealth of the Nation; the National Balance Sheet of the United Kingdom, 1957–1961*, Cambridge Univ. Press, London.

Richardson Report (1964). *Report of the Committee on Turn-Over Taxation*, Cmnd. 2300, HMSO, London.

Rubenstein, W. D. (1974). 'Men of Property: Some Aspects of Occupation, Inheritance and Power among Top British Wealth-Holders' in P. Stanworth and A. Giddens (eds.), *Elites and Power in British Society*, Cambridge Univ. Press, London.

Sabine, B. E. V. (1966). *A History of Income Tax*, Allen & Unwin, London.

Sandford, C. T. (1971). *Taxing Personal Wealth*, Allen & Unwin, London.

—— (1973). *Hidden Costs of Taxation*, IFS, London.

—— Willis, J. R., and Ironside, D. J. (1975). *An Annual Wealth Tax*, Heinemann Educational Books, London.

—— et al. (1982). *Costs and Benefits of VAT*, Heinemann, London.

Sandilands Report (1975). *Report of the Inflation Accounting Committee*, Cmnd. 6225, HMSO, London.

Sandmo, A. (1976). 'Optimal Taxation—An Introduction to the Literature', *Journal of Public Economics*, **6**.

Select Committee on Tax Credit (1973). *Report and Proceedings of the Committee*, HMSO, London.

Sen, A. K. (1974). 'Informational Bases of Alternative Welfare Approaches; Aggregation and Income Distribution', *Journal of Public Economics*, **3**.

Shoup, C. S. (1969). *Public Finance*, Weidenfeld & Nicolson, London.

Simons, H. C. (1938). *Personal Income Taxation*, Univ. of Chicago Press, Chicago.

Smith, S. R. (1986). *Britain's Shadow Economy*, Oxford Univ. Press, Oxford.

Social Services Committee (1985). *Seventh Report, 1984-5*, HC 451, HMSO, London.

Stanworth, P. and Giddens, A. (eds.) (1974). *Elites and Power in British Society*, Cambridge Univ. Press, London.

Starkie, D. N. M. and Thompson D. J. (1985). *Privatising London's Airports: Options for Competition*, IFS Report Series No. 16, London.

Statistical Abstract of US (Annual). US Department of Commerce, Washington, DC.

Stern, N. H. (1976). 'Taxation and Labour Supply—A Partial Survey' in *Proceedings of a Conference on Taxation and Incentives*, IFS, London.

—— (1977). 'The Marginal Valuation of Income' in M. J. Artis and A. R. Nobay (eds.), *The Proceedings of the Association of University Teachers of Economics, Edinburgh, 1976*, Basil Blackwell, Oxford.

Tanzi, V. (1982). *The Underground Economy in the United States and Abroad*, D. C. Heath, Lexington, Mass.

Titmuss, R. M. (1962). *Income Distribution and Social Change*, Allen & Unwin, London.

Townsend, P. (1979). *Poverty in the United Kingdom*, Penguin, London.

Travers, A. (1982). 'Block Grant: Origins, Objects and Use', *Fiscal Studies*, Vol. 3, No. 1.

US Treasury (1977). *Blueprints for Basic Tax Reform*, US Government Printing Office, Washington.

—— (1984). *Tax Reform for Fairness, Simplicity and Economic Growth*, US Government Printer, Washington.

Vision (1977). No. 75, Feb.

Whalley, J. and Piggott, J. R. (1977). 'General Equilibrium Investigations of UK Tax Subsidy Policy' in M. J. Artis and A. R. Nobay (eds.), *The Proceedings of the Association of University Teachers of Economics, Edinburgh, 1976*, Basil Blackwell, Oxford.

Wheatcroft, G. S. A. (1965). 'Proposals for a System of Estate and Gift Taxation' in G. S. A. Wheatcroft (ed.), *Estate and Gift Taxation: A Comparative Study*, Sweet & Maxwell, London.

Whittington, G. (1983). *The Theory of Inflation Accounting*, Cambridge Univ. Press.

Worswick, G. N. D. (1971). 'Fiscal Policy and Stabilization in Britain' in A. Cairncross (ed.), *Britain's Economic Prospects Reconsidered*, Allen & Unwin, London.

Zabalza, A., Pissarides, C., Piachaud, D., and Barton, M. (1979). 'Social Security and the Choice between Full-Time Work, Part-Time Work and Retirement', paper presented to NBER/SSRC Conference on Econometric Studies in Public Finance, Cambridge, mimeo.

Index